IMAGES
of America

MURRAY

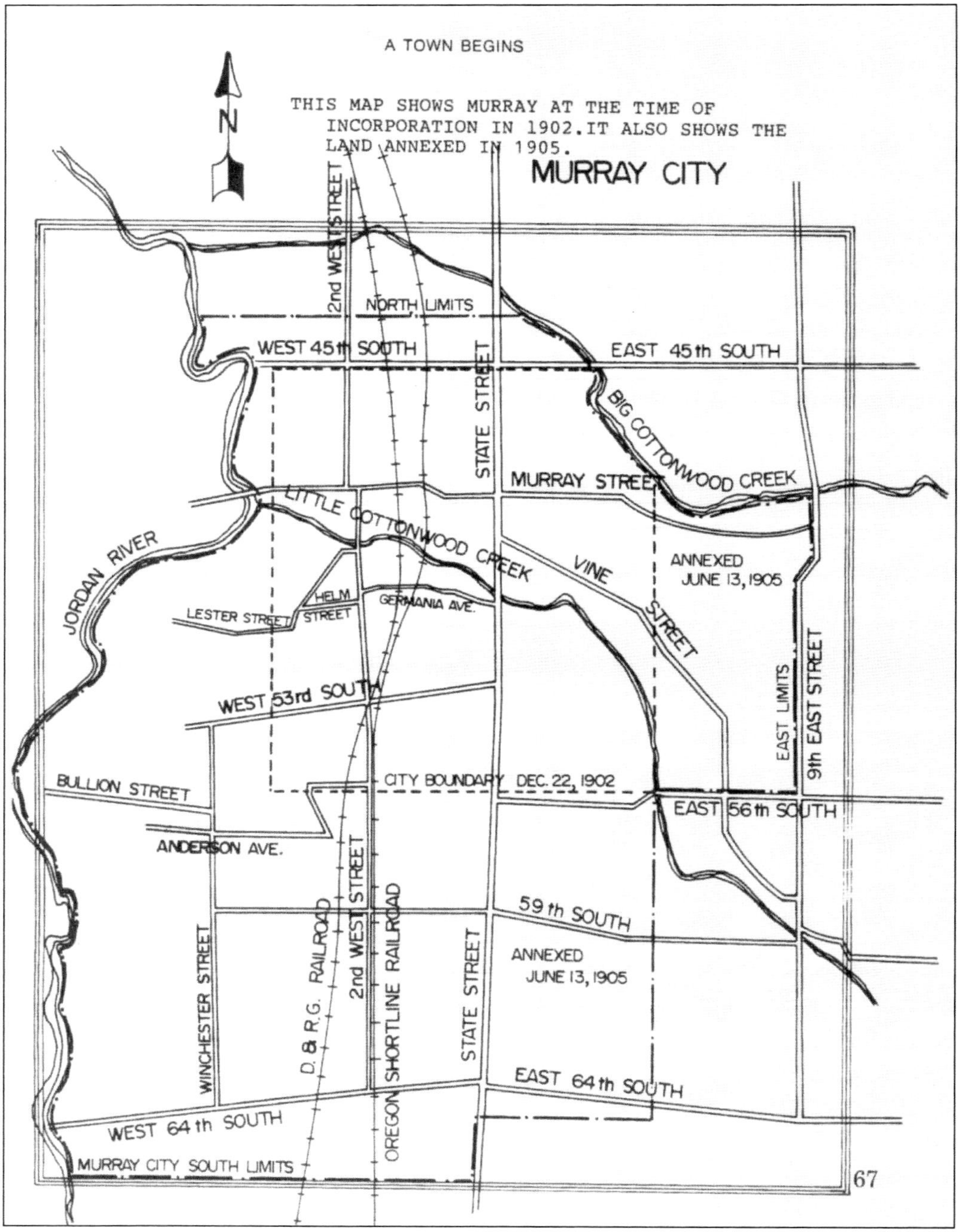

This map is included in *The History of Murray*, published for the nation's bicentennial in 1976. It illustrates the boundaries at the time of incorporation in 1903 and the first annexation in 1905. (Courtesy of the Murray City Corporation.)

On the Cover: Murray citizens love a parade. This photograph from the early 1920s shows the commercial district along State Street. Today, only the buildings at the far right are still standing. (Courtesy of the Murray City Museum.)

IMAGES
of America

MURRAY

Korral Broschinsky

ARCADIA
PUBLISHING

ISBN 978-1-4671-3322-7

Published by Arcadia Publishing
Charleston, South Carolina

Printed in the United States of America

Library of Congress Control Number: 2014952483

For all general information, please contact Arcadia Publishing:
Telephone 843-853-2070
Fax 843-853-0044
E-mail sales@arcadiapublishing.com
For customer service and orders:
Toll-Free 1-888-313-2665

Visit us on the Internet at www.arcadiapublishing.com

To Mike, Krystopher, Kamryn, Kourtlyn, Zach, and Riley, for giving me love when I most needed it

Contents

Acknowledgments

The majority of photographs in this book can be found in the photograph collection of the Murray City Museum (MCM), therefore first and foremost my thanks go to the hundreds of Murray residents who donated their precious family photographs to Murray City over the years. Mary Ann Kirk, the city's cultural-arts director, has been the driving force behind cataloging the collection and making it available to the public. She has also made available a collection of historical photographs from various agencies within Murray City. These and many more photographs can be found on the website of the Murray City Library. I owe a debt of gratitude to Bunny Ankney, the curator of the museum, for her valuable aid in accessing the collection. A thank-you goes to Murray City for the use of these photographs.

Other photographs were obtained from the following archives and are used with permission: the Utah State Historical Society (USHS), the Church History Library of the Church of Jesus Christ of Latter-day Saints (CHL), the International Daughters of Utah Pioneers (IDUP), and the Salt Lake County Archives (SLCA). Thanks go to the staff of these institutions for their expertise in maintaining these irreplaceable resources.

I wish to thank the many historians of Murray City, past and present, who have helped me re-create the people and places of Murray in my mind. These historians include Ethel Bradford, Judson Callaway, Reed Clegg, Vere McHenry, R. Ray Rasmussen, Su Richards, David Schirer, the contributors to the 1976 *History of Murray*, the participants in Murray's oral history project, and the anonymous journalists of the *Murray Eagle*.

I am grateful to my editors at Arcadia Publishing for their patience and support. Lastly, I wish to thank my family for always making Murray feel like home.

INTRODUCTION

Every story of Murray City begins with its place near the center of the Salt Lake Valley. Following the footpaths of the Native Americans who traversed the valley before them, a group of hardy Mormon pioneers camped near a creek eight miles south of the newly established Salt Lake City in the spring of 1848. Named for the cottonwood trees that lined its banks, the Little Cottonwood Creek cut a diagonal path from an eastern mountain canyon to the Jordan River and on to the Great Salt Lake. The settlers dug ditches, planted crops, and built log cabins on a one-square-mile tract of land. Within a few years, more tracts were surveyed, following the path of the Big Cottonwood Creek to the north, and the community of scattered farmsteads was organized into the South Cottonwood Ward.

The religious and social center of South Cottonwood was an adobe meetinghouse near the rest stop for wagons that hauled granite blocks from a quarry at the mouth of Little Cottonwood Canyon and was about halfway between the quarry and the temple site in Salt Lake City. This granite trail established the path of present-day Vine Street to the Territorial Road (later State Street), the main arterial connecting Salt Lake City to other Mormon settlements along the Wasatch Mountains. By the time the Utah Southern Railway reached South Cottonwood in 1870, there was a cluster of businesses near the intersection of Vine Street and Territorial Road. The arrival of the railroad and the discovery of valuable minerals in the mountain canyons changed the landscape dramatically. With Big and Little Cottonwood Creeks only a mile apart near the rail corridor, the presence of abundant water and branch rail lines to the mines spurred the construction of eight smelters by 1880. As the new boomtown emerged, community identification became important, and the local postmaster submitted for consideration the name Murray, after Utah's territorial governor Eli H. Murray. One early resident referred to the town as a "dirty little place with only two stores and a number of saloons."

Murray developed three distinct populations: the farmers living on the outlying agricultural lands, the merchants living near the business district, and the smelter workers, living in boardinghouses and shanty towns. The smelters drew hundreds of immigrants, mostly single men from Southern and Central Europe and Scandinavia. The influx of workers steadily increased, particularly after the American Smelting and Refining Company (ASARCO) built a massive lead smelter at State Street just south of the Little Cottonwood Creek. For a time in the late 19th and early 20th centuries, Murray was the most ethnically diverse community in Salt Lake County. ASARCO's two colossal smokestacks, visible from every part of the valley, would dominate Murray's skyline through the 20th century.

A campaign for incorporation began after a confrontation between "a group of cowboys, fresh from sheep shearing, and smelter workers on payday" resulted in robbery, riots, and the burning of a brewery and dance hall. For several years, the residents were divided into opposing camps, with one side hoping incorporation would help manage growth and rising social unrest and the other side fearful of burdensome taxation and lack of control. The vote for incorporation took place on November 18, 1902, with 294 votes in favor and 235 votes against. Murray became a third-class city when the official declaration was published on January 3, 1903.

From the beginning, Murray was fiercely independent. Resisting pressure from Salt Lake County to be included in a consolidated high school district, the city council annexed additional farmland to increase the population, allowing the city to form its own school district. Murray was designated a second-class city in July 1905. The new boundaries extended to approximately 4500 South on the north, 6400 South on the south, 900 East on the east, and the Jordan River on the west. Within a few years of incorporation, the city had its own school district, power plant, waterworks, and police and fire departments. A city hall was built on State Street in 1907. The burgeoning city built new schools, constructed a library, established a city park, and acquired the South Cottonwood Ward cemetery.

During the Great Depression, city officials took advantage of public funds to expand its electrical system, improve the city park, and build a new elementary school. Murray was a place where kids "could go down to the tracks by the river and talk to the hoboes." On the outskirts were the "enormous farms," with dairies along the east boundary and grains and sugar beets near the Jordan River to the west. Many of the immigrants married and settled in Murray to raise their families. The ethnic diversity spread from the industrial corridor as naturalized citizens purchased land for truck farms or started businesses. The storefronts along the State Street corridor began advertising their central location as the "Hub of Salt Lake County." The county agreed when it chose a site adjacent to Murray City Park for the location of the county fairgrounds.

With the city growing steadily, two subdivisions were platted just north of the downtown business district, but further development was curtailed by the onset of World War II. In the postwar years, Murray's central location and stable infrastructure were ideal for returning veterans eager to use their GI benefits to start families. During the 1950s, the *Murray Eagle* noted month after month of record-breaking numbers for city building permits. The school district expanded three and constructed six new school buildings during the suburban boom. Murray City annexed additional land to develop a second shopping center in the southeast quadrant of the city not far from the site of South Cottonwood Ward's old adobe meetinghouse on Vine Street. In 1958, city hall was moved to a new location farther south on State Street as the population center shifted.

Even before ASARCO closed its smelting operations in 1950, Murray City had replaced its tax base with a new economic model based on automobile dealerships, supermarkets, discount stores, and specialized agriculture and industry. The Interstate 15 freeway and the I-215 belt route reached Murray in the 1960s and 1970s respectively, making it easier to get "anywhere from anywhere in 15 minutes." Murray adopted "Hub of Salt Lake County" as its official motto. Fashion Place Mall opened in 1972 at the south end of the city. City hall moved once again in 1980 to a high-profile location adjacent to the city park. Murray's formula for success was a combination of its central location and a high quality of life for its residents. Throughout Murray's transformation into a bedroom community for Salt Lake City, the leaders and citizens remained independent and consistently rejected all attempts to merge government services with either the county or other municipalities.

As Murray City approached its centennial celebration, two large annexations increased the physical size of the city. These east side neighborhoods included the original one-square-mile settlement survey, bringing the city full circle. On August 6, 2000, the landmark stacks, the last remnants of the smelter era, were demolished in a spectacular implosion of smoke and brick. The former slag heap was cleaned up and replaced by a light-rail station and a state-of-the-art medical center. For more than a century, Murray City has been a shining example of cooperation between agriculture, business, industry, and government. The city provides its residents with more educational, recreational, and cultural opportunities than other communities its size. Murray's latest motto, "There's More to Murray," pays homage to the community's past while looking forward to its bright future.

One

From South Cottonwood to Murray

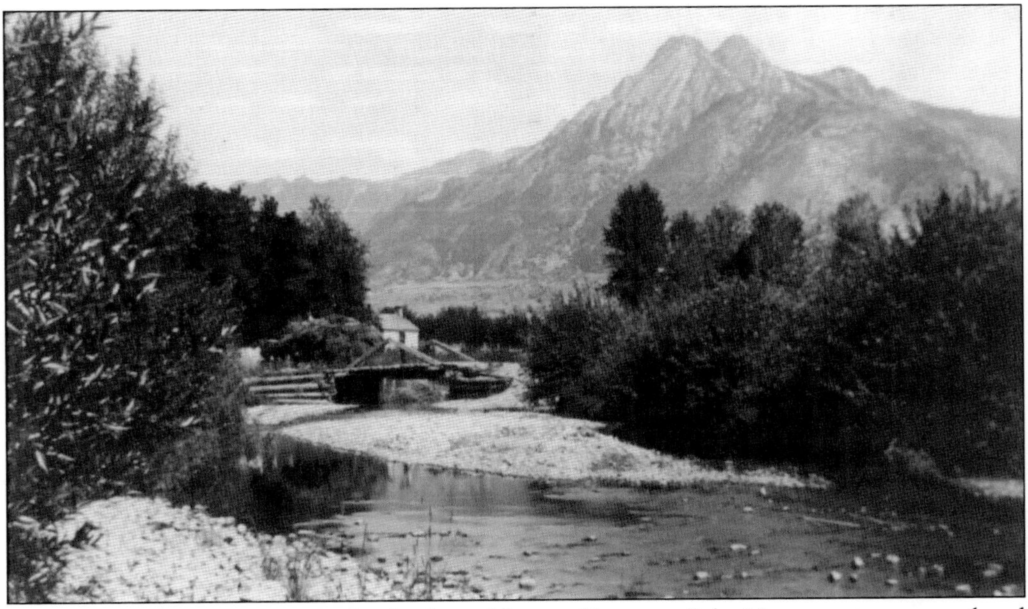

Tasked by Brigham Young to "make the desert blossom like a rose," the Mormon pioneers explored the streams that flowed through the Salt Lake Valley to the Jordan River. By the early 1850s, numerous farmsteads were located along the banks of the Big and Little Cottonwood Creeks. This undated photograph shows an early home and log bridge built to link the farmsteads scattered between the cottonwoods. (USHS.)

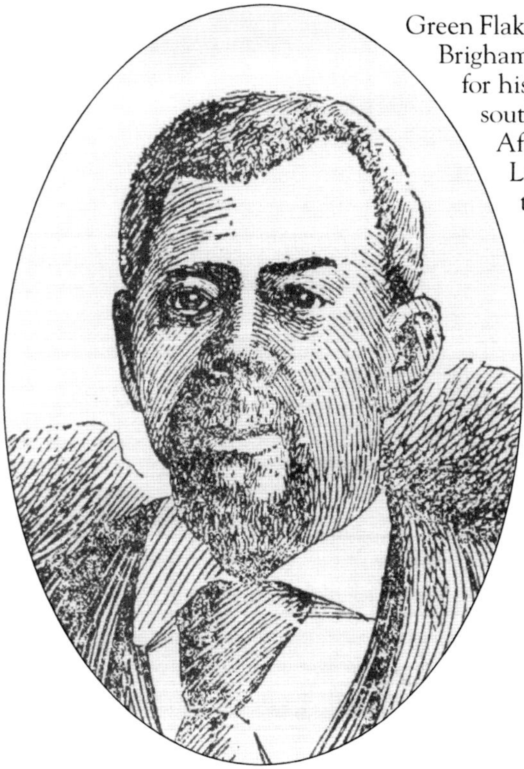

Green Flake, an enslaved African American, traveled with Brigham Young's company in 1847. He built a log cabin for his owner, James M. Flake. The cabin was in the southeast corner of Murray's current boundaries. After obtaining his freedom, Flake married Martha Lay and settled in Union, Utah. He later moved to Idaho but returned to Utah as an honored guest at the 50-year Pioneer Day celebration in 1897. (IDUP.)

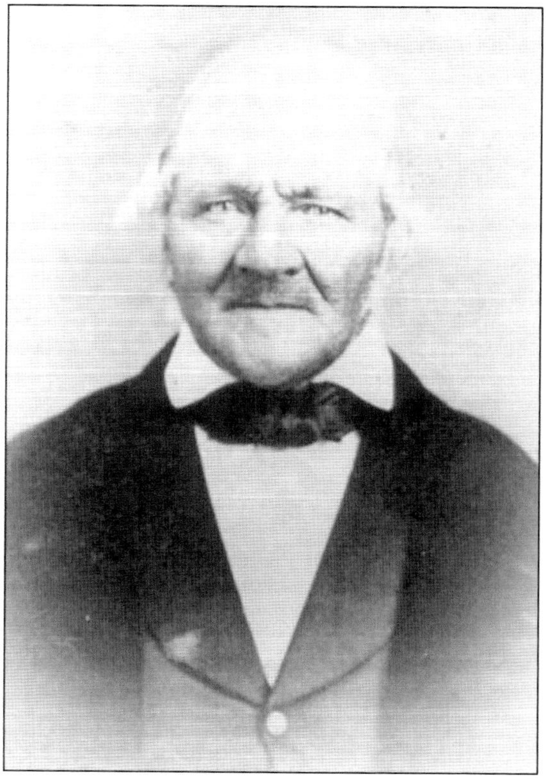

John Benbow came to Utah in September 1848 and built a dugout on the Little Cottonwood Creek. The following spring, he built a log cabin for his wife, Rosetta Wright King Peacock. John raised oats on the family farm. At his death on May 12, 1874, he became the first settler to be buried in the South Cottonwood Cemetery (later Murray Cemetery). (MCM.)

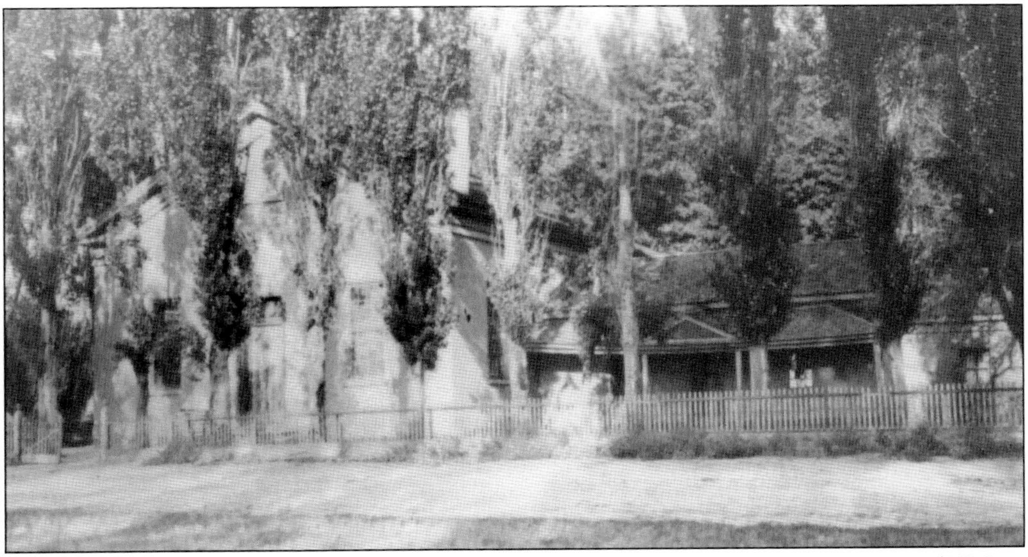

In the early 1850s, the members of the Church of Jesus Christ of Latter-day Saints (LDS or Mormon Church) were organized as the South Cottonwood Ward. Vine Street and 5600 South became the religious and social center of the community. This c. 1900 photograph shows the adobe meetinghouse built in 1856 (right) as well as an addition built in 1869 (left). The ward cooperative store is visible in the right background. (CHL.)

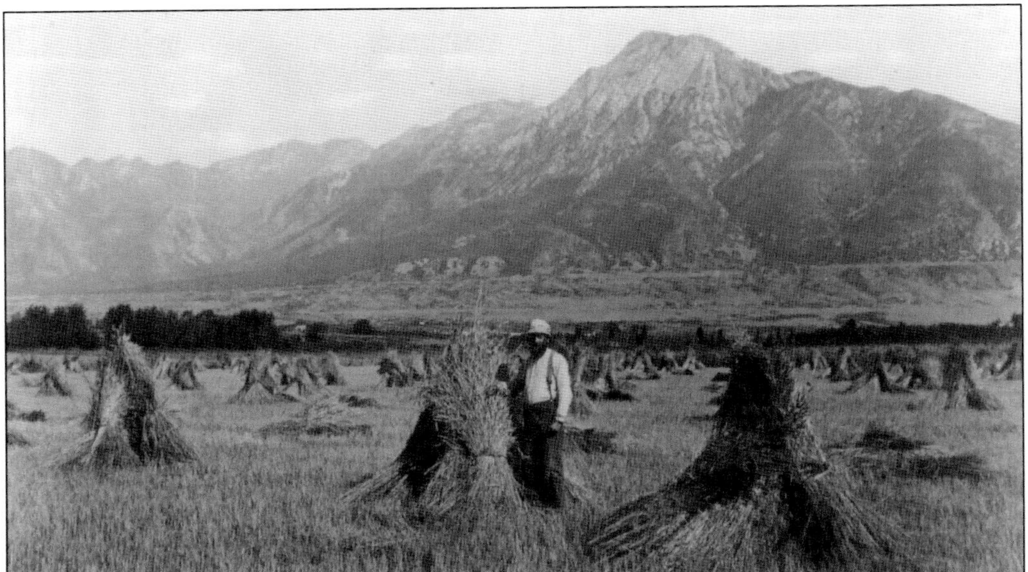

By the 1870s, a communal system of canals and ditches drawing water from the Jordan River and the Cottonwood Creeks allowed many farmers to move from subsistence to production agriculture. Salt Lake County farmers were also known for their early experiments in dry farming. This photograph is of the Christensen wheat farm in the early 1880s. (USHS.)

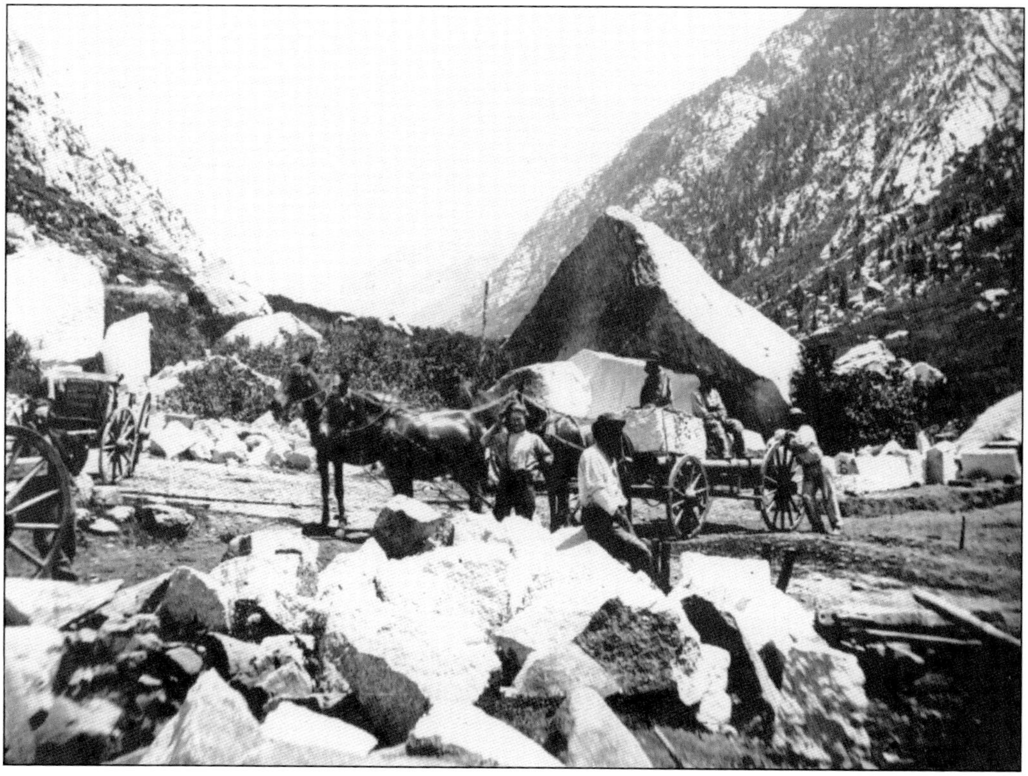

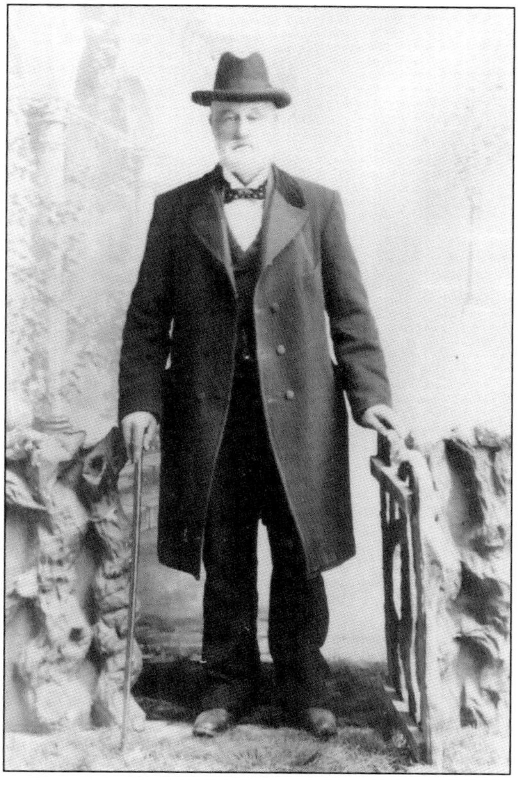

This photograph by Charles W. Carter was taken at the temple quarry in Little Cottonwood Canyon. The wagons are loaded with granite bound for the LDS temple site in Salt Lake City. An overnight campground for the teamsters who hauled the granite was located 600 feet north of the South Cottonwood Ward meetinghouse. (CHL.)

Dyre Amundsen, a Norwegian convert to the LDS Church, used his personal team and wagon to haul granite blocks from the canyon to the temple. Around 1867, he homesteaded a large farm in south Murray near today's Fashion Place Mall. He and his wife, Marie Sophia Person Amundsen, lived in an adobe house before finishing a brick house with a foundation made from cast-off granite blocks. (IDUP.)

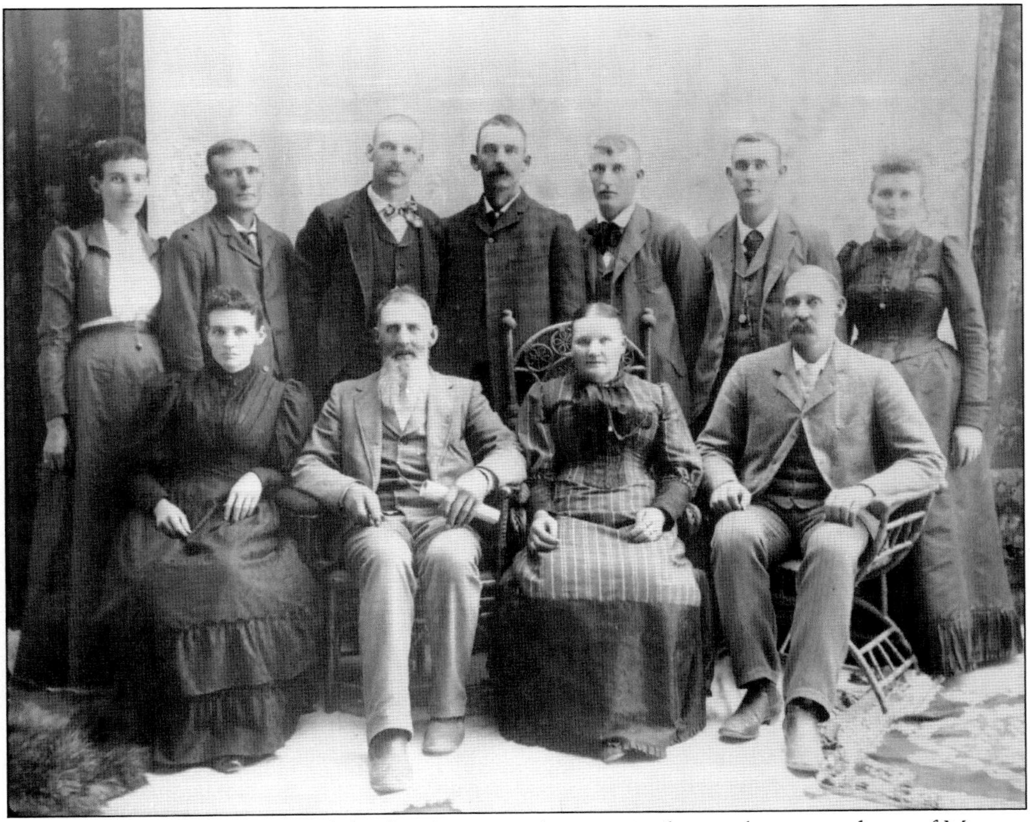

James Winchester was granted the first homestead patent in the southwest quadrant of Murray. James was a self-trained veterinarian and instrumental in starting the first school in the area. His wife, Elizabeth Jane Crismon Winchester, was a nurse-midwife and could often be seen harnessing her horse to her black-top buggy day or night. The Winchesters raised nine children, including an Indian boy who was found hiding under a bed. (IDUP.)

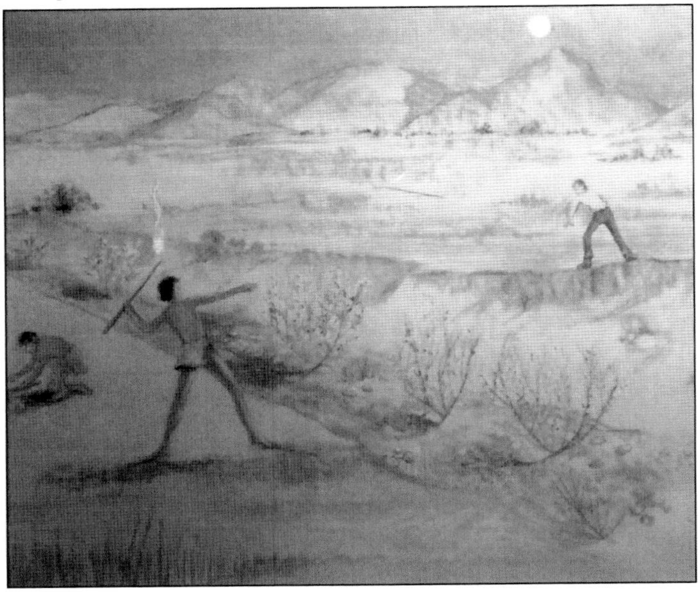

The early settlers interacted with the nomadic Shoshone and Ute tribes who established camps in the area. The Mormon pioneers traded sugar, tea, and beans for the Native Americans' tanned hides and fresh game. Indian and white boys played a game that involved throwing and dodging fire-tipped willow sticks back and forth across the Jordan River, as depicted in this illustration by Kathleen Pulsipher. (MCM.)

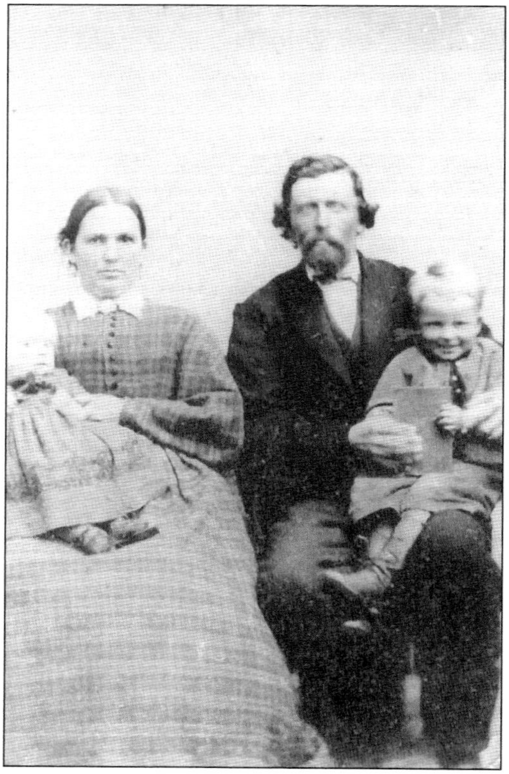

In 1852, Jonas Erekson married Mary Powell and moved from the Millcreek area to South Cottonwood. He raised sheep and cattle on a ranch in Tooele County. When Jonas decided to enter into plural marriage in 1869, he took Mary with him to court John Benbow's daughter Isabella. Mary's feelings expressed to Isabella were typical: "I'm not particularly anxious to have Jonas take a second wife, but if he has to do it, I'd rather it be you than anyone I know." Mary is pictured in 1867 holding Norman Wines Erekson, and Jonas is holding James Theodore Erekson. (MCM.)

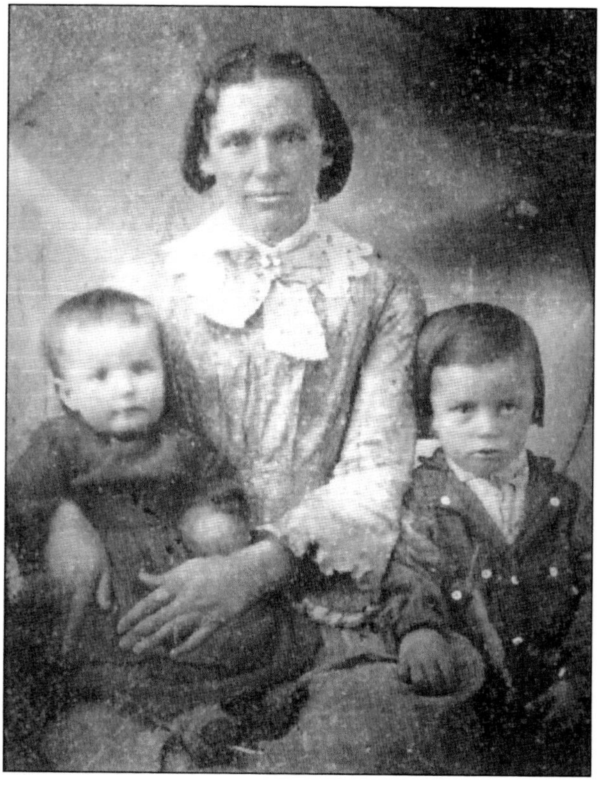

Isabella Benbow Erekson poses with her two sons, William Benbow Erekson (left) and John Benbow Erekson, in 1879. (MCM.)

When James Theodore Erekson married Janet Brown McMillan in 1890, the couple moved into the adobe house where he had been born. The family-owned Erekson Dairy was in operation longer than any of the eight dairies on Murray's east side in the late 19th and early 20th centuries. Pictured here around 1910 are, from left to right, James, Janet, and their daughter Mary Fern Erekson. (MCM.)

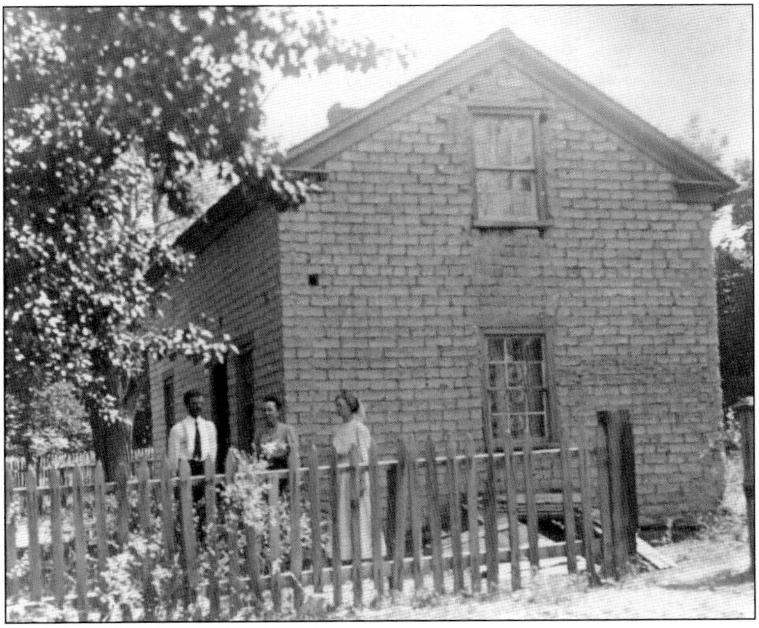

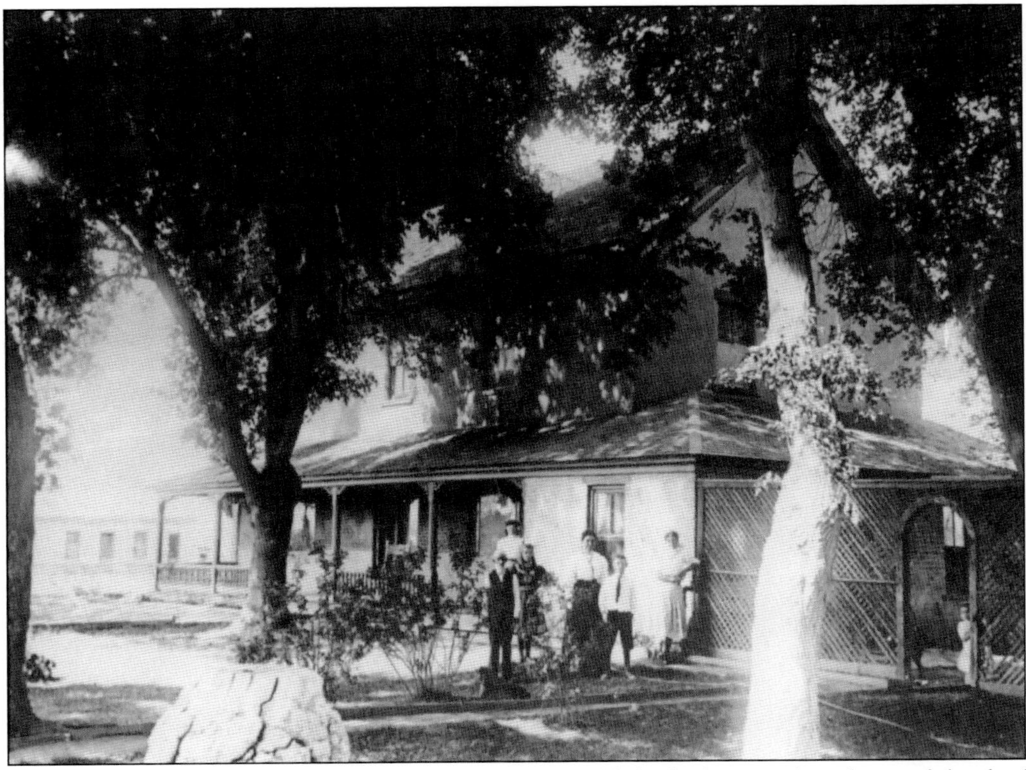

Ruben Miller and his wife, Rhoda Ann Letts Miller, established a farmstead on the north bank of the Big Cottonwood Creek in the early 1850s. Although Ruben was associated with the Millcreek Ward as a bishop, five of their sons were Murray businessmen. Ruben is credited with introducing alfalfa to the Salt Lake Valley. Rhoda and her daughters raised silkworms. This photograph of the farmhouse was taken around 1908. (MCM.)

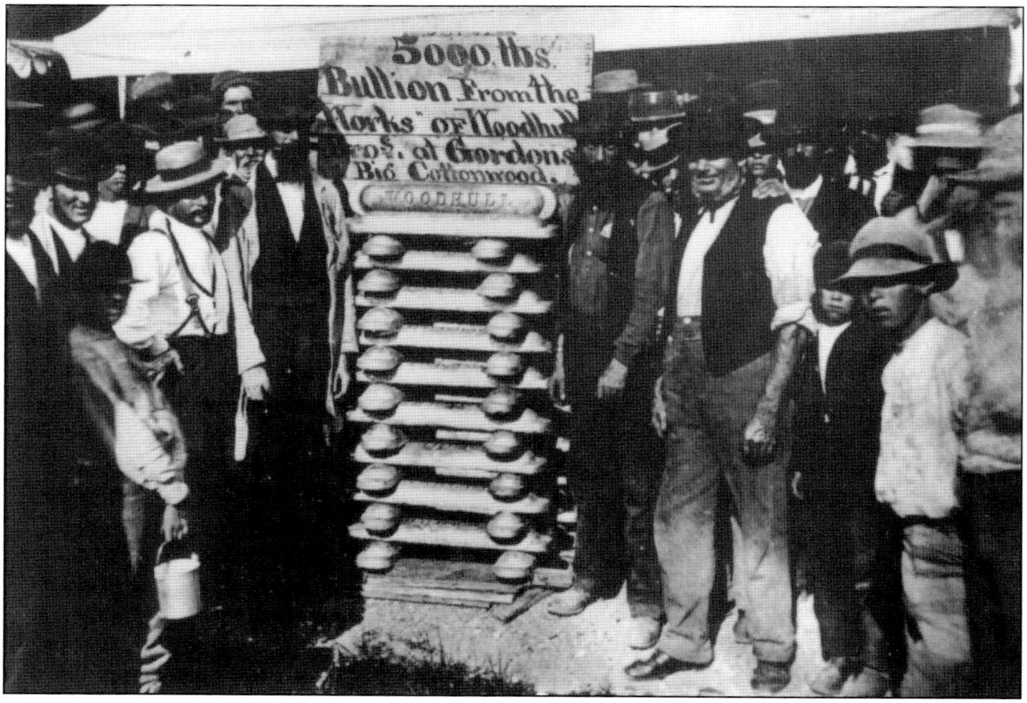

The transition of South Cottonwood from agricultural outpost to industrial boomtown began with the discovery of valuable minerals in the mountain canyons in the 1860s. In 1869, the first smelter, Woodhull Brothers, was established where the Big Cottonwood Creek crossed the Territorial Road (later State Street), Murray's main north-south corridor. (USHS.)

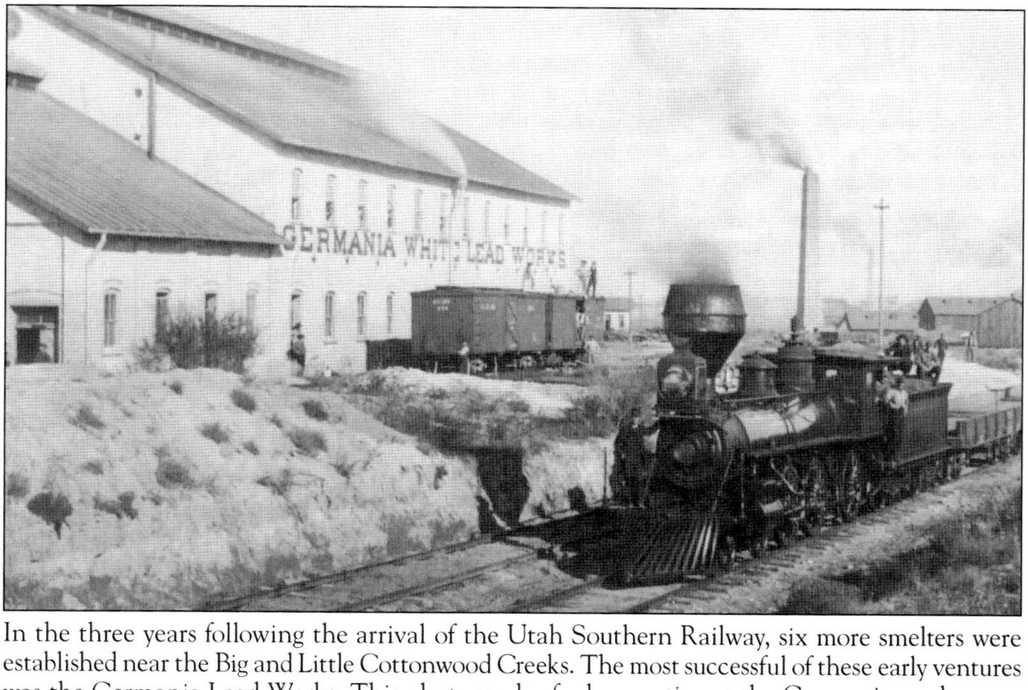

In the three years following the arrival of the Utah Southern Railway, six more smelters were established near the Big and Little Cottonwood Creeks. The most successful of these early ventures was the Germania Lead Works. This photograph of a locomotive at the Germania smelter was taken by noted Utah photographer Charles R. Savage around 1880. (CHL.)

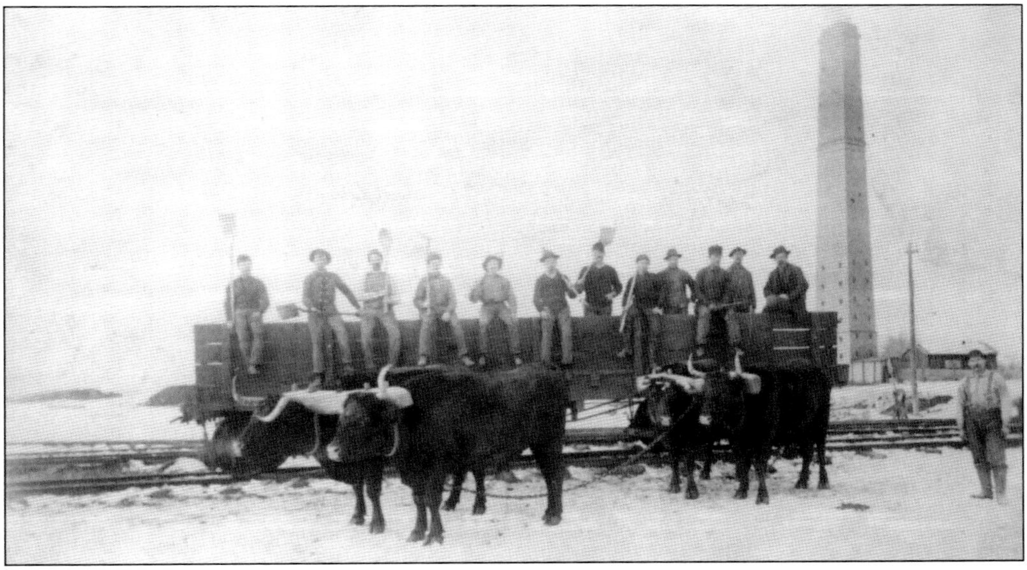

For 21 years, two brothers, James W. and Joseph C. Cahoon, had a contract for handling the ore at Germania. Pictured here around 1890 are the oxteams that were used to switch the railcars. The workers shoveled all the ore by hand. Pictured on the wagon, James is at far right and Joseph is third from right. (USHS.)

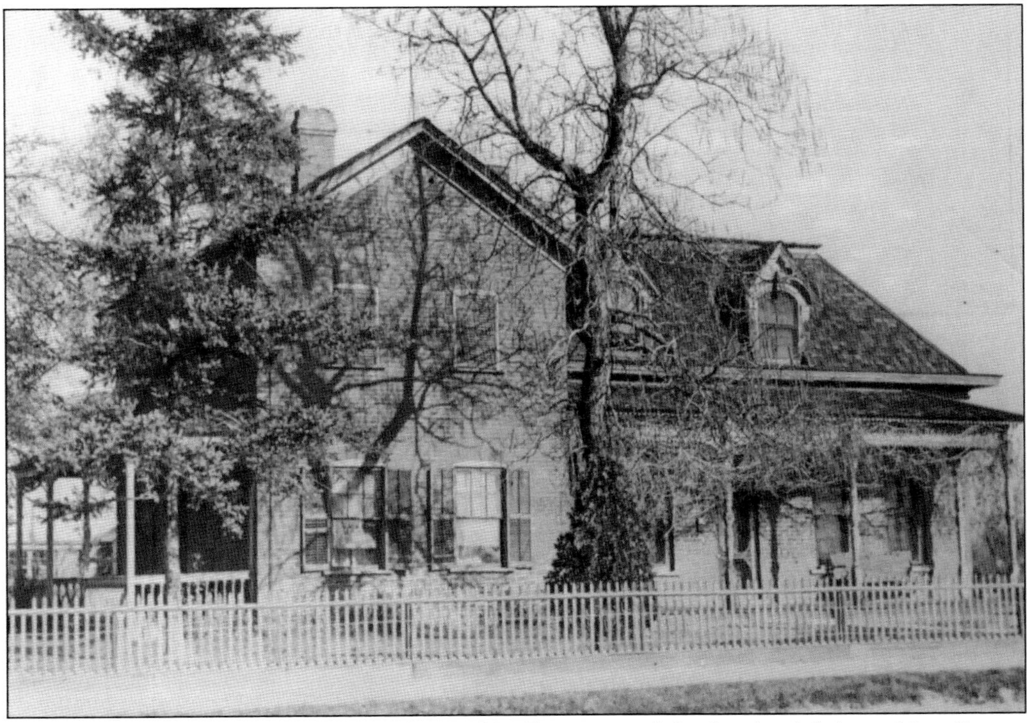

Simeon Atwood and his two sons Walter and William started the first brick kiln on Vine Street. Walter Atwood built the first fired-brick residence in South Cottonwood. The two-story house, built in 1864, had separate entrances for his wives, Deidamia Stickney and Julia Dibble. Noted dignitaries such as Brigham Young and John Taylor stayed at the Atwood Mansion, which also served as a community center for parties and dances. (USHS.)

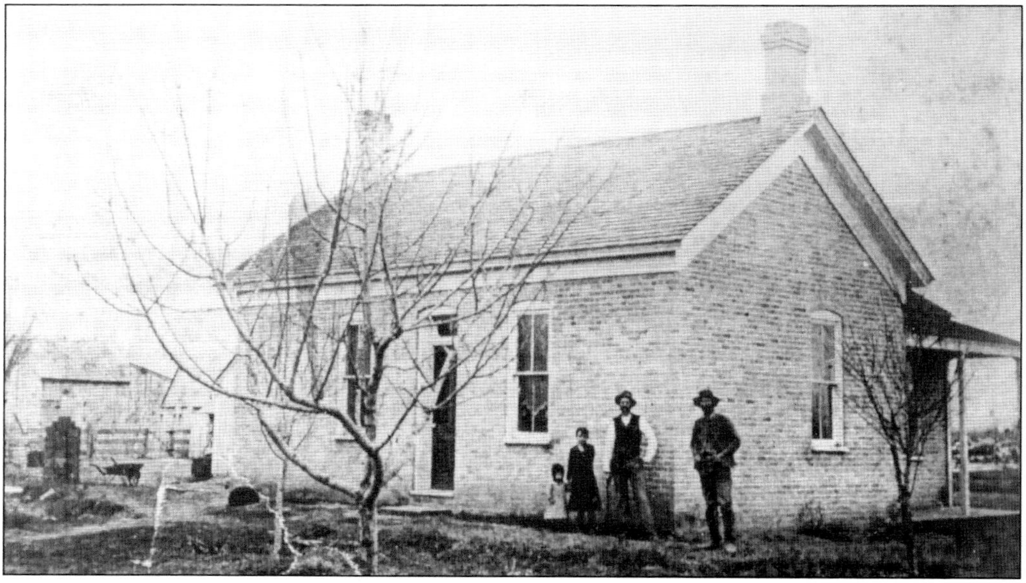

William Atwood built a more modest brick house farther east on Vine Street. Atwood bricks were used to build four of the Murray-area smelters. The Atwood brothers donated land on the south side of Vine Street for a district school and an LDS meetinghouse. This photograph taken around 1875 is believed to show Walter and William and his eldest daughters. (MCM.)

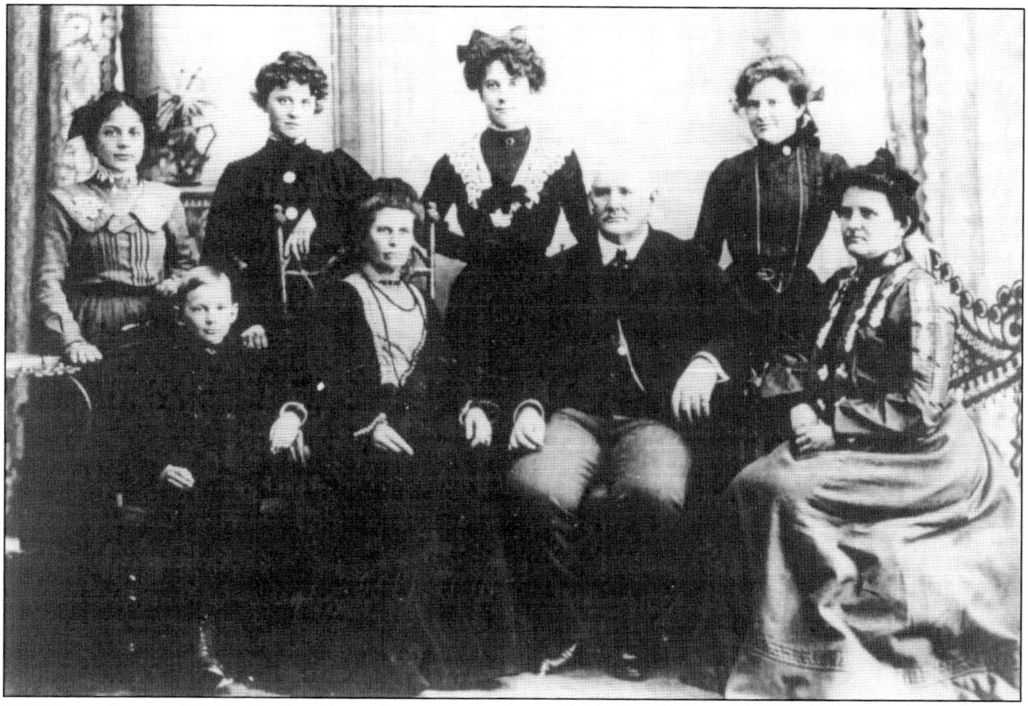

William Atwood left the brick industry to start a coal, lumber, and hardware business. This photograph of his family was taken around 1900. Pictured are, from left to right, (first row) Roscoe Atwood, Sarah Jane Atwood, William Turrell Atwood, and Oralie Melissa Atwood Baker; (second row) Wilma Fay Atwood Mackay, Nina Vivien Atwood Brockbank, Ione Lizette Atwood, and Royola Adna Atwood. (MCM.)

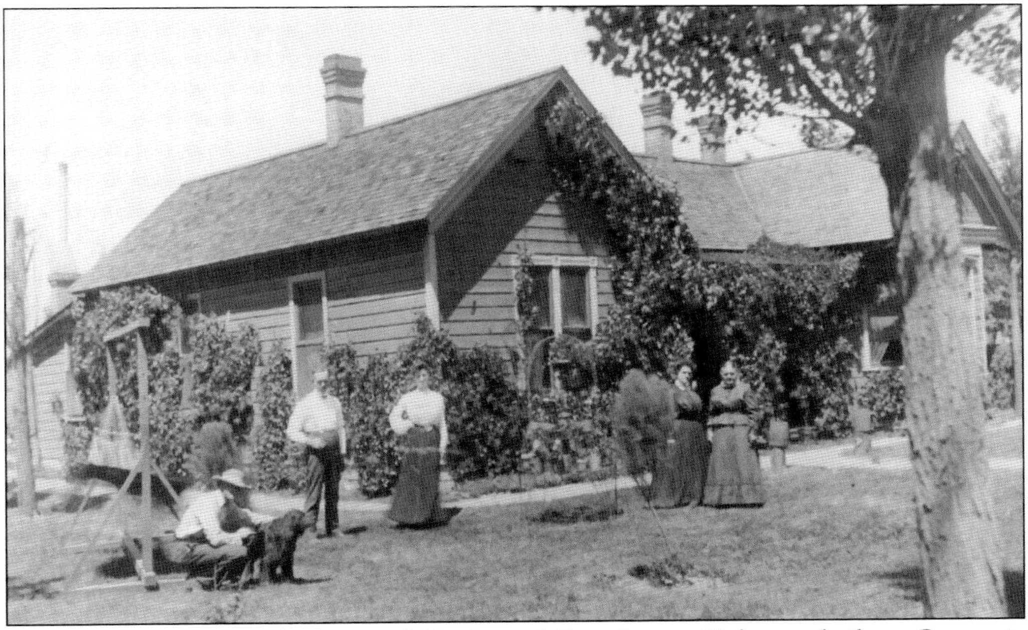

Sometime in the 1870s, the house of Charles and Ilene Iverson Holm was built on Germania Avenue, just west of the smelter where Charles worked as an assayer. The Holms raised 11 children and operated a small grocery store adjacent to the house (pictured around 1890). Charles presided over the local Scandinavian branch of the LDS Church between 1884 and 1893. (MCM.)

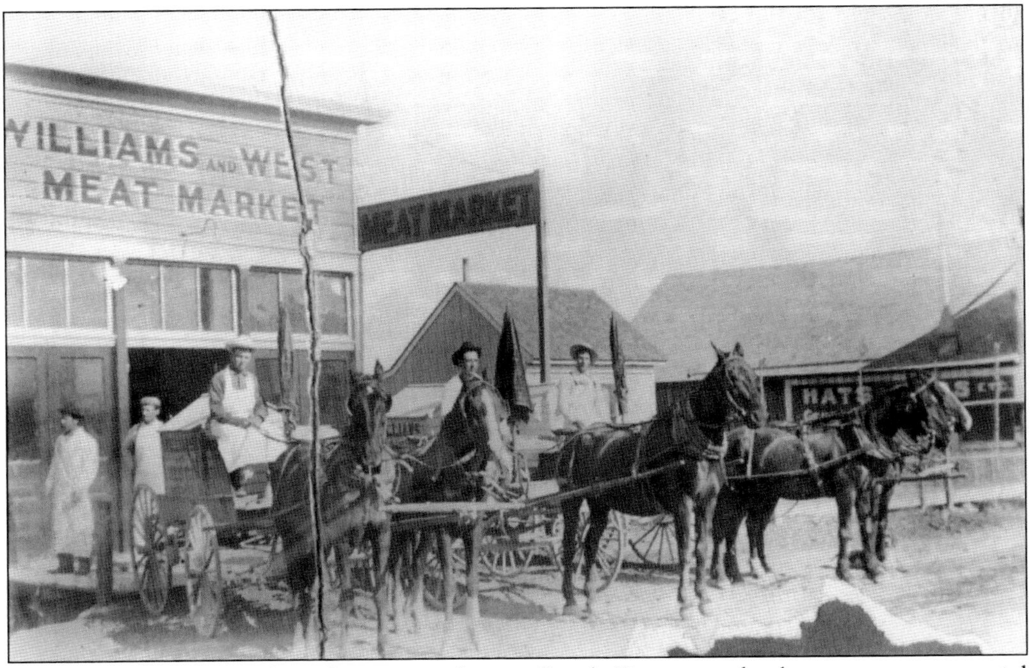

As the smelter industry brought more workers to South Cottonwood, a boomtown commercial district grew along the Territorial Road (State Street). The Williams and West Meat Market, owned by Lorenzo Williams and Charlie West, was located north of today's 4800 South, which ran west to Taylorsville and east to Holladay. (MCM.)

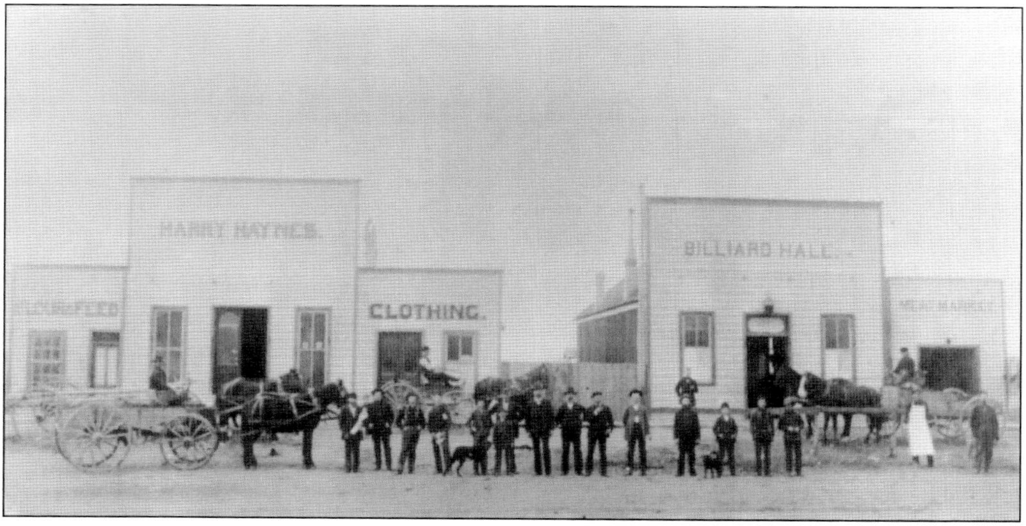

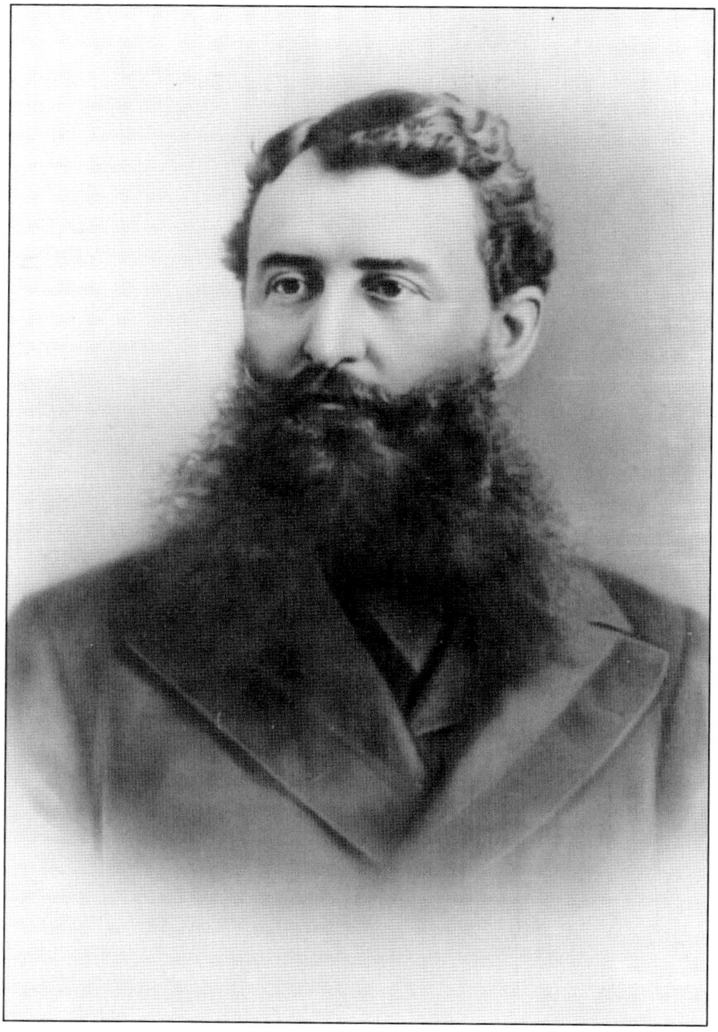

Harry Haynes was a Union veteran of the Civil War who came to Utah in 1870. He married a local girl, Jane Elizabeth Cahoon. Haynes built a row of commercial buildings on the west side of State Street (seen above in 1881). He was appointed postmaster in October 1882. As postmaster, Haynes was faced with competing interests for the identity of the emerging community. The farmers preferred the name South Cottonwood, while business leaders wanted to use one of the smelter names. Haynes submitted two names to the postmaster general: Custer, for the popular late general George Armstrong Custer, and Murray, for then territorial governor of Utah Eli H. Murray (pictured at left). Murray became the official postal designation in March 1883. (Both, MCM.)

Two

INDUSTRY AND DIVERSITY

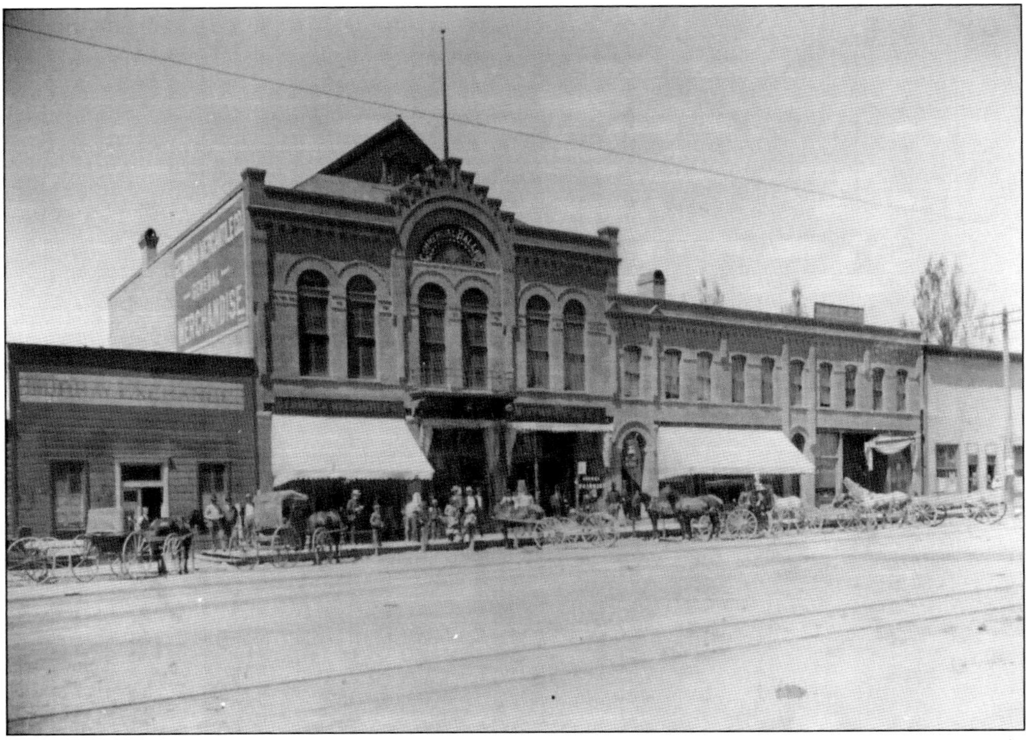

The imposing two-story Commercial Hall building had a large auditorium and was commonly known as the Murray Opera House. Built in 1893, the building was the first commercial block in Murray to have both steam heat and electric light. The electricity was supplied by an on-site generator, making it the most modern building outside of Salt Lake at the time. (MCM.)

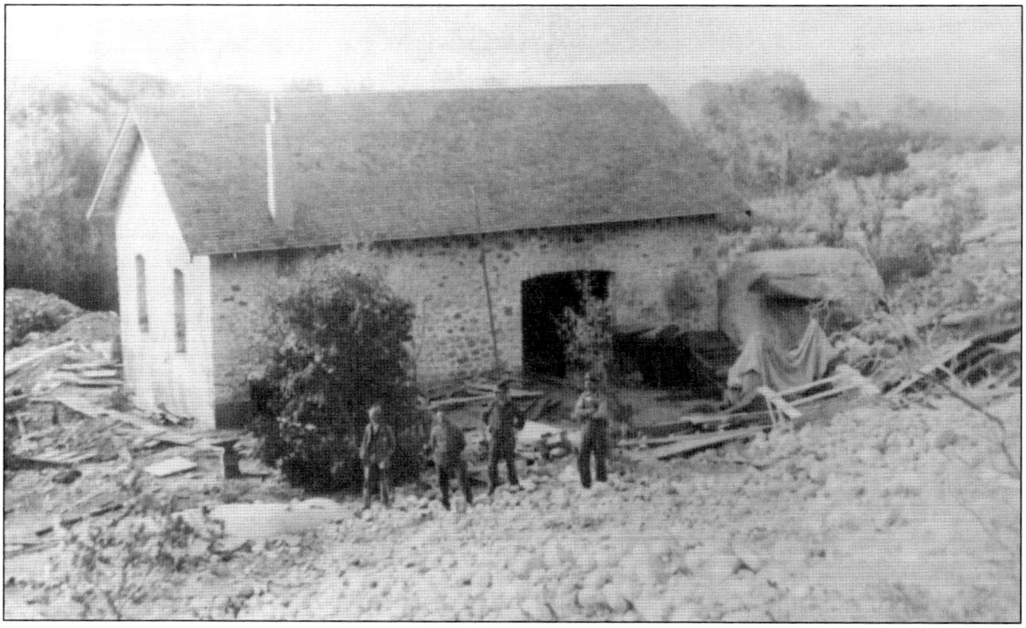

The Progress Company supplied power to Murray businesses and residences until 1913, when Murray City built a municipal power plant in Little Cottonwood Canyon (pictured during construction). Harry Haynes and John P. Cahoon, owners of the Murray Opera House, and three others had organized the Progress Power Company in 1897. By 1924, the city had obtained all of the private company's facilities. (MCM.)

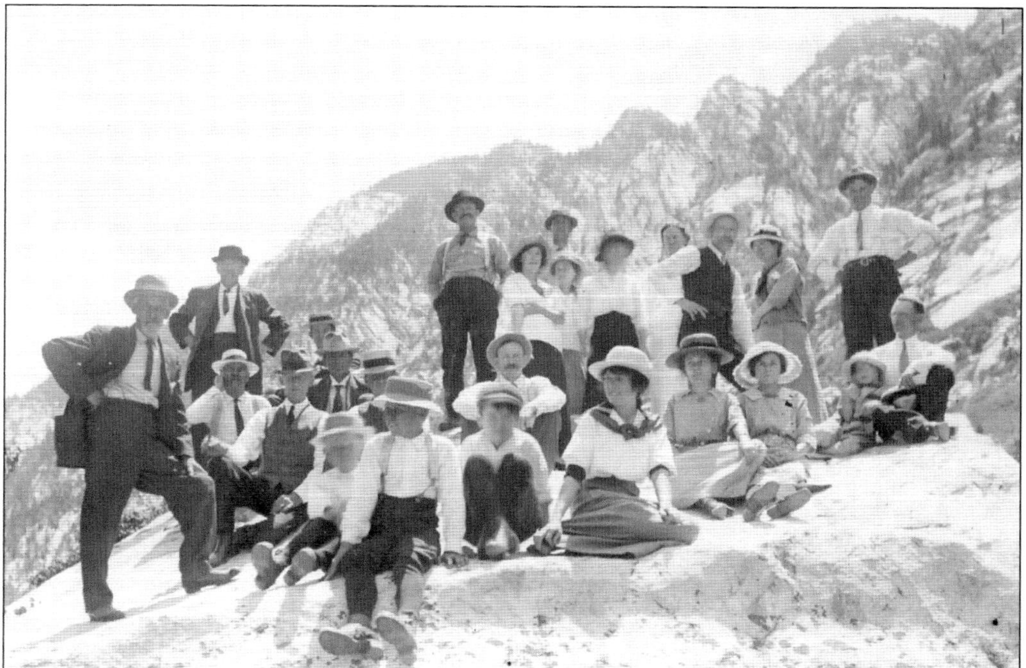

A group of Murray citizens poses atop an outcrop during an outing for the dedication ceremony of the Murray Power Plant, most likely in the late summer or fall of 1913. The location was at the mouth of the Little Cottonwood Canyon on the granite boulders near the water flume. (MCM.)

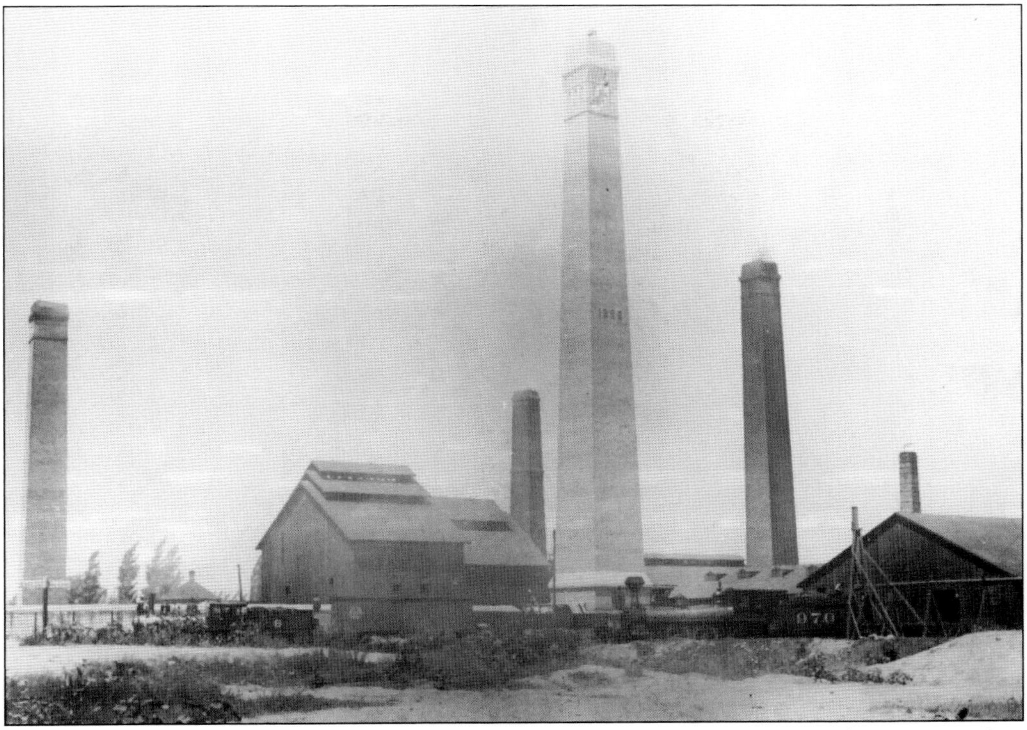

Improvements in electricity and rail transportation allowed the Germania Smelter to expand its operations in the late 19th century. The 175-foot "Germania Tower" smokestack was designed in 1896 to replace the numerous smaller chimneys at the plant. The construction cost $70,000 and used half a million bricks. The plant was sold to the American Smelting and Refining Company (ASARCO) in 1899. (USHS.)

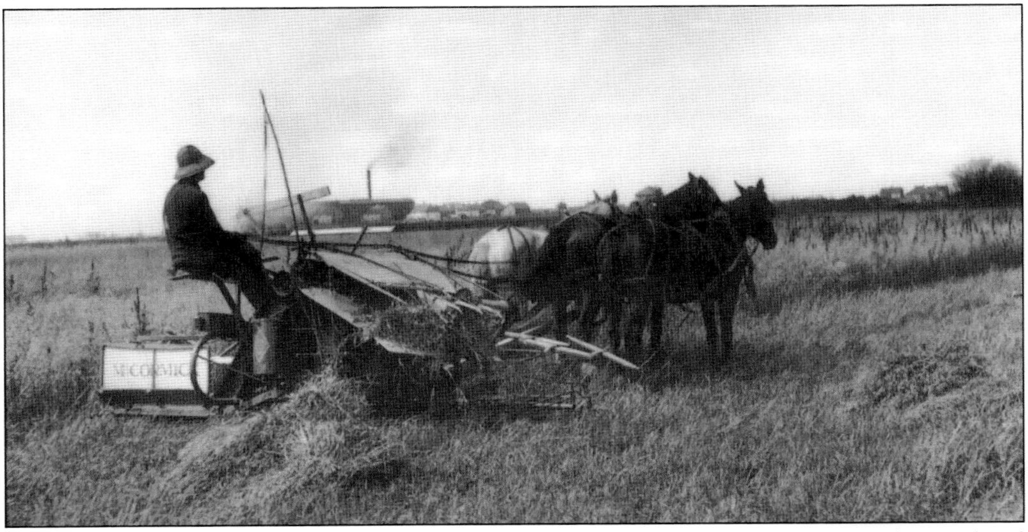

Toxins released by area smelters damaged crops and sickened livestock. In 1904 and 1906, local farmers won lawsuits against the heaviest polluters. The Highland Boy Smelter, located near the Jordan River, was forced to close in 1907. All that remains is the name of Bullion Street on Murray's west side. Highland Boy is pictured here in 1906 as seen from the farm of John Evans, one of the litigants. (USHS.)

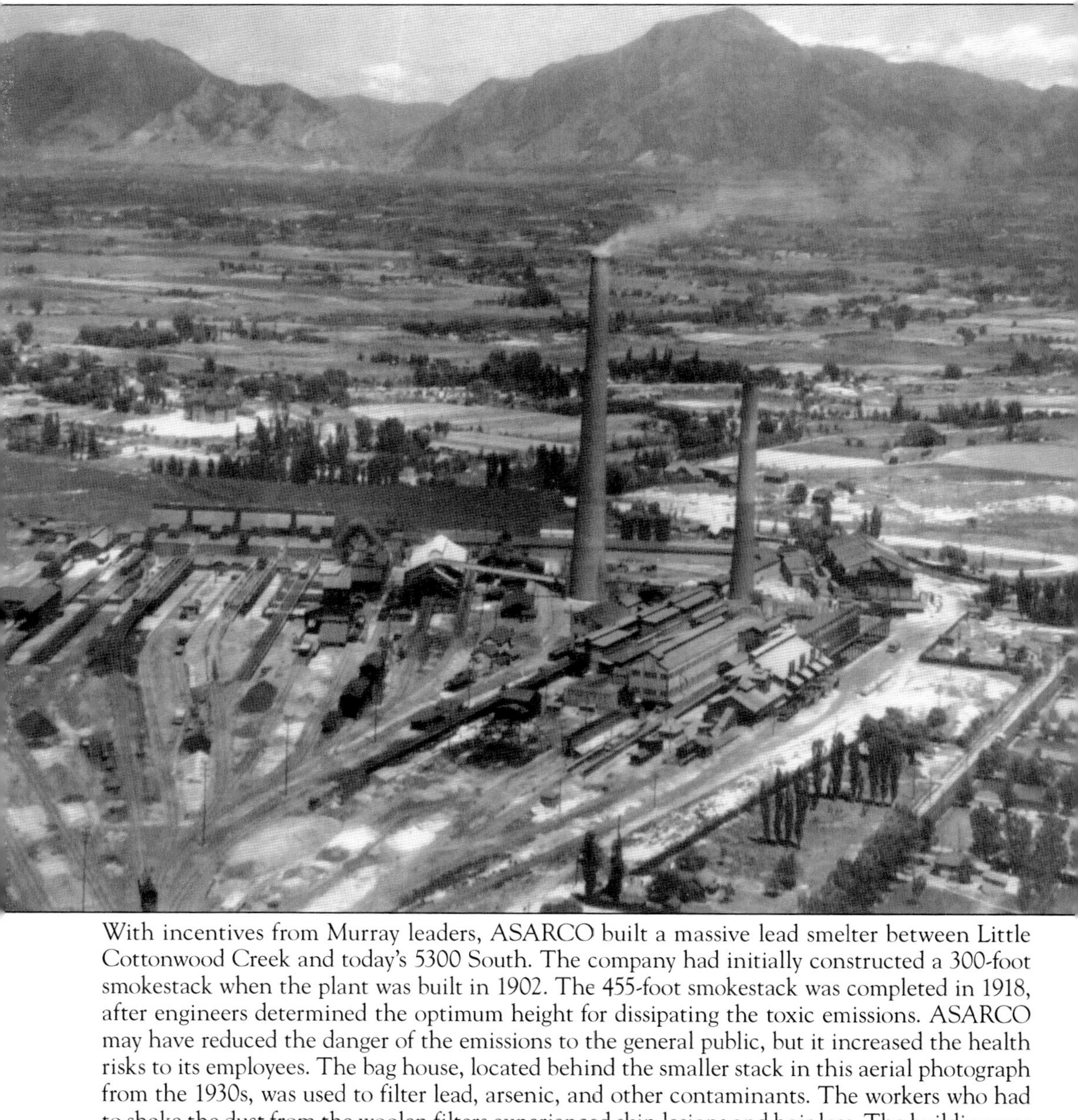

With incentives from Murray leaders, ASARCO built a massive lead smelter between Little Cottonwood Creek and today's 5300 South. The company had initially constructed a 300-foot smokestack when the plant was built in 1902. The 455-foot smokestack was completed in 1918, after engineers determined the optimum height for dissipating the toxic emissions. ASARCO may have reduced the danger of the emissions to the general public, but it increased the health risks to its employees. The bag house, located behind the smaller stack in this aerial photograph from the 1930s, was used to filter lead, arsenic, and other contaminants. The workers who had to shake the dust from the woolen filters experienced skin lesions and hair loss. The building was nicknamed "Hell Hole" for good reason. (USHS.)

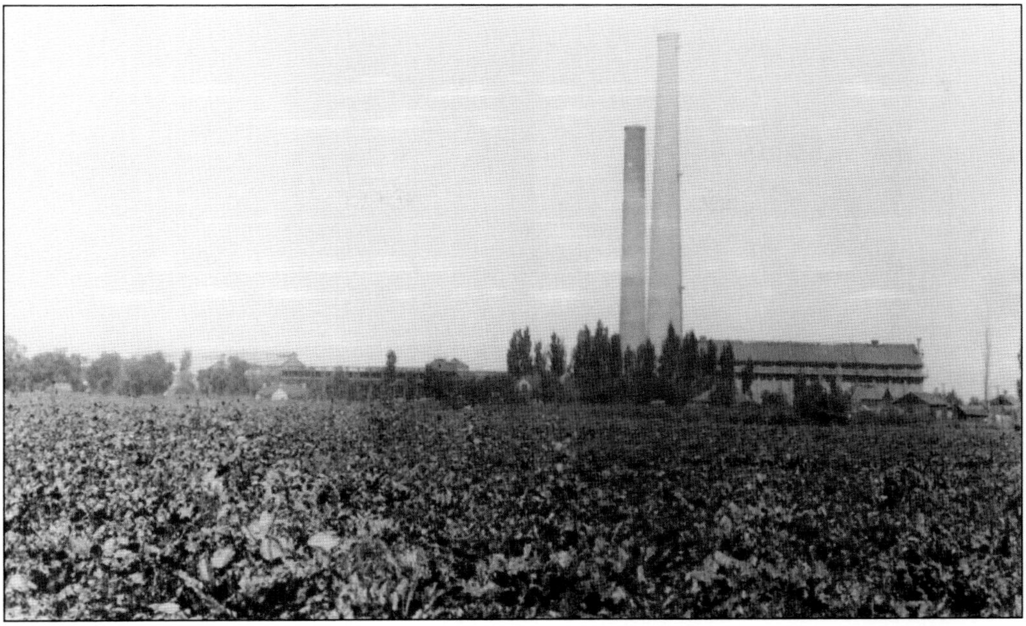

Smelter scientists conducted regular testing on crops and established experimental farms for observation and demonstration in the 1910s and 1920s. The former Winchester homestead between Murray and Midvale was one example. This photograph shows affected sugar beet fields just south of ASARCO. The sugar beet was one of the most important cash crops in the early 20th century. Beets grown in Murray were shipped to West Jordan for processing. (MCM.)

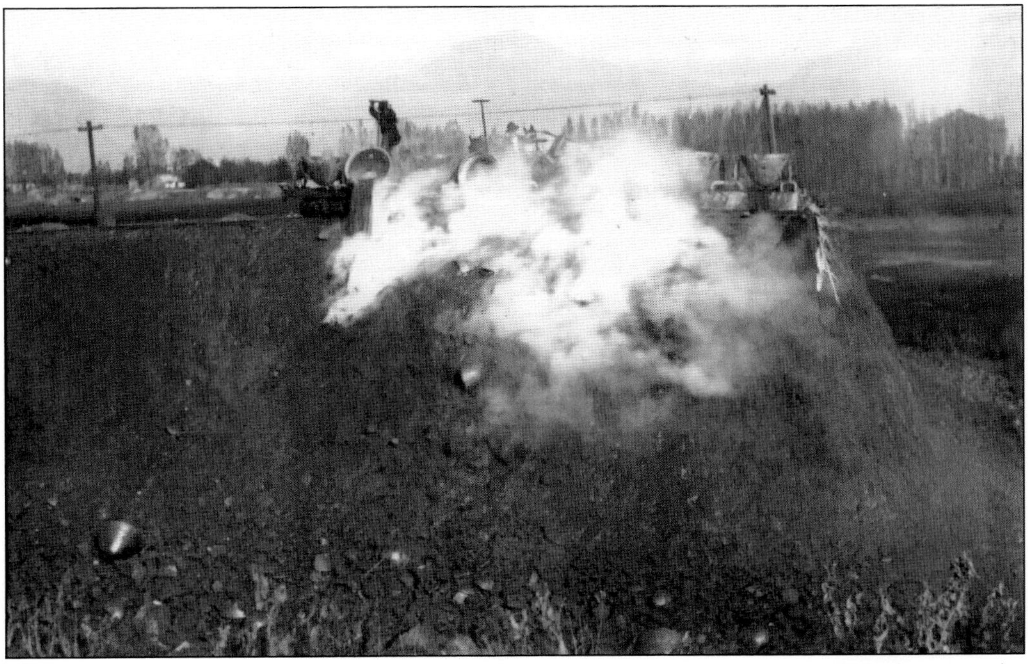

For many years, one of the most exciting scenes in Murray was the sight of workers dumping the molten by-products of ore processing onto the growing slag heap north of the smelter on the west side of State Street. Particularly at night, the molten slag would glow orange against the purple-black night—colors Murray High School would later adopt. (USHS.)

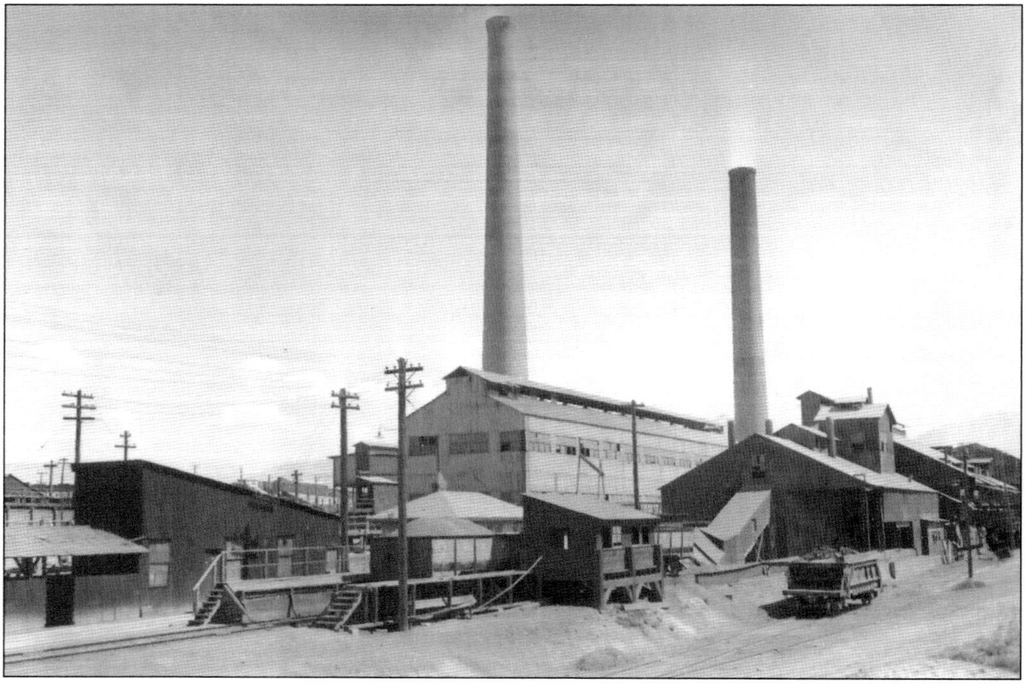

In the early 1900s, ASARCO's Murray plant (pictured in 1939) was the most up-to-date and largest lead smelter in the world, with a capacity of 1,200 tons of lead per day processed in eight blast furnaces. The ore smelted at the facility came from Utah mining districts as well as mines in all of the western United States. (USHS.)

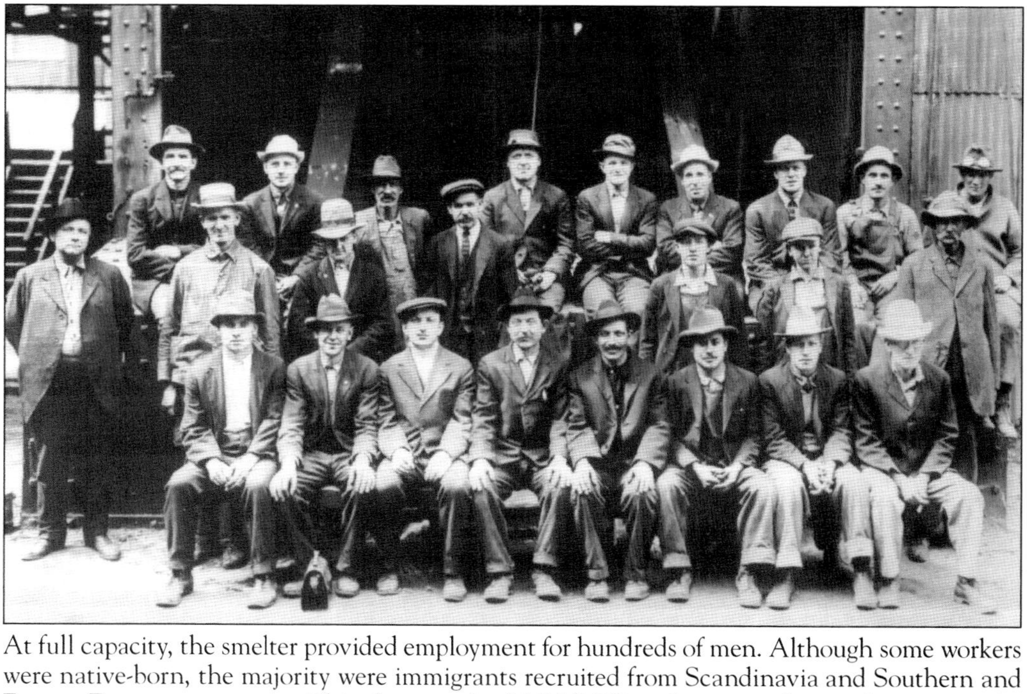

At full capacity, the smelter provided employment for hundreds of men. Although some workers were native-born, the majority were immigrants recruited from Scandinavia and Southern and Eastern European countries. This photograph of ASARCO workers was taken in the 1910s at the peak of immigration from Greece, Italy, Sweden, Austria, and the Slavic countries. (MCM.)

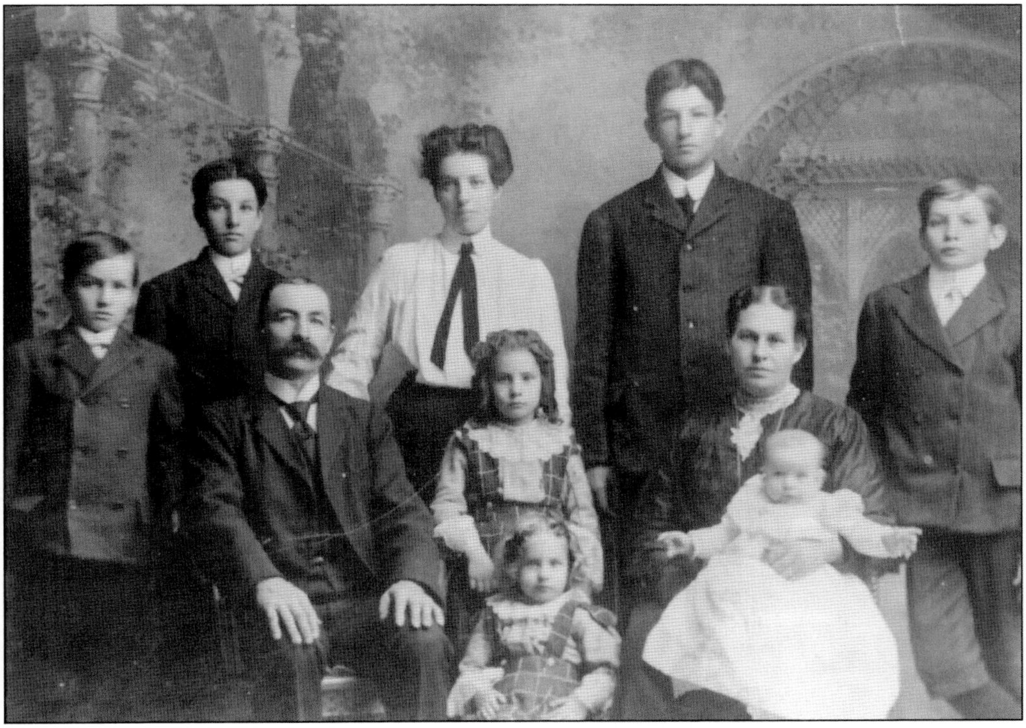

Anna Melvina Johnson was born in South Cottonwood. She married Rangvald Carlsen in 1886, and they lived in the Fort Union area south and east of Murray. This photograph, taken in 1909, shows the family with eight of their 12 children. Rangvald worked for the US Smelter in Midvale for 41 years. Three of their sons became smelter workers in Murray. From left to right are Ernest, Rudolf, and Archie Carlsen, pictured around 1910 while working for either the Midvale or Murray smelter. Rudolf married Clara Eckman in 1907, and they built a home on State Street near the south border of Murray. Rudolf worked at the ASARCO for 34 years before transferring to the Midvale smelter for 10 more years. (Both, MCM.)

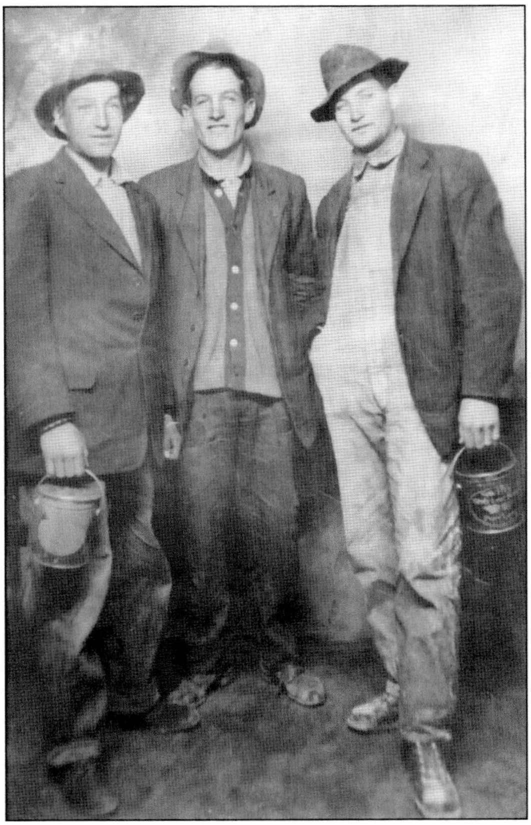

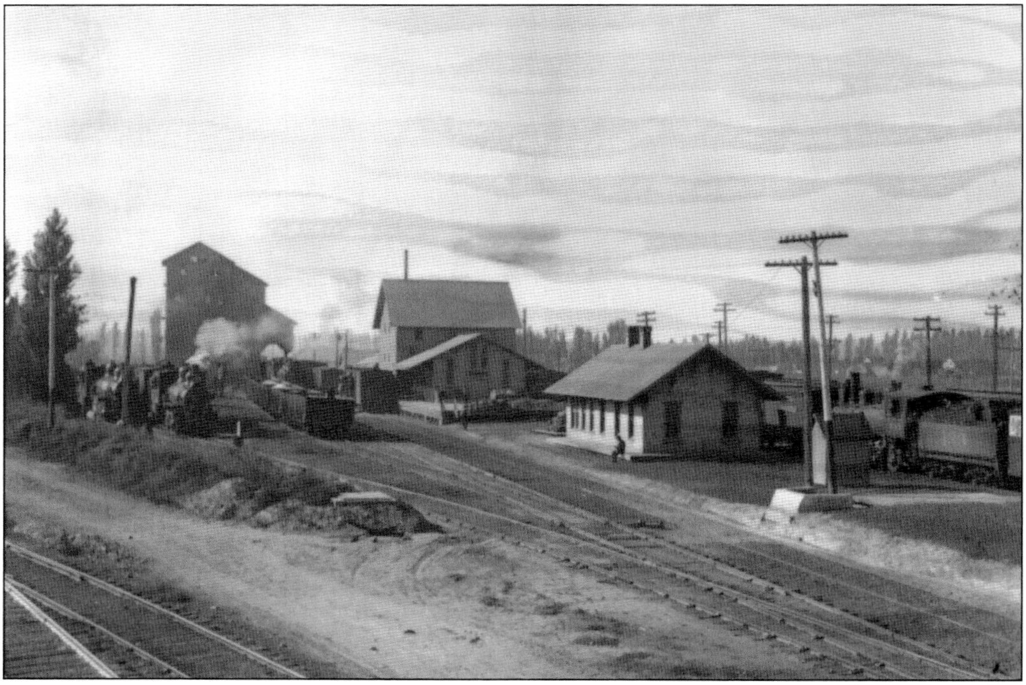

A 1906 photograph of the Taylor & Brunton ore sampling mill by noted Utah photographer Harry Shipler shows the vital importance of the railroad to the smelting industry in Murray. Train cars filled with ore would be brought to this facility to be evaluated and sorted before processing at the ASARCO smelter. (USHS.)

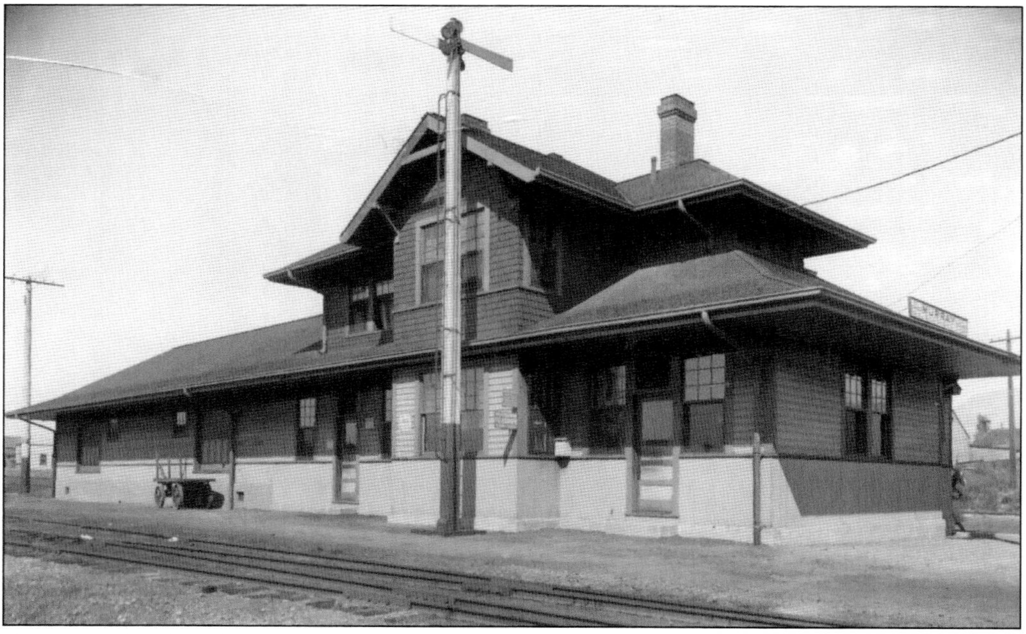

Harry Shipler also photographed the Murray City Depot of the Denver & Rio Grande Western Railroad around 1910. Built for both passengers and freight, this building was larger and grander than the older Oregon Short Line Depot, located on the parallel tracks to the east. Both depots were located near today's 4800 South. (USHS.)

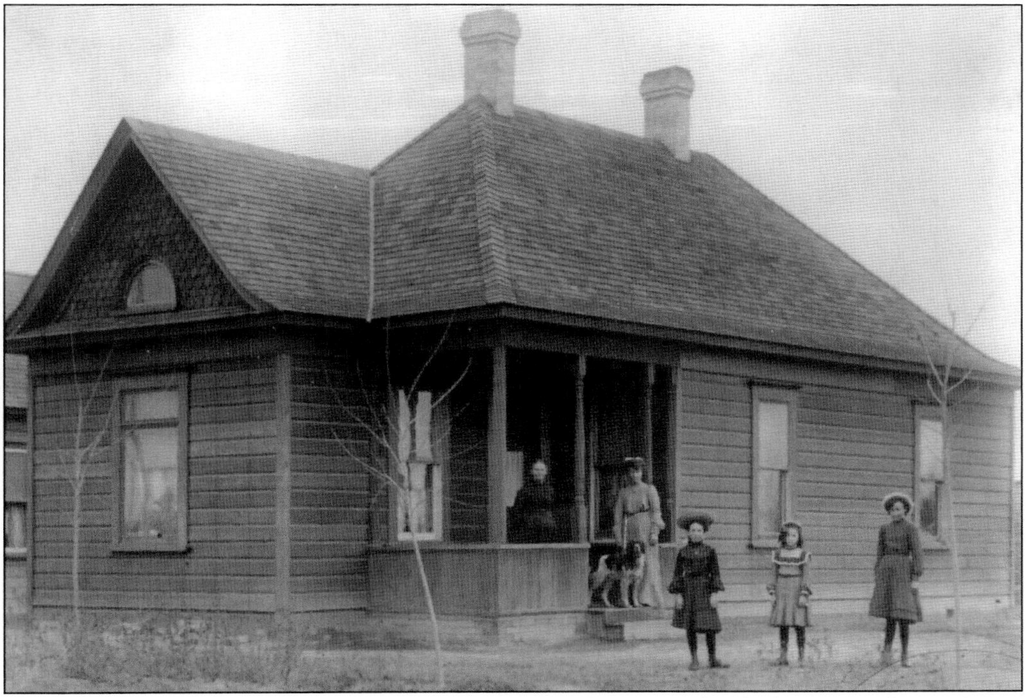

Edwin and Desdemona Fox Brown originally lived on the Brown family farm east of State Street but later moved to 4800 South and 200 West, where they built a boardinghouse for railroad and smelter workers. This photograph of their family home, with Desdemona Brown on the porch, was taken around 1900. (MCM.)

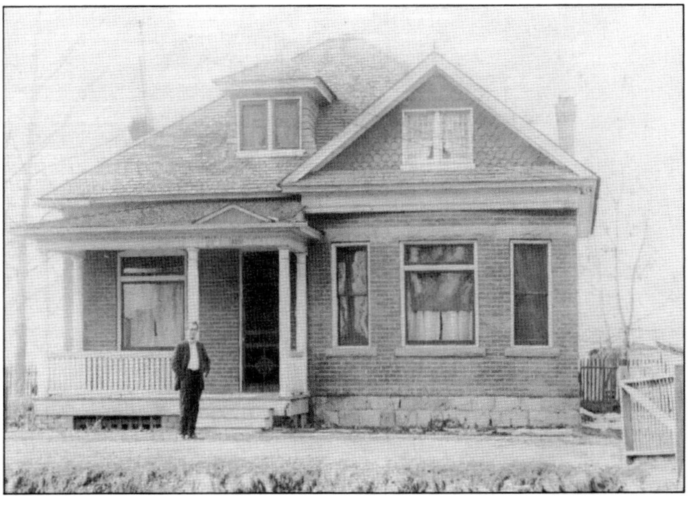

Daniel Towler, and his wife, Sarah Ann Dunford, ran a boardinghouse near their home on State Street, at the northern boundary of Murray. In the 1900 census, 16 men are listed as living at the boardinghouse, mostly employed as day laborers. By the 1910 census, the Towlers had retired with a comfortable income. In this photograph, Daniel stands in front of the family home around 1905. (IDUP.)

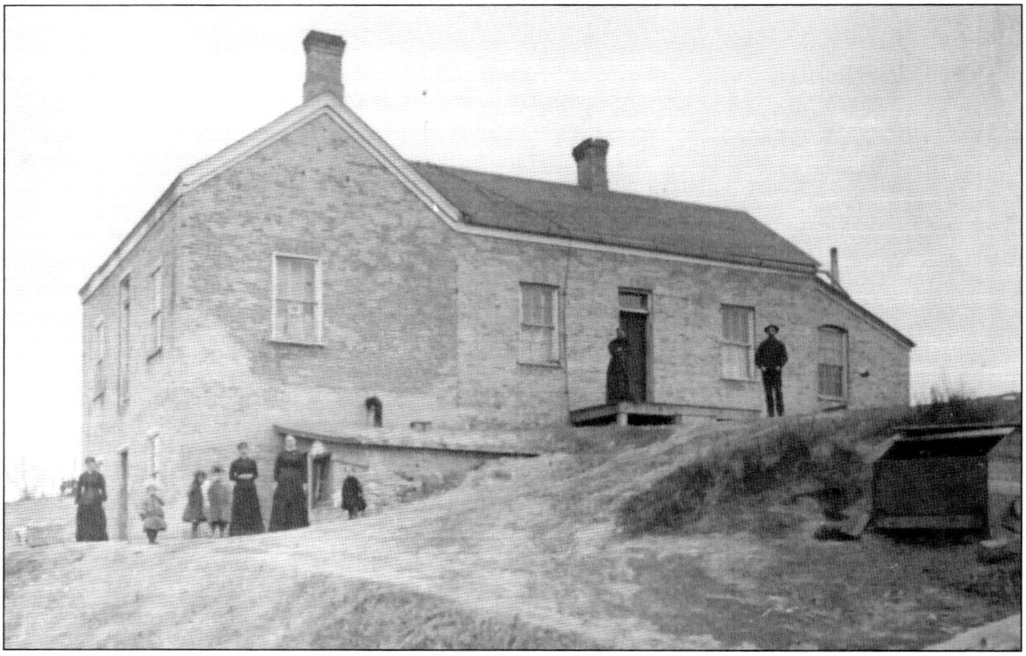

John Berger, a son of early Swiss settlers Christian and Magdalena Zaugg Berger, built a group of homes on a hill at the southwest corner of State Street and 5300 South. The house pictured here around 1900 was later occupied by John Glavas, a Greek immigrant who married John Berger's daughter Alice. John Glavas worked at the smelter but was also a tailor. (MCM.)

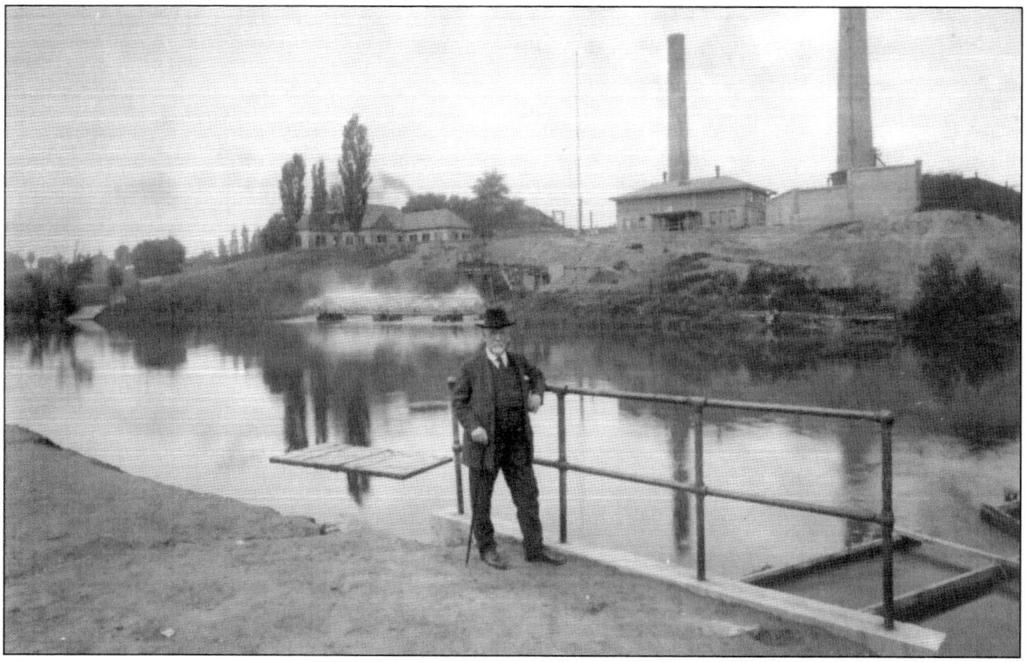

This photograph from about 1910 features John Wood posing in front of the smelter pond on State Street. His former home, which was used for the smelter office after ASARCO purchased his land, sits on the hill above him. Chris Glavas remembers trying to catch perch in the smelter pond as a young boy. (MCM.)

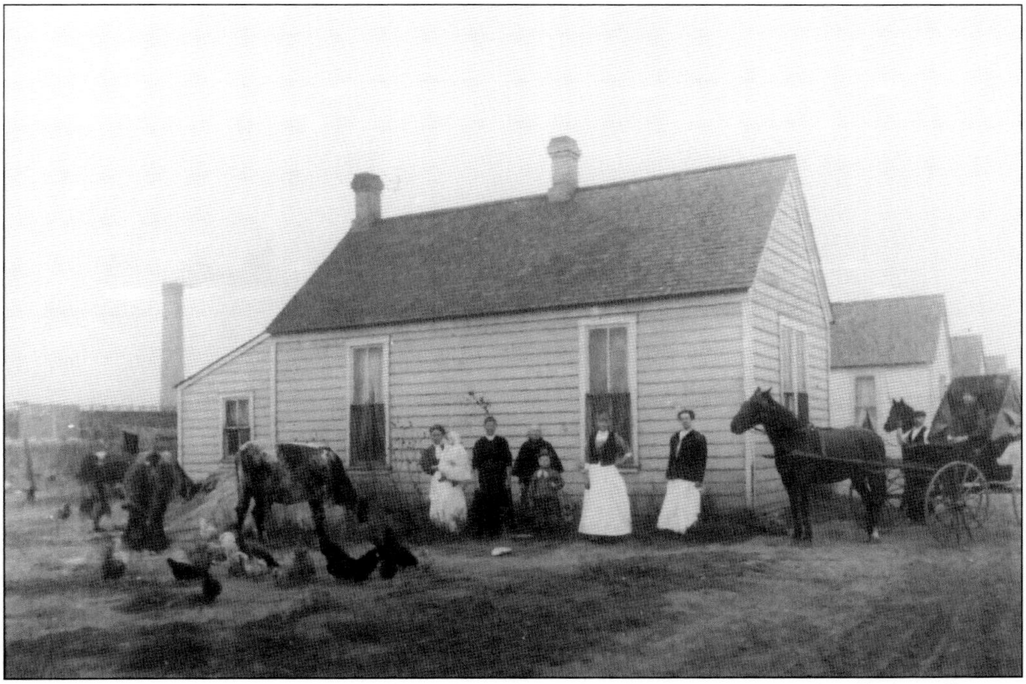

Many of Murray's immigrant families lived in substandard housing. In an early effort to alleviate the problem, the Berger family built 20 cottages and a recreation hall north of the Germania Lead Works. In 1910, John Wood built 12 cottages south of the ASARCO smelter. This photograph shows the cottages on Woodrow Street soon after construction. Only a handful of the homes survive today. (MCM.)

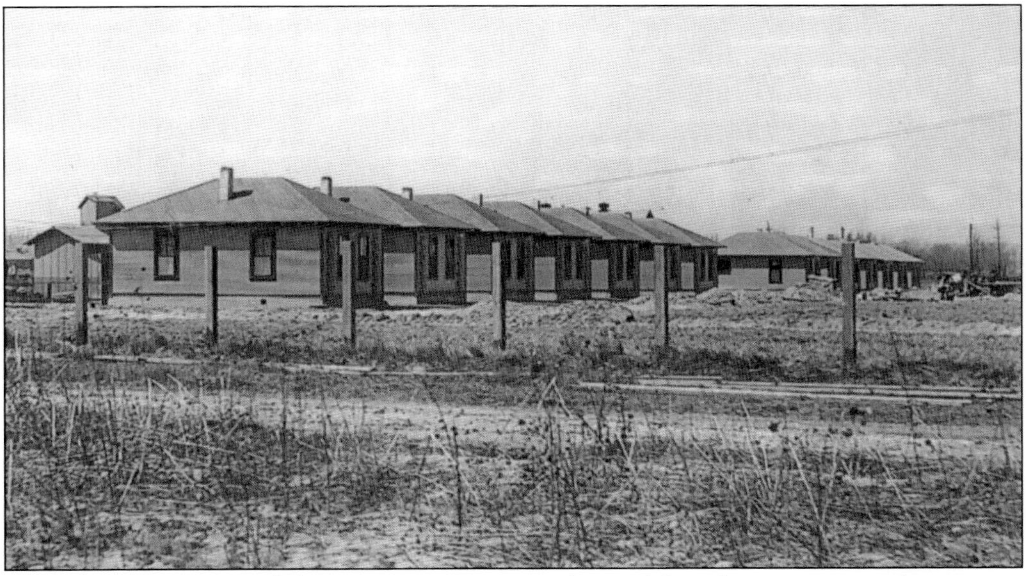

In 1911, ASARCO responded to community outrage at the squalid conditions present in shantytowns nestled near the slag heap by building 14 worker cottages on land west of Woodrow Street, nicknamed the community center (shown in 1918). The company provided the residents with a clubhouse and garden plots. In the early years, residents were not obligated to pay rent when the smelter was idle. (MCM.)

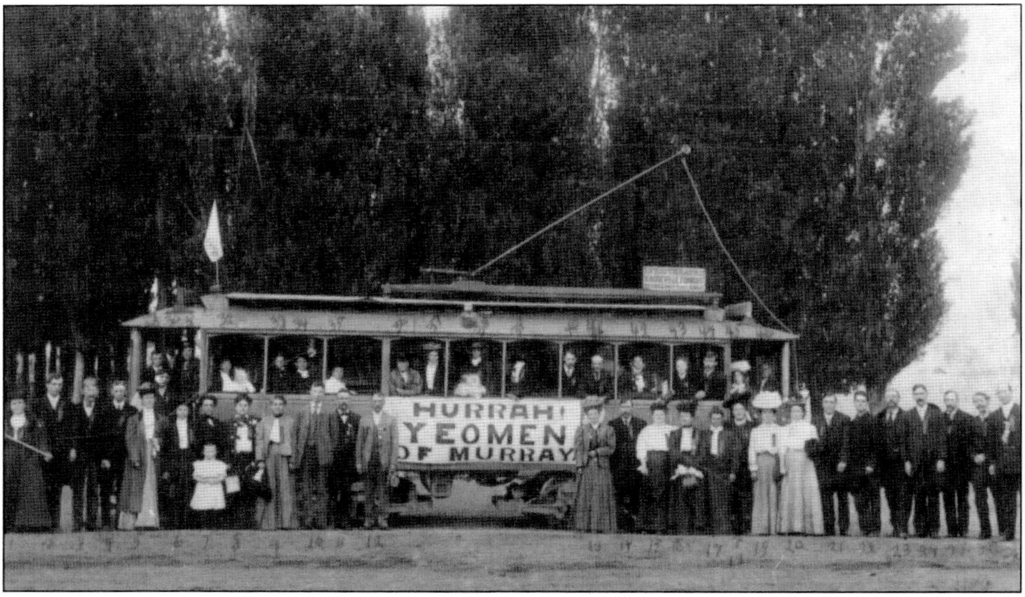

The electric streetcar, or trolley, line connected Murray to Salt Lake City between 1893 and 1933. Olga Johnson Reading remembered dodging both the streetcar and herds of longhorn cattle during her walk to school on State Street as a little girl in the late 1890s. The Yeomen of Murray are pictured here around 1900 on an outing to Salt Lake City. (MCM.)

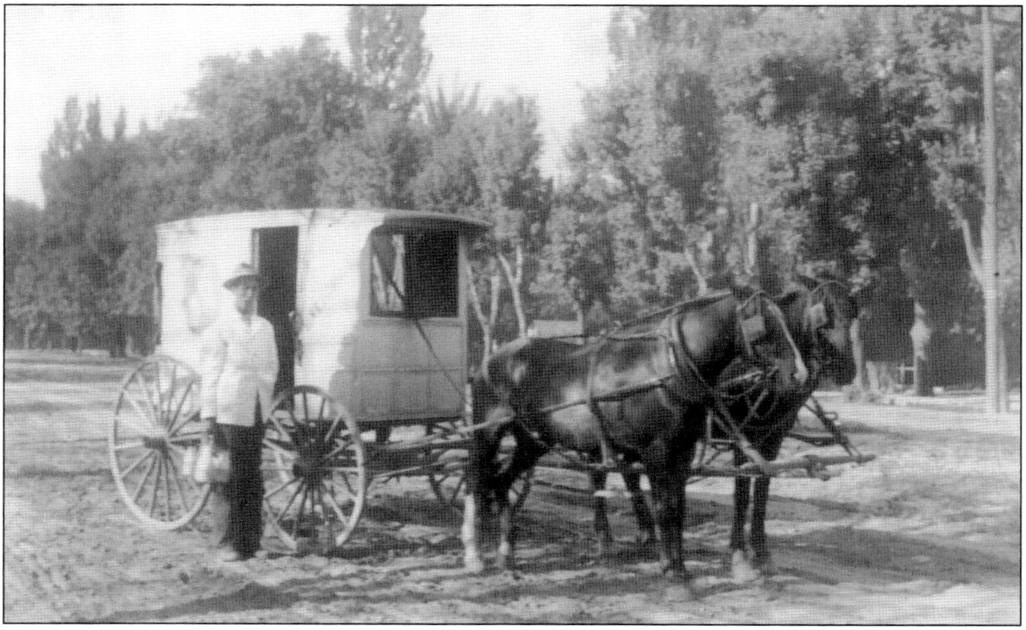

While State Street was a hive of activity at the turn of the 20th century, the east side of Murray transformed into a corridor of dairy farms. The farms were operated by a number of families, many of whom were related—Erekson, Wheeler, Howe, Huffaker, Jensen, Daw, Herman, and Gerrard to name a few. Pictured here around 1900 is an unidentified man delivering ice and milk. (MCM.)

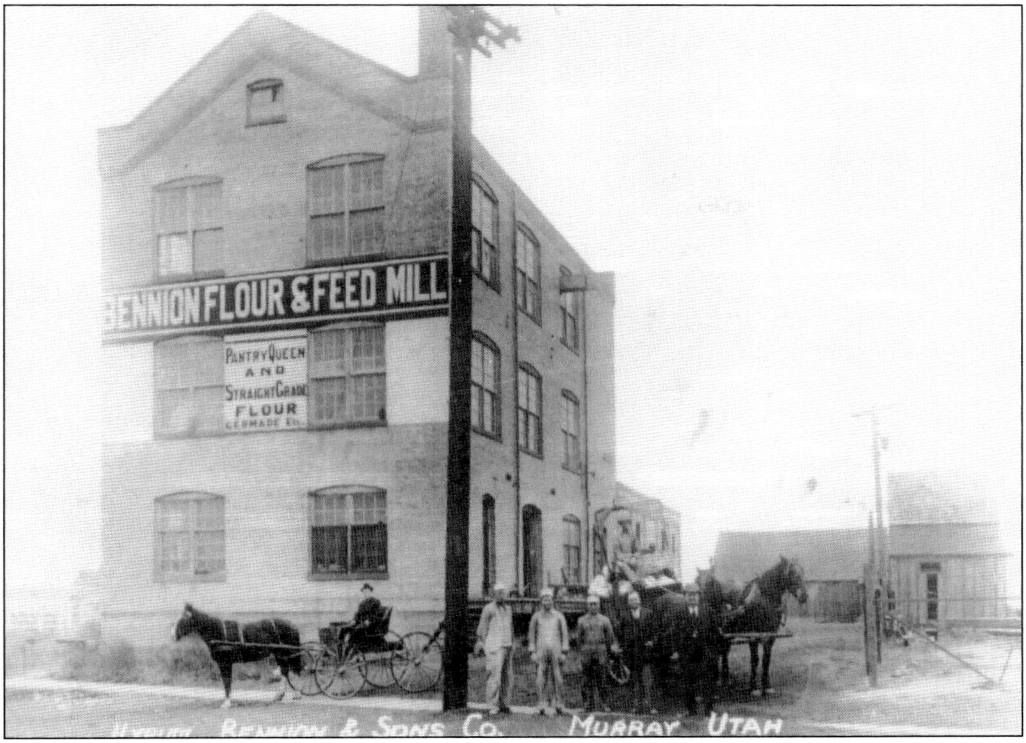

After a fire destroyed his flour mill on the Jordan River in Taylorsville, Hyrum Bennion built a brick mill near the railroads on 4800 South in Murray in 1909. A small hydroelectric plant at the former river site was used to power the mill. Bennion used the excess electricity to light his Taylorsville home along with several neighboring houses. The Bennion Flour & Feed Mill (pictured above around 1910) switched to Murray City power in 1913 and was one of the city's first industrial customers. The Jones-Olson & Company Coal & Lumber Company (pictured below around 1915) was the first of a number of early businesses located on the north side of 4800 South, east of the Bennion mill. (Above, USHS; below, MCM.)

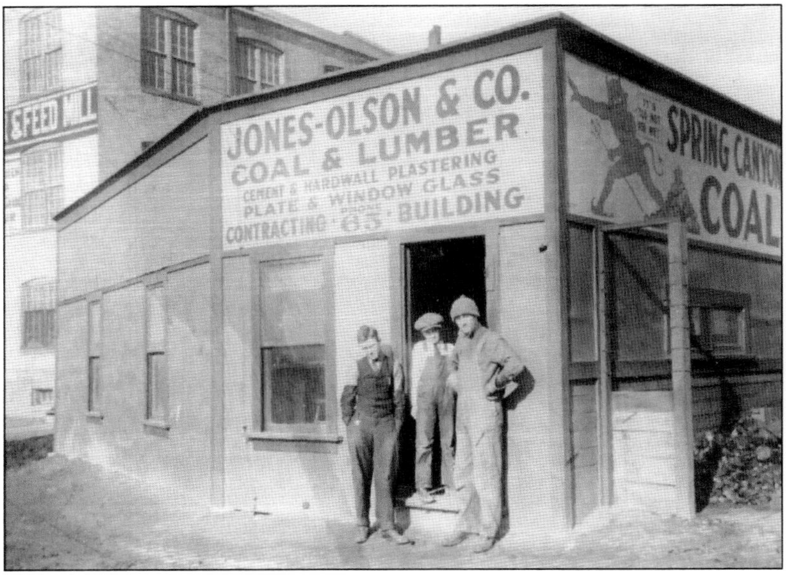

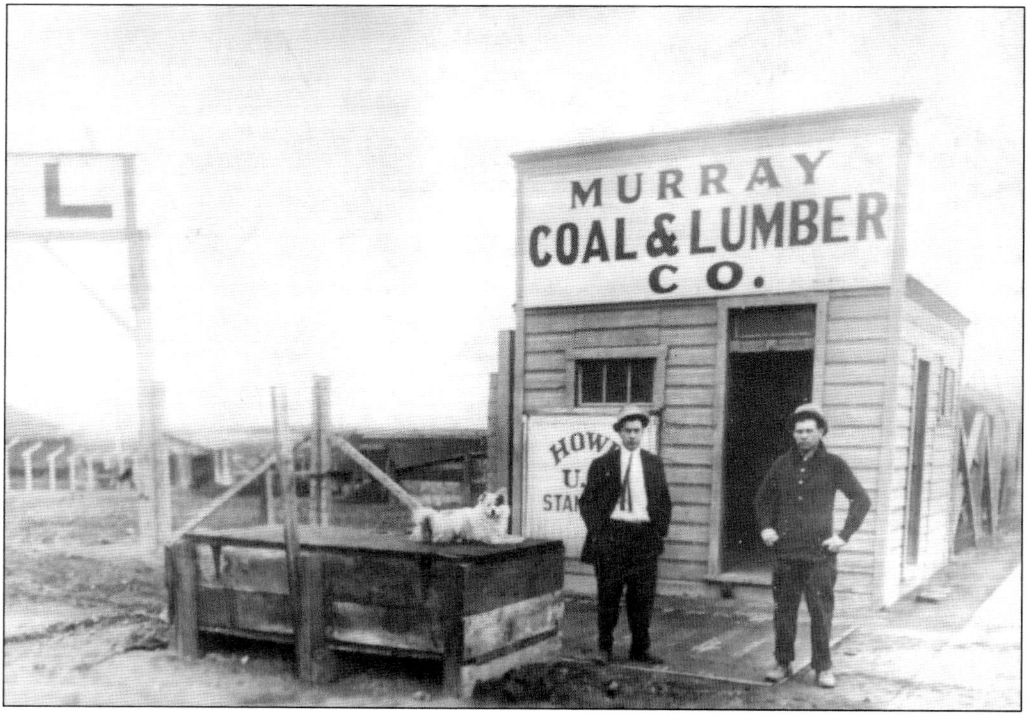

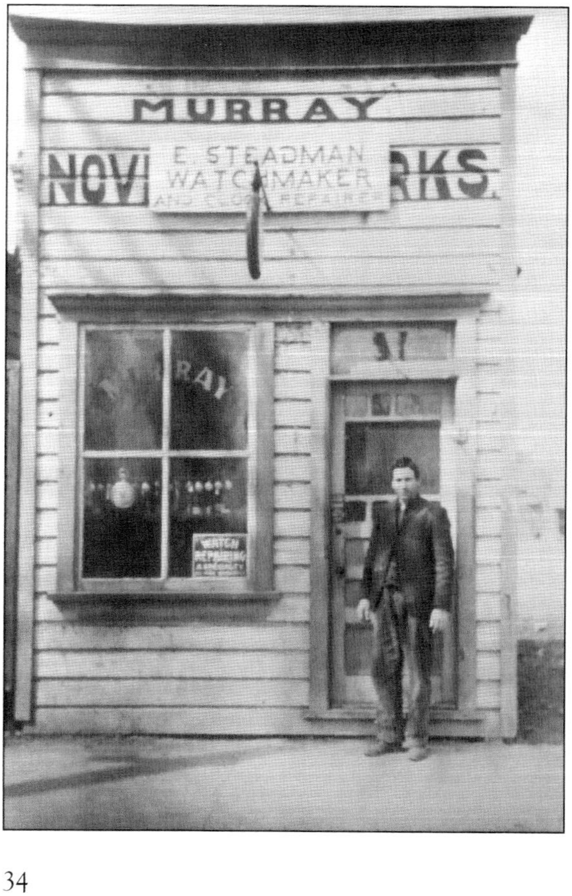

Like many businessmen, Frank C. Howe made use of the Murray name when he built the rival Murray Coal & Lumber Company yard on the south side of 4800 South. At least four lumberyards operated in this area. Howe's employee Arthur Hobbs (right) and an unidentified friend and dog are pictured here around 1915. (MCM.)

Taylorsville resident Edward Steadman was a self-taught watch- and clockmaker. He opened a shop in Murray on 4800 South in 1904. His son Virgil continued the family business in a more prestigious location, in the Harker Building on State Street. Today, Steadman Jewelry is still in business on West 4800 South in Taylorsville. (MCM.)

The Utah Fireclay Company's brickyard in Murray made specialty bricks. This photograph of workers and kilns was taken around the time Alexander Wilson became the superintendent in 1914. He managed Murray Fireclay until its closure in the 1930s. The former brickyard site is now an apartment complex near the Murray North light-rail line. (MCM.)

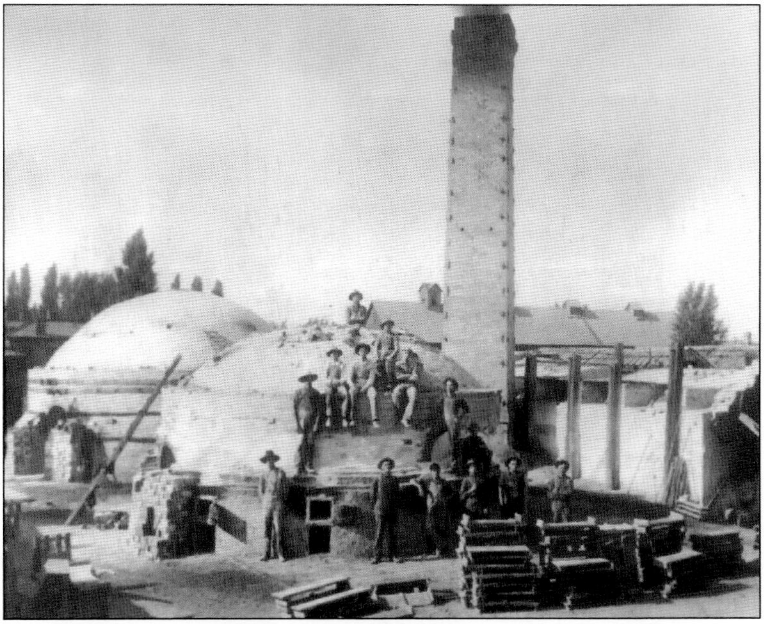

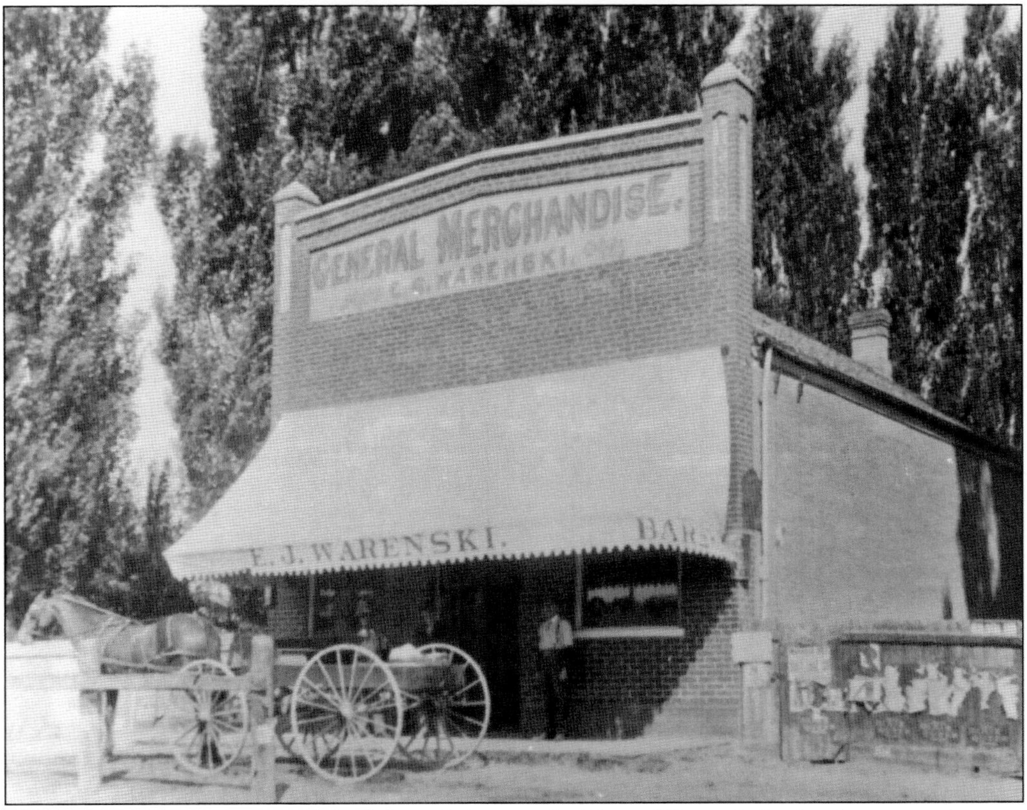

English Polish immigrants Edward C. and Susannah Albion Warenski built a home on the east side of State Street in 1856, in an area that would later be the center of the historic downtown. Edward and his son E.J. Warenski operated a general merchandise store and saloon in one of the earliest brick storefronts in the city, pictured here around 1895. (MCM.)

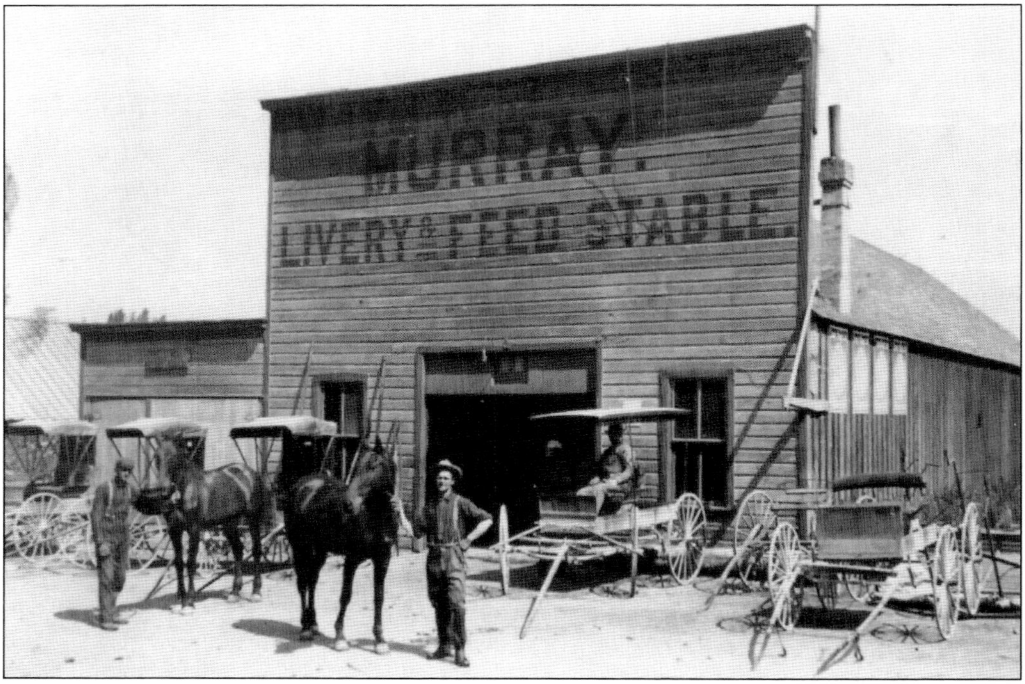

Murray was an enterprising town with name recognition. George W. Granter called his business the Murray Livery & Feed Stable in 1902. His sister Sarah Jane Granter married James P. Freeze, who donated much of the land for the Murray City Park. The livery business was on State Street, where the main entrance to the park is currently located. (MCM.)

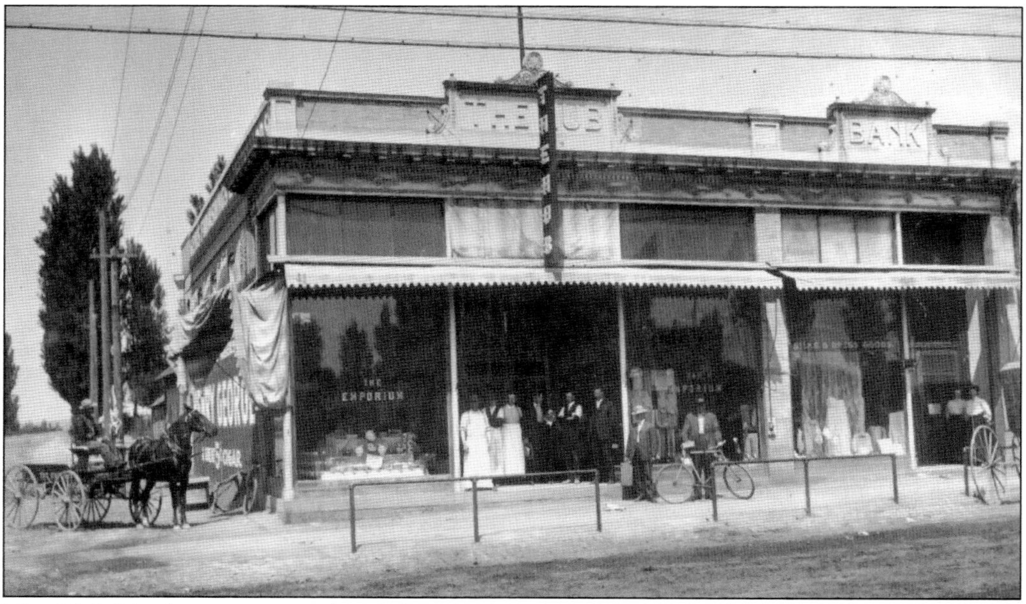

The Hub Block was a general merchandise store and bank, built in 1902–1903, located at approximately 5000 South on State Street. The building featured large plate-glass windows and a "shifting" electric sign. This photograph was taken after 1906, when the company was sold and renamed the Emporium. By this time, the store had expanded into the vacated bank space. (MCM.)

Pictured here in 1900, the family of William S. and Flora Bullock Turner was typical of Murray's small holding farm families. The Turners lived on 4500 South near Atwood Boulevard (formerly Bullock Lane). The family owned a large team of horses they used to help the community dig canals, build roads, and level land for the Murray City Cemetery. (MCM.)

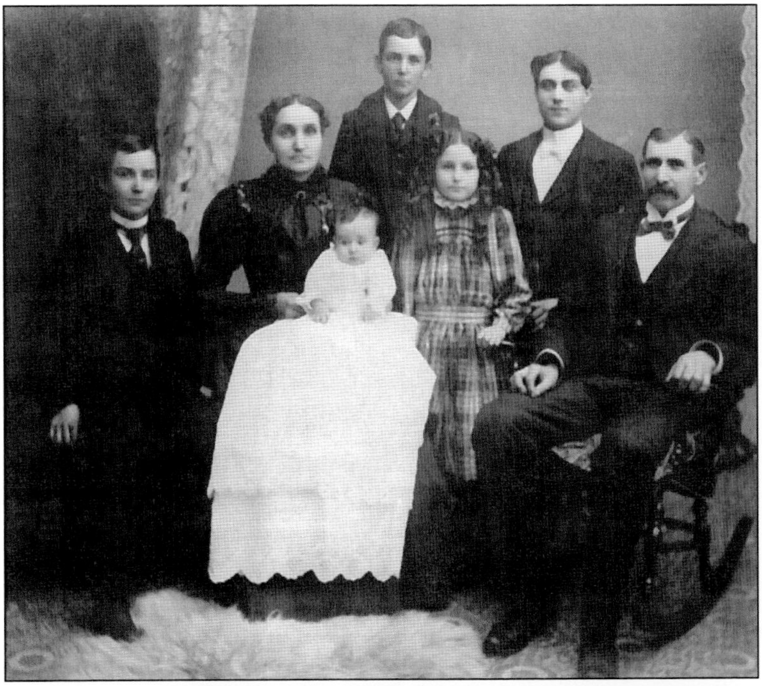

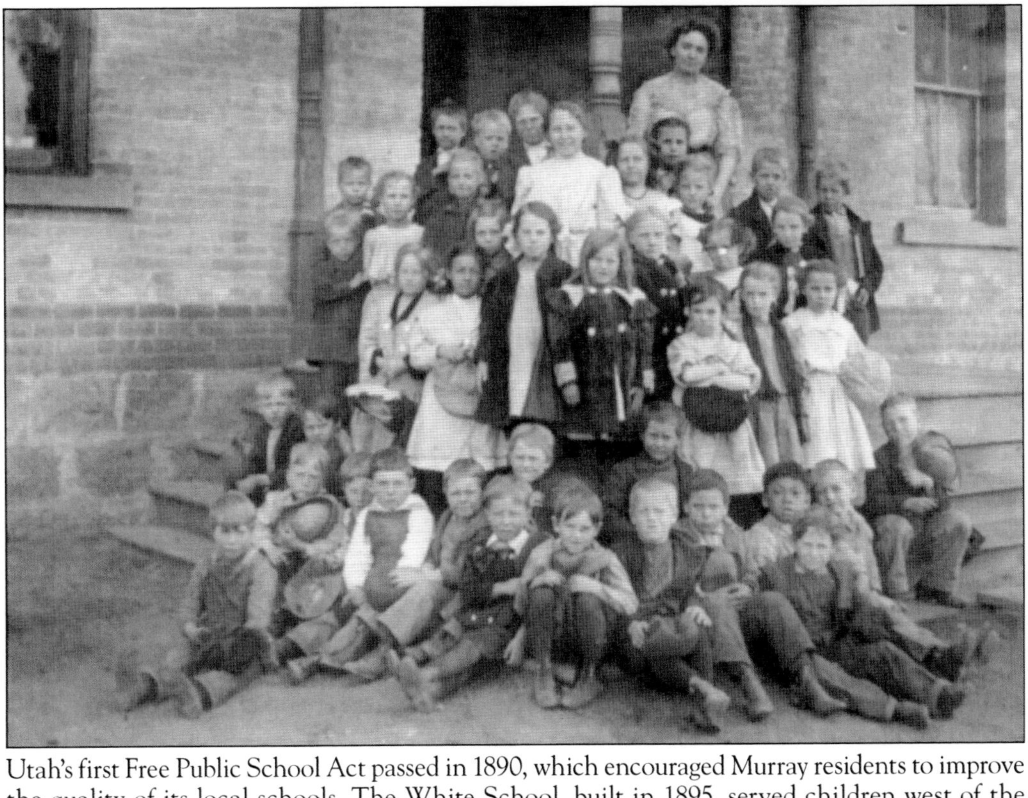

Utah's first Free Public School Act passed in 1890, which encouraged Murray residents to improve the quality of its local schools. The White School, built in 1895, served children west of the railroad tracks at approximately 5200 South and 300 West. This photograph was taken in 1907, one year after it was renamed the Pioneer School. (MCM.)

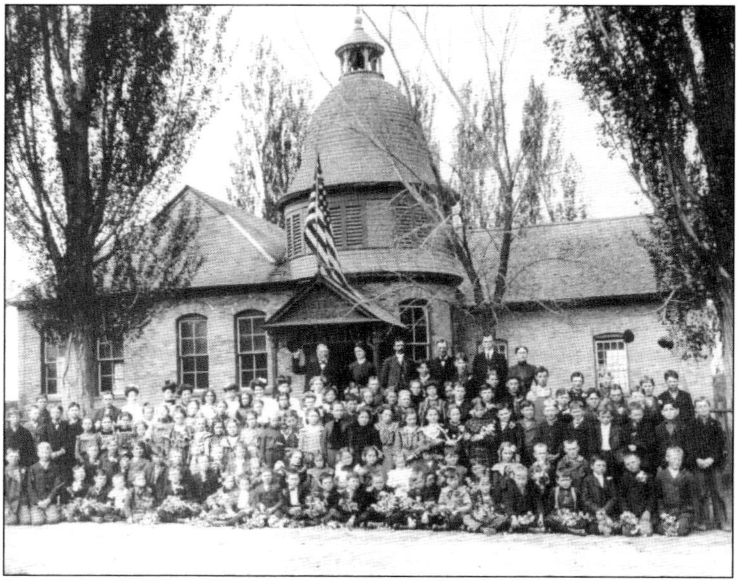

Shown here in the 1890s, the 26th District School, later called Woodstock, was the first of four school buildings located at 1300 East and Vine Street. The most recent Woodstock Elementary School was completed in 2011. Originally farmland, the surrounding neighborhoods were annexed into Murray between 2001 and 2003, but the school remains in the Granite School District. (MCM.)

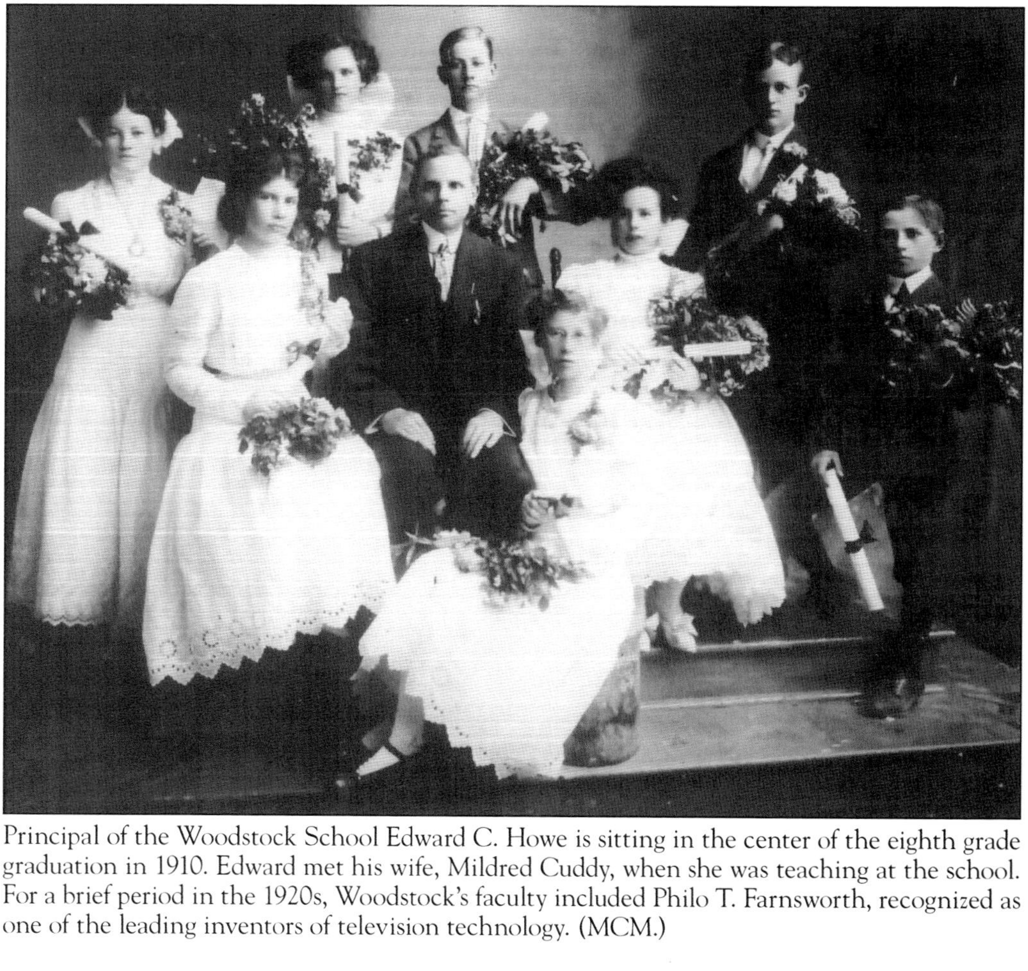

Principal of the Woodstock School Edward C. Howe is sitting in the center of the eighth grade graduation in 1910. Edward met his wife, Mildred Cuddy, when she was teaching at the school. For a brief period in the 1920s, Woodstock's faculty included Philo T. Farnsworth, recognized as one of the leading inventors of television technology. (MCM.)

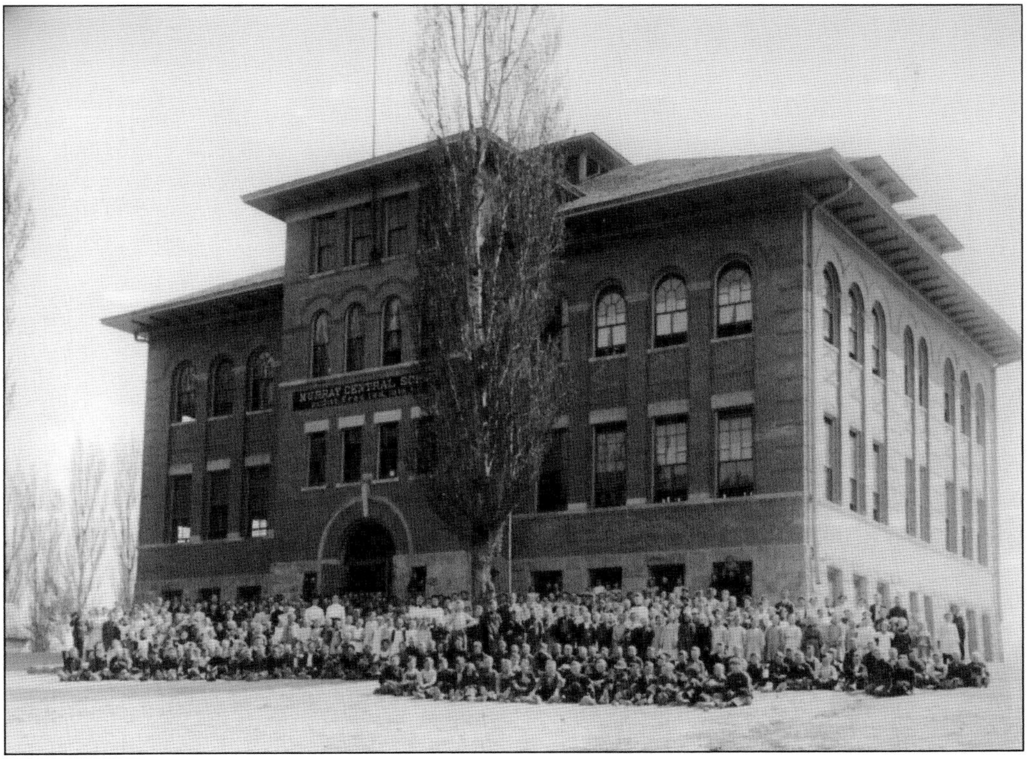

The imposing three-story Murray Central School was built to replace the overcrowded 25th District School in 1899. This photograph of the students and faculty may have been taken around 1903, when the building was finally completed. After the Murray School District was organized in 1905, a contest was held to rename the school. The name Arlington was chosen. (MCM.)

In this 1903 photograph, a Mr. Stephenson's fifth- or sixth-grade students sit quietly at their desks in the Murray Central School. Julia Vicchrilli remembered lining up for cod liver oil as a student. Although the building was reasonably comfortable, with electric lights and steam heat, Merle Hobbs did not have fond memories of the privies in a separate building that required a long wait until recess or dismissal. (MCM.)

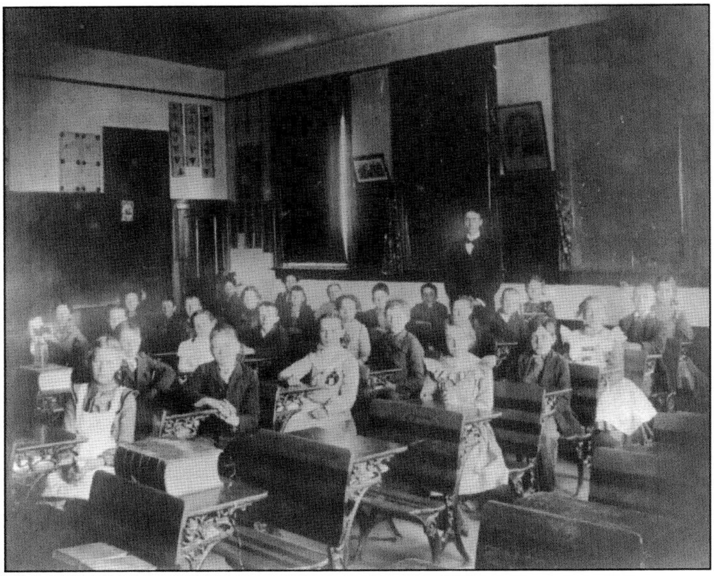

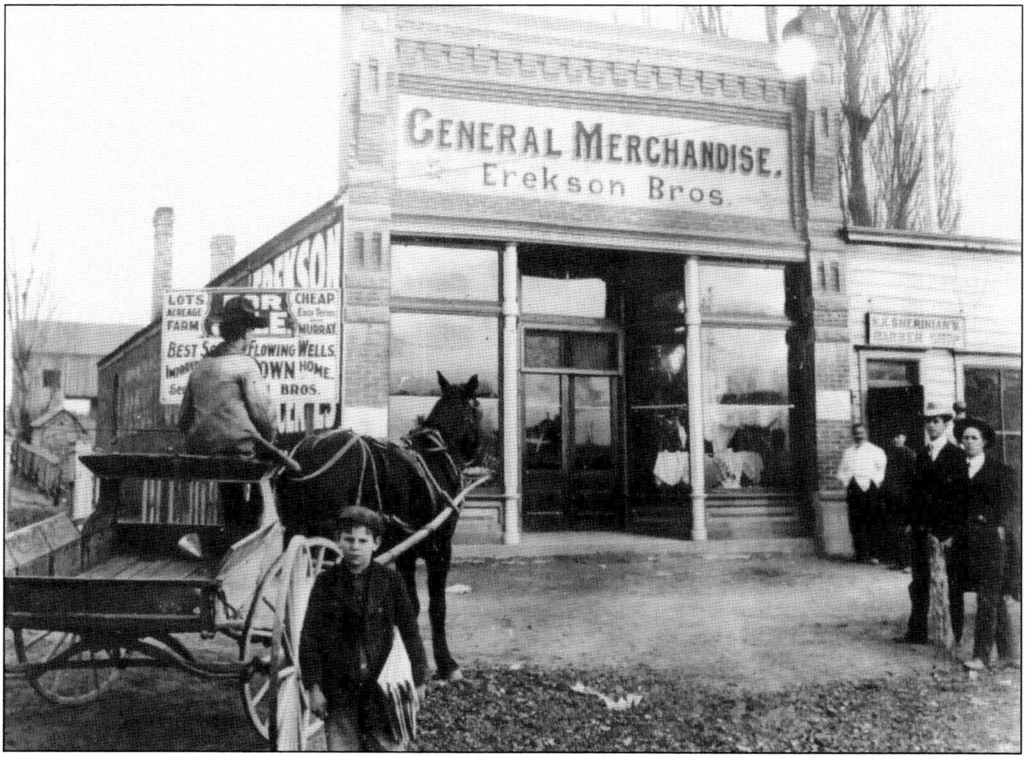

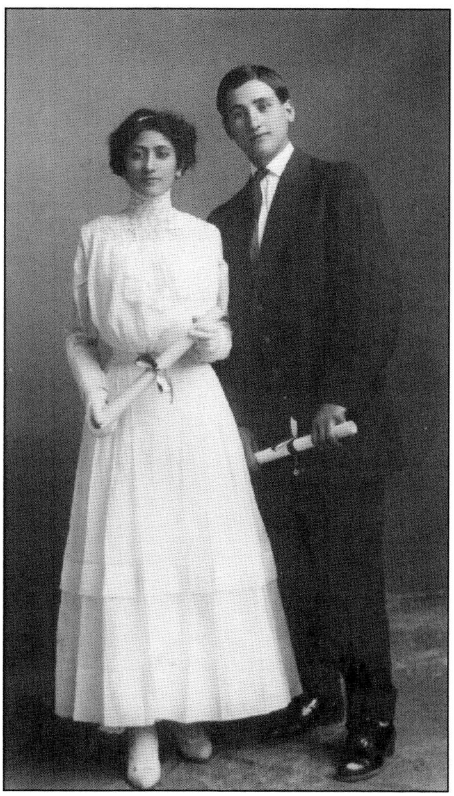

As longtime members of the LDS Church, the Armenian family of Nishan and Rebecca Sheranian emigrated from Turkey in 1902. Nishan "N.K." Sheranian established a barbershop next to the Erekson Bros. store (at right above). The family lived near 4800 South and 200 West. Six of the children attended Murray schools. Two of their eldest children, Arick (left) and Herond (right), are pictured at left at their eighth-grade graduation from Arlington School. Arick married Armanang Kezerian, who came to Murray in 1910 and worked at the smelter for 30 years. Herond earned pocket money by driving the buggy for Murray's first professional physician, Dr. Ferrebee. To help finance his education while attending medical school, Herond worked in the Murray smelter bag house for a short time. (Both, MCM.)

Joseph Sharich emigrated from Gospic in Croatia to work in the smelting industry with his brothers in 1907. He married Annie Margeras in 1918. In 1933, he quit the smelter to operate the UP Bar. Pictured here around 1925 are, from left to right Joseph, his brother Marko, friend Paul, and brother Matt (seated). (MCM.)

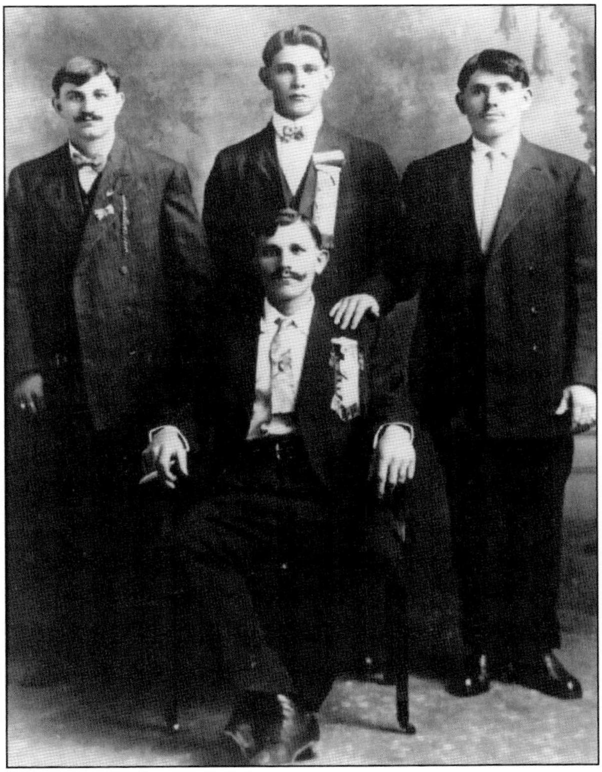

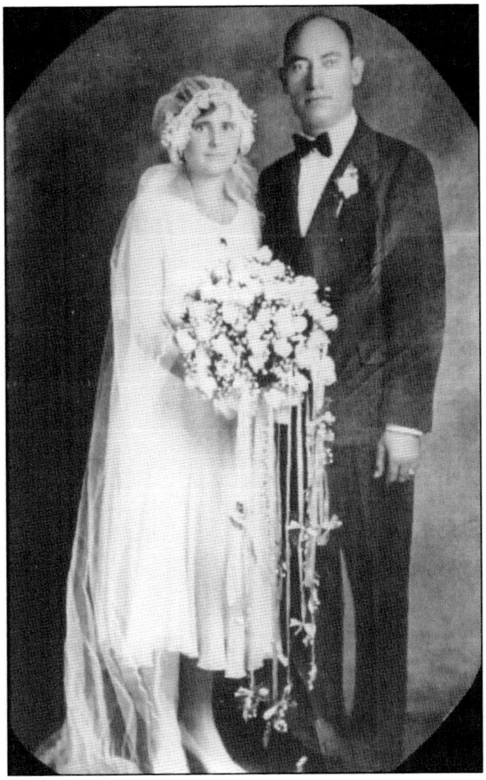

When George Petrogiannis relocated his wife and four children from Greece to Murray in 1909, the Greek population was primarily single men. The family Americanized their name to Peters. Their young son Tom learned English in three months and acted as interpreter for many of the newer immigrants. In 1930, Tom traveled to Cuba for a prearranged marriage with a girl from Greece, Angeline Polychronopoulous. They are pictured here. (MCM.)

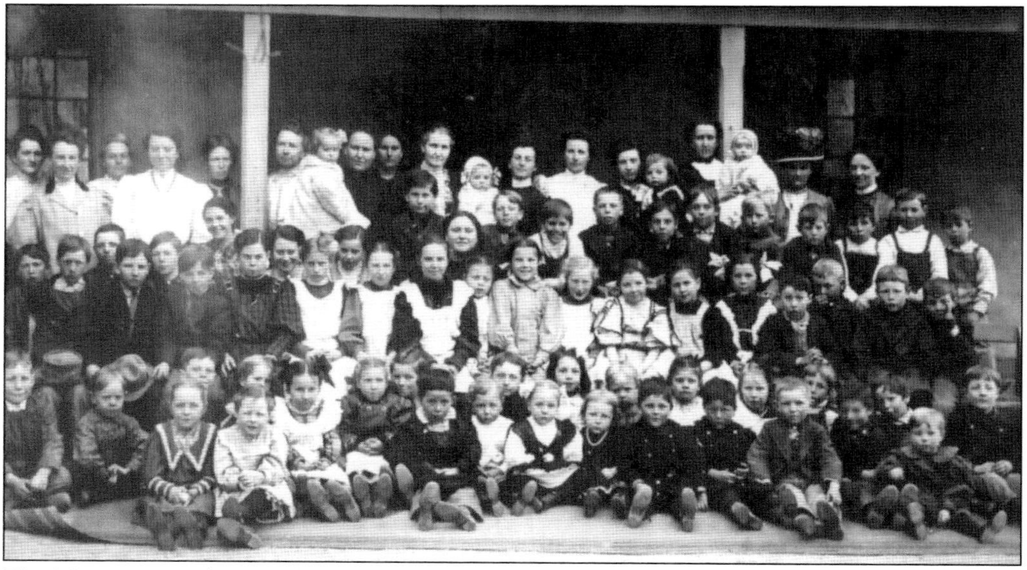

The Mormon population of Murray continued to increase through both immigration and a high birthrate, as seen in this 1908 photograph of the South Cottonwood Ward Primary, the LDS Church's religious program for young children. New buildings were built for the Murray First and Murray Second Wards in 1906 and the Grant Ward in 1912. For a time, an unofficial Swedish branch met on Murray's west side. (MCM.)

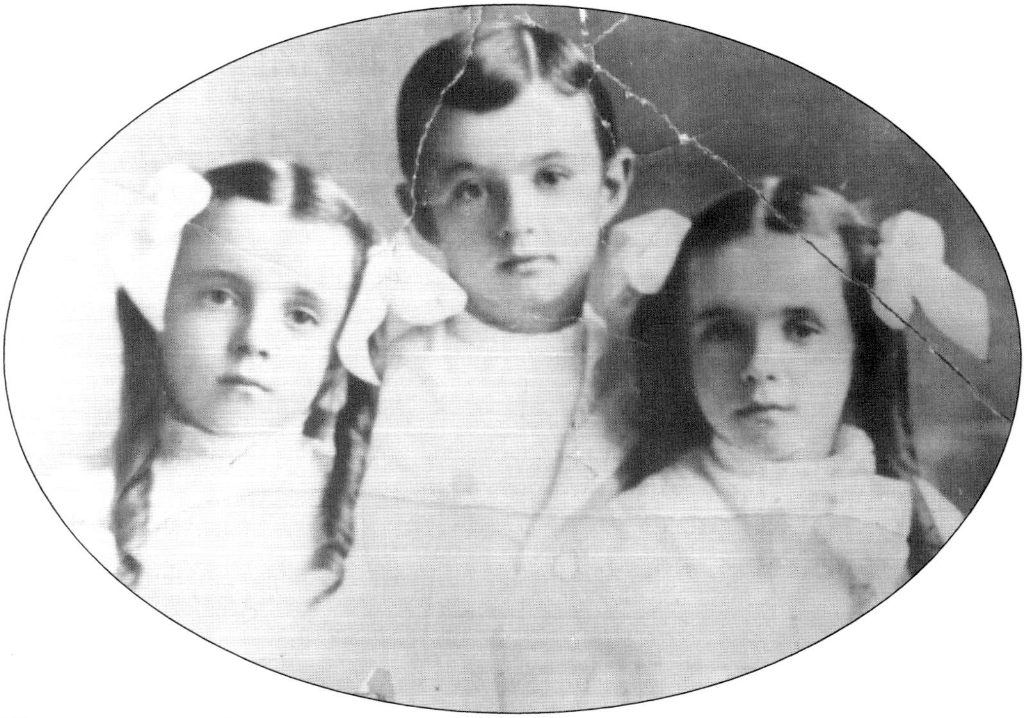

When premature triplets were born to Michael and Charlottie Mauss in August 1900, their father placed them in a shoebox on the family stove to keep them warm. The Mauss triplets were exhibited at the Utah State Fair in 1907, when this photograph was taken. Remarkably, Velma Mauss (Torp) (left), Vinal Mauss (center), and Vilda Mauss (Hughes) lived into their 90s. (MCM.)

Three

The Independent City

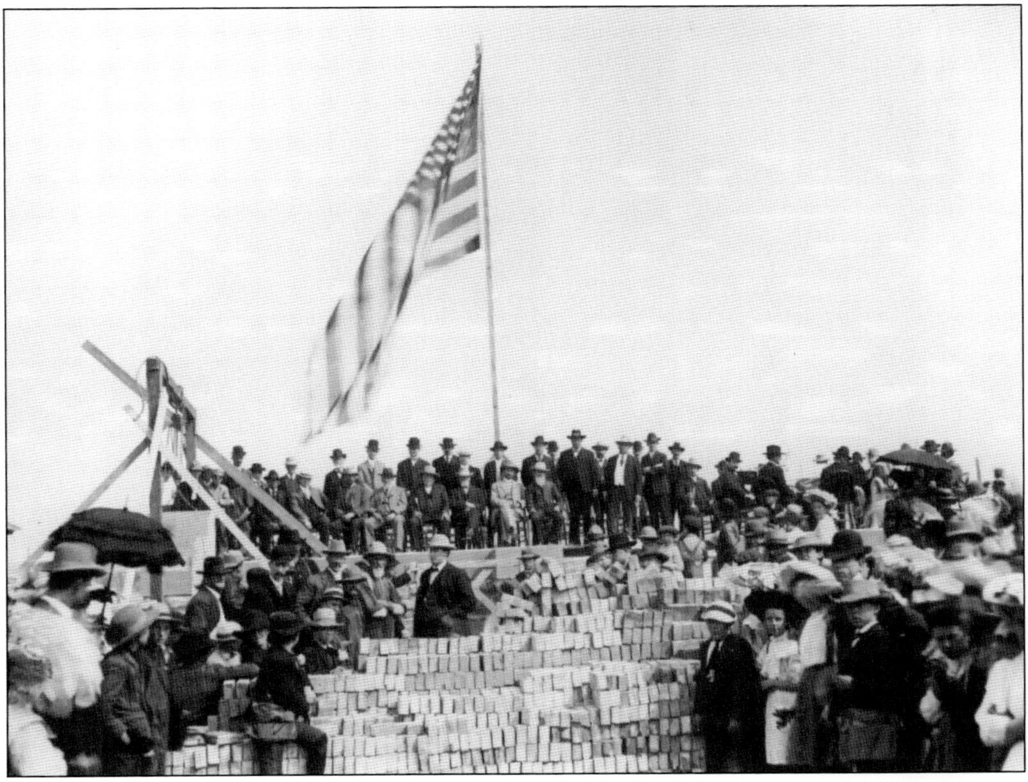

Three years after the city was incorporated, a cornerstone ceremony was held for the first city hall. Completed in 1908, Murray City Hall on the east side of South State Street at approximately 4900 South was a symbol of the emerging independent city. A copy of this photograph was one of the items sealed in a copper time capsule in the foundation. (MCM.)

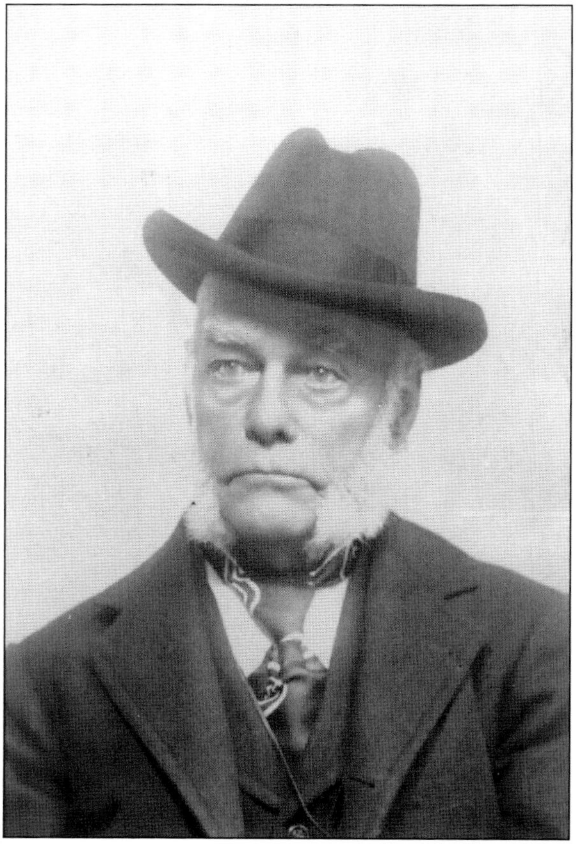

Andrew Cahoon (pictured), one of Murray's first settlers and a major property owner in the city center, sided with the smelter owners in the fight against incorporation. Cahoon believed that city taxes would burden residents and curtail industry. His major opponent was Martin A. Willumsen, the editor of the local newspaper, the *American Eagle*, who believed incorporation was necessary to control the rowdy element attracted by the smelters. (MCM.)

With over 40 saloons prior to incorporation, the unofficial town motto was "If anybody went dry on State Street in Murray, it was his own fault." Women were forbidden from entering the front door of the U.P. Saloon on 4800 South, near the tracks. The building had a family entrance on the east side and a special room where women were allowed. (MCM.)

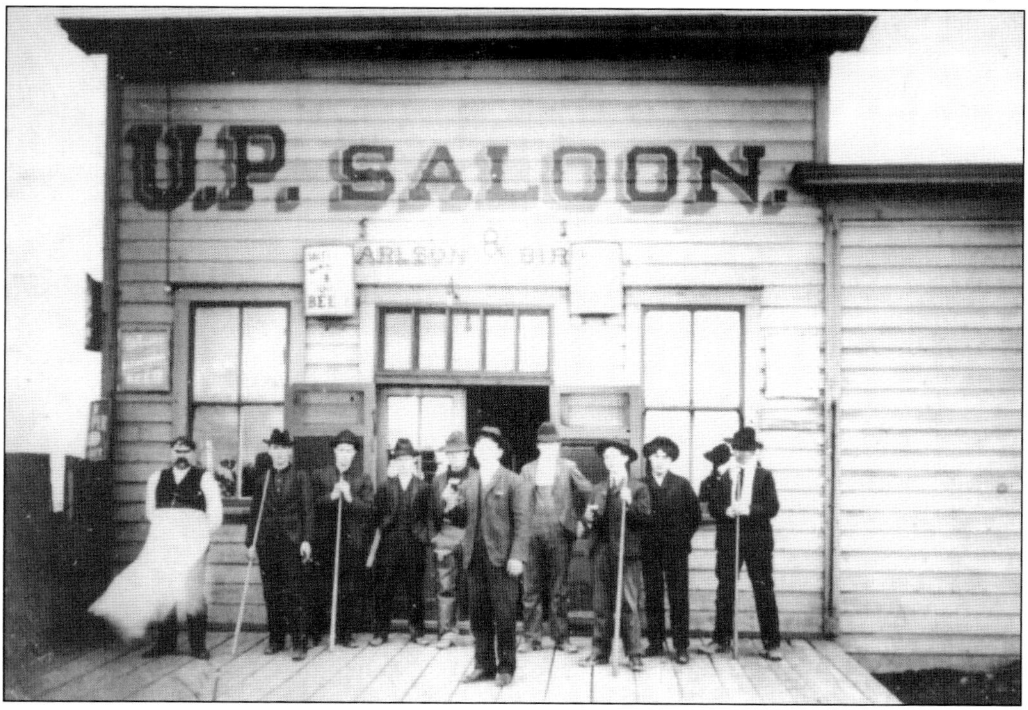

Murray was declared a third-class city on January 3, 1903. Chillion L. Miller (pictured) was elected as Murray's first mayor. The city's first 14 mayors served only one to three years each. In 1905, Murray annexed the adjacent farmlands in order to become a second-class city and form its own school district, which it did in 1906. (MCM.)

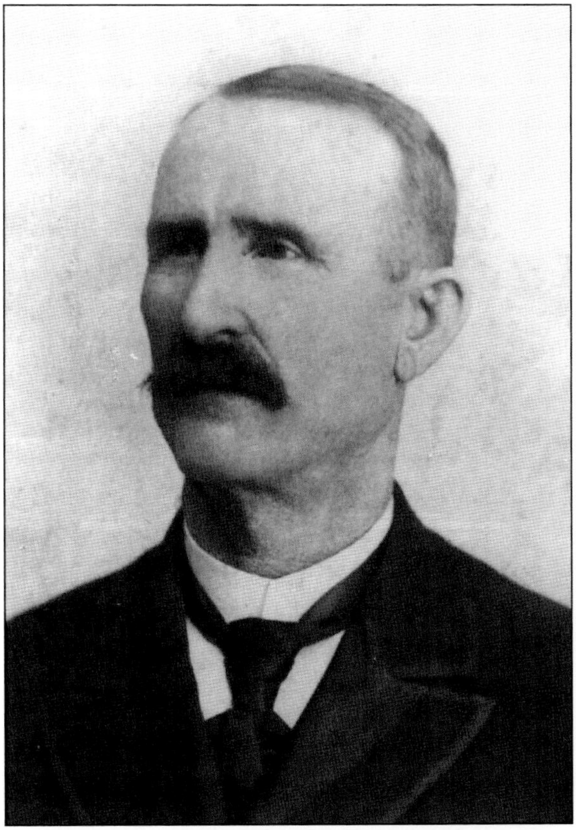

Murray City Hall was dedicated on May 14, 1908. This photograph taken in September 1908 shows the recorder's office. Will J. Warenski (left) was the second city recorder, serving from 1904 to 1911. Michael Mauss (standing behind the man with the book) was the city marshal between 1902 and 1914. (MCM.)

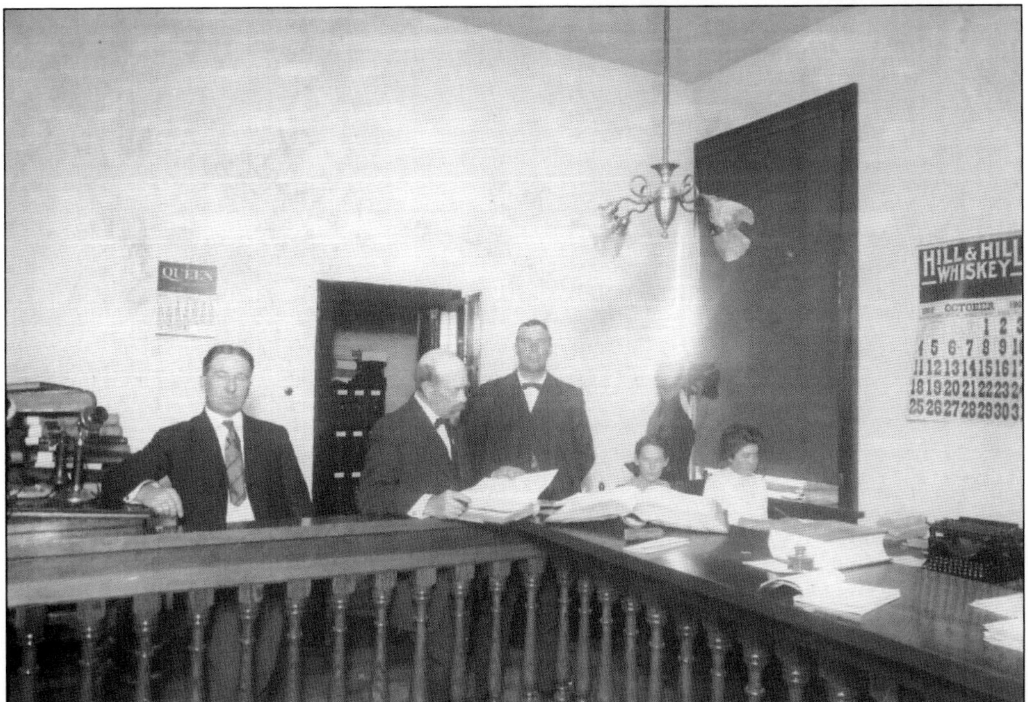

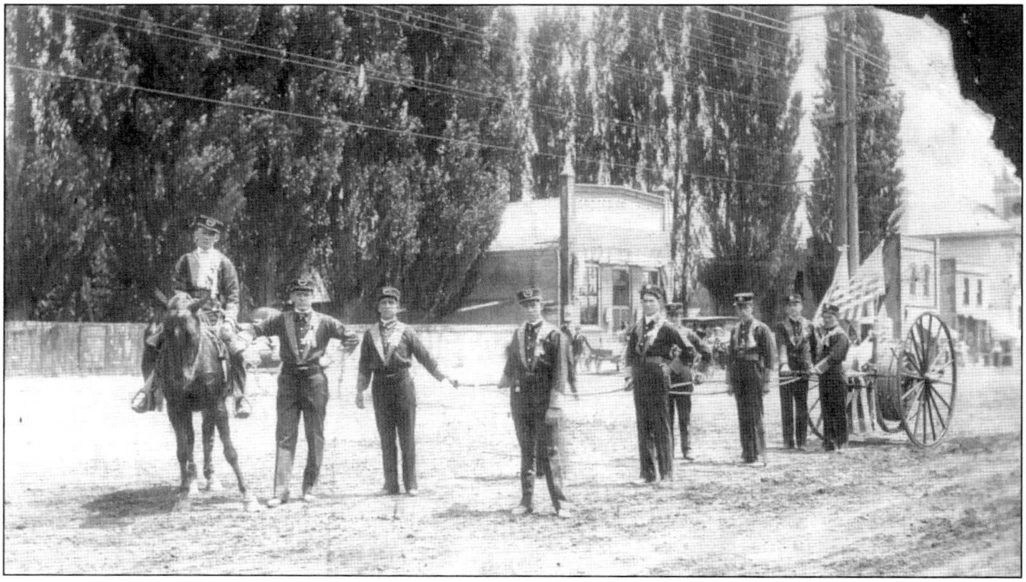

The Murray City Fire Department was organized in 1906. The first allocation of money purchased two hose carts, one chemical engine, one hook-and-ladder vehicle, four shutoff nozzles, and seven aluminum hats. In this June 1908 photograph, members of the volunteer fire department in their parade uniforms can be seen pulling one of the hose carts. (MCM.)

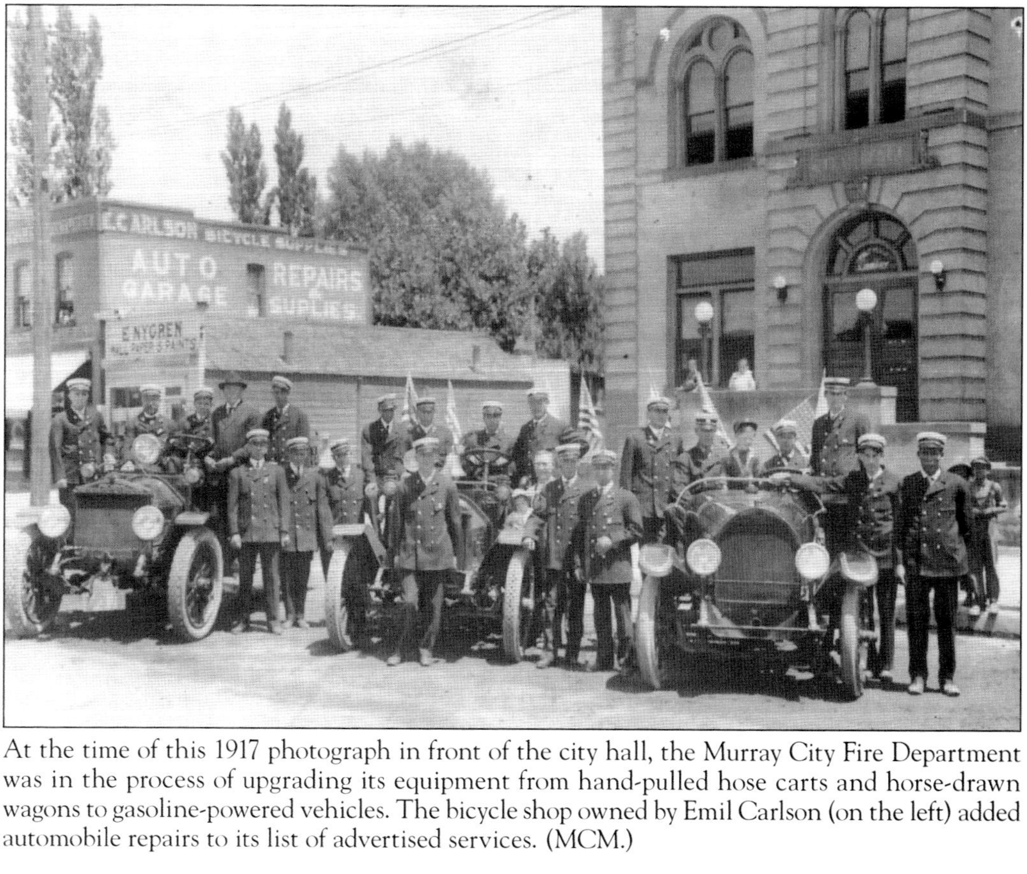

At the time of this 1917 photograph in front of the city hall, the Murray City Fire Department was in the process of upgrading its equipment from hand-pulled hose carts and horse-drawn wagons to gasoline-powered vehicles. The bicycle shop owned by Emil Carlson (on the left) added automobile repairs to its list of advertised services. (MCM.)

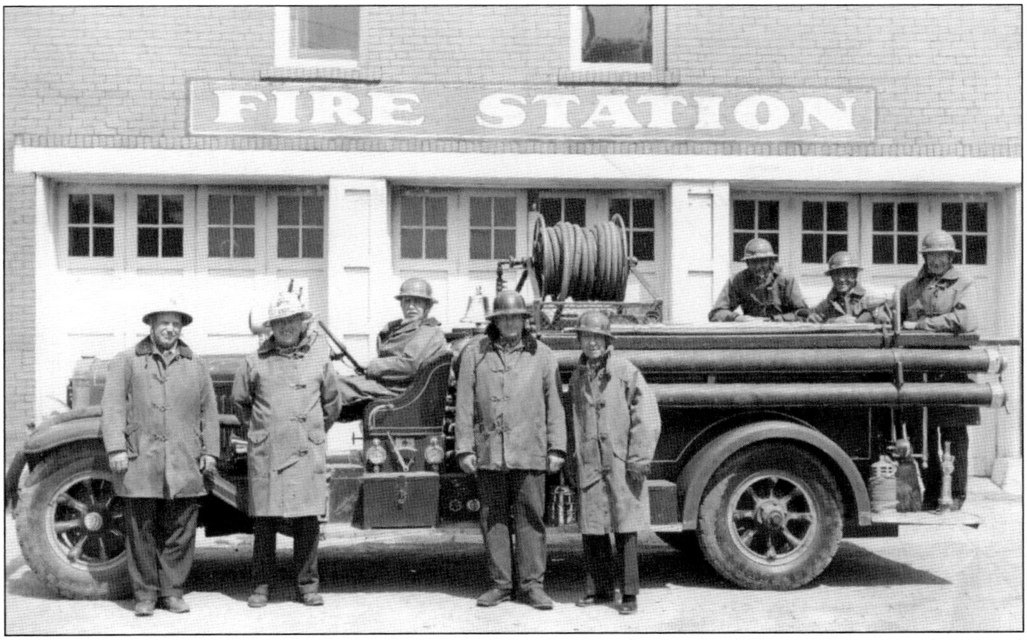

The first Murray fire station was built in 1908 to house the horse-drawn equipment. Pictured here around 1930, the building has been modified for modern fire engines. The building still stands at the rear of a strip mall built in 1962 at 4901 South State Street. The main level of the old fire station has been modified for retail use, but the meeting hall on the top floor is mostly intact. (MCM.)

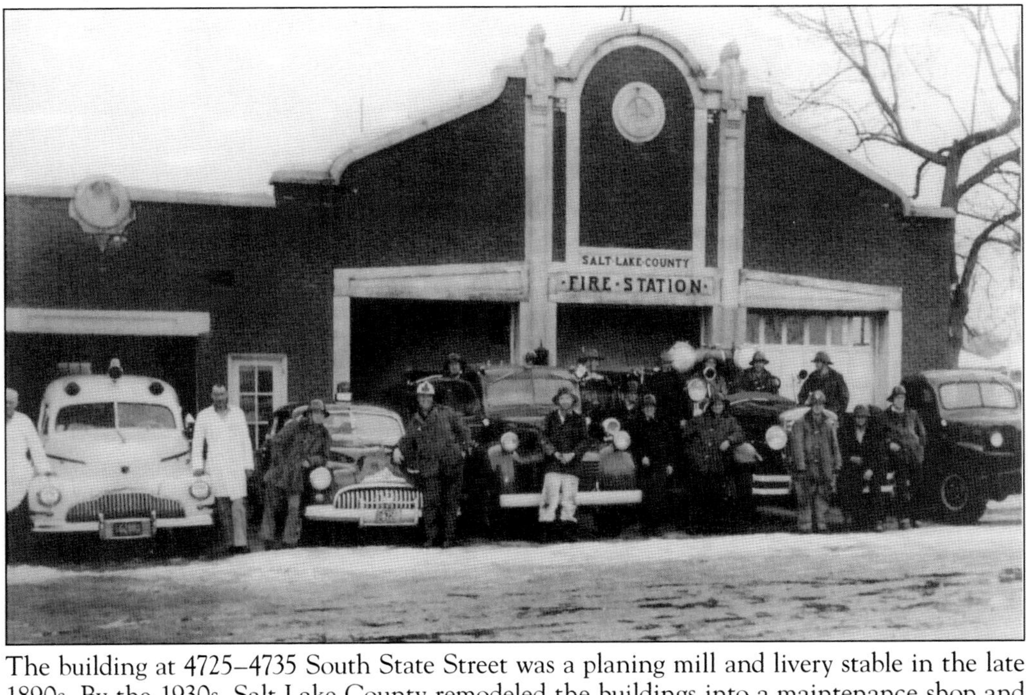

The building at 4725–4735 South State Street was a planing mill and livery stable in the late 1890s. By the 1930s, Salt Lake County remodeled the buildings into a maintenance shop and fire station. Murray City used the building as a fire station between 1958 and 1974. Today, it is the BMW of Murray dealership. (MCM.)

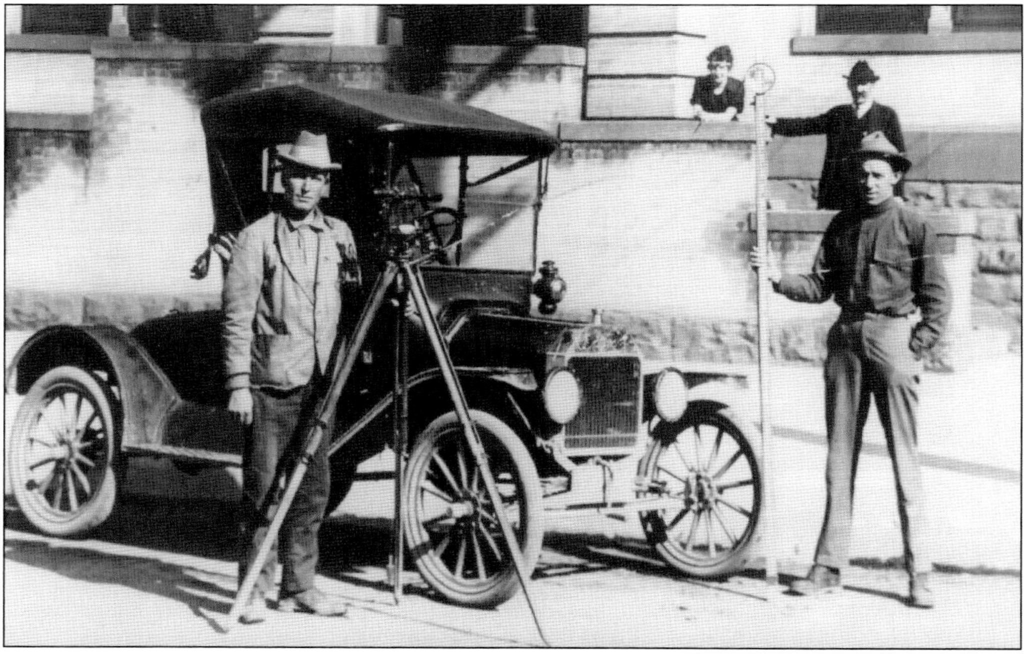

Thomas McDonald (left), Murray city engineer, poses in front of city hall with his surveying equipment and an assistant (around 1918). Thomas was in the first class of graduates at the University of Utah's engineering department. He and his wife, Ada Pearl Russell McDonald, lived on Wasatch Street in the neighborhood directly east of city hall. Ada McDonald was a member of the Mormon Tabernacle Choir. (MCM.)

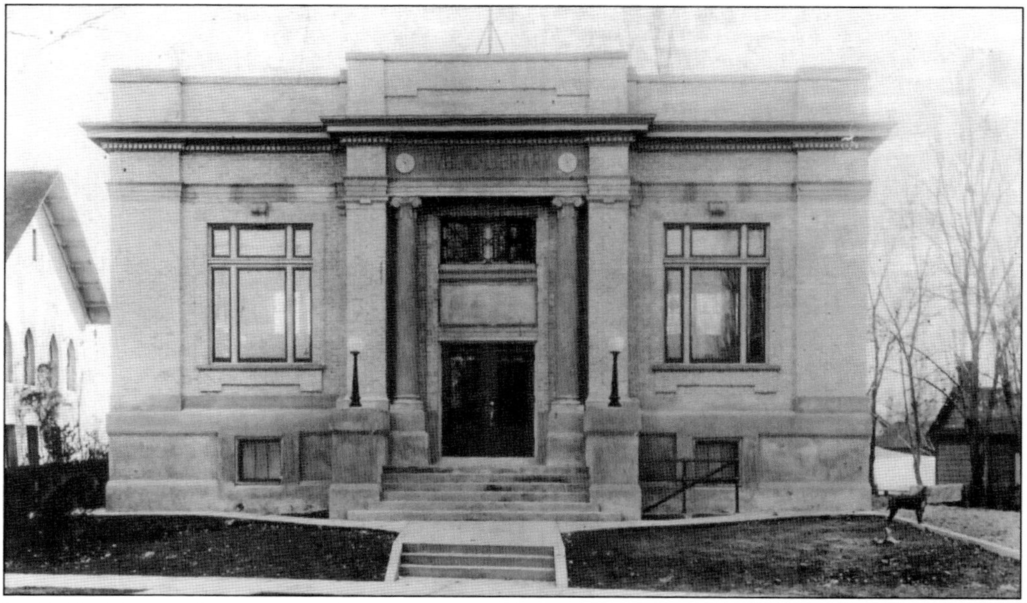

In 1912, Murray City accepted a grant from the Carnegie Corporation of New York for the construction of a library building. The Neoclassical building was completed in 1916 and served as the only library in the city for 50 years. The building was remodeled and expanded in 1970. The building is now part of the Mount Vernon Academy complex, a private school located at 184 East Vine Street. (MCM.)

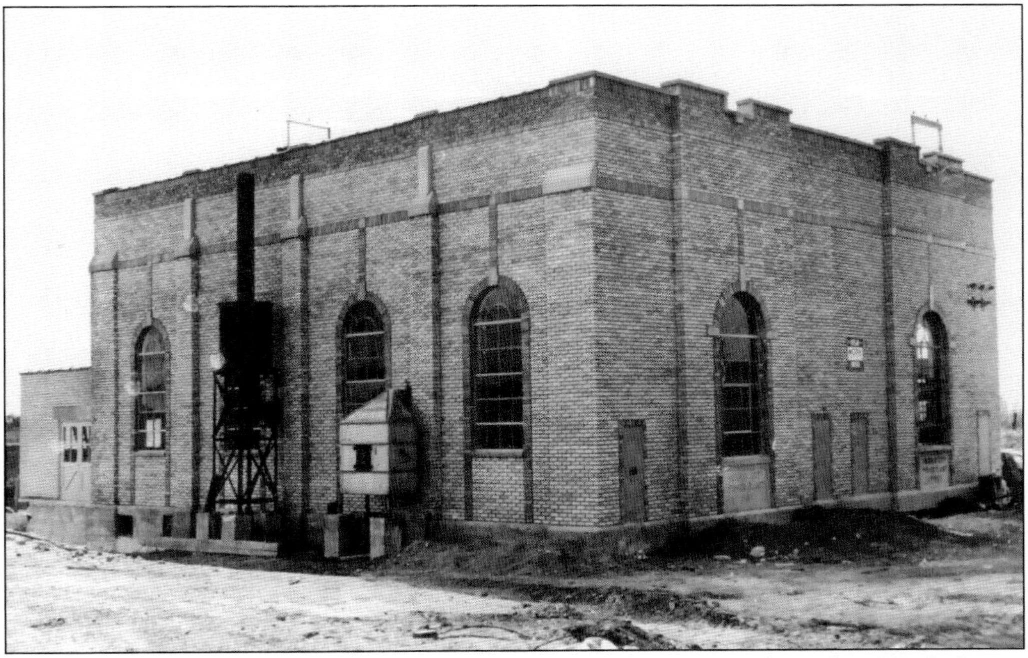

Murray City ramped up its power capacity after business leaders requested a "White Way" of street lighting along State Street in 1926. The following year, the Murray City Power Department built a plant to house a diesel generator at 157 West 4800 South. This photograph of the plant was taken soon after a 1934–1935 expansion, which doubled the capacity but retained the architectural character of the 1927 building. (MCM.)

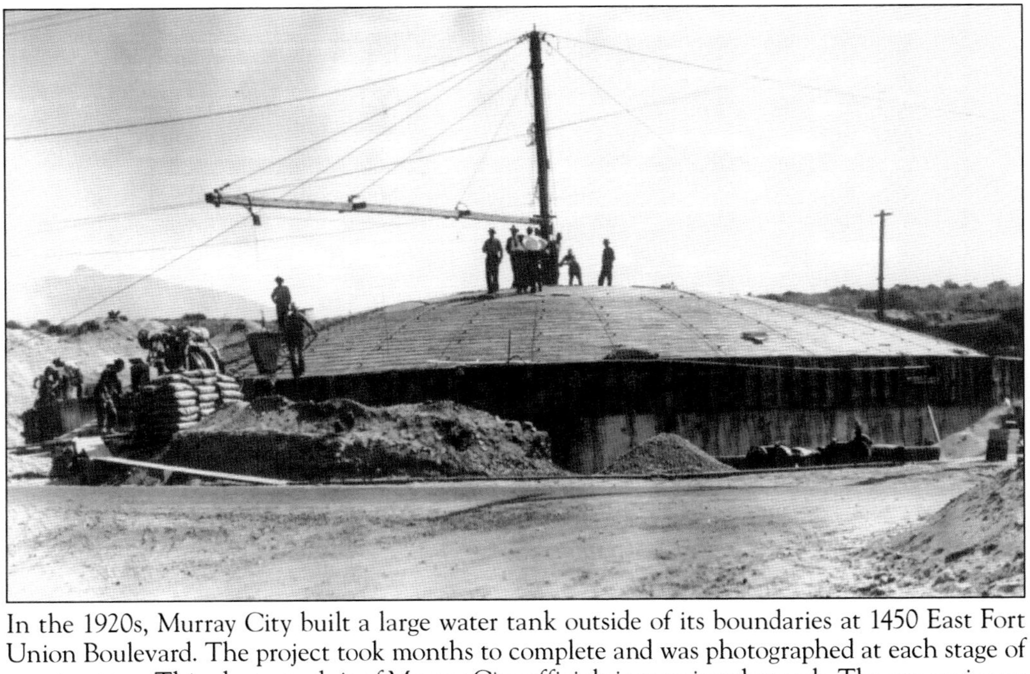

In the 1920s, Murray City built a large water tank outside of its boundaries at 1450 East Fort Union Boulevard. The project took months to complete and was photographed at each stage of construction. This photograph is of Murray City officials inspecting the work. The reservoir was upgraded in 1964 and is still a public water facility, now within the boundaries of Cottonwood Heights. (MCM.)

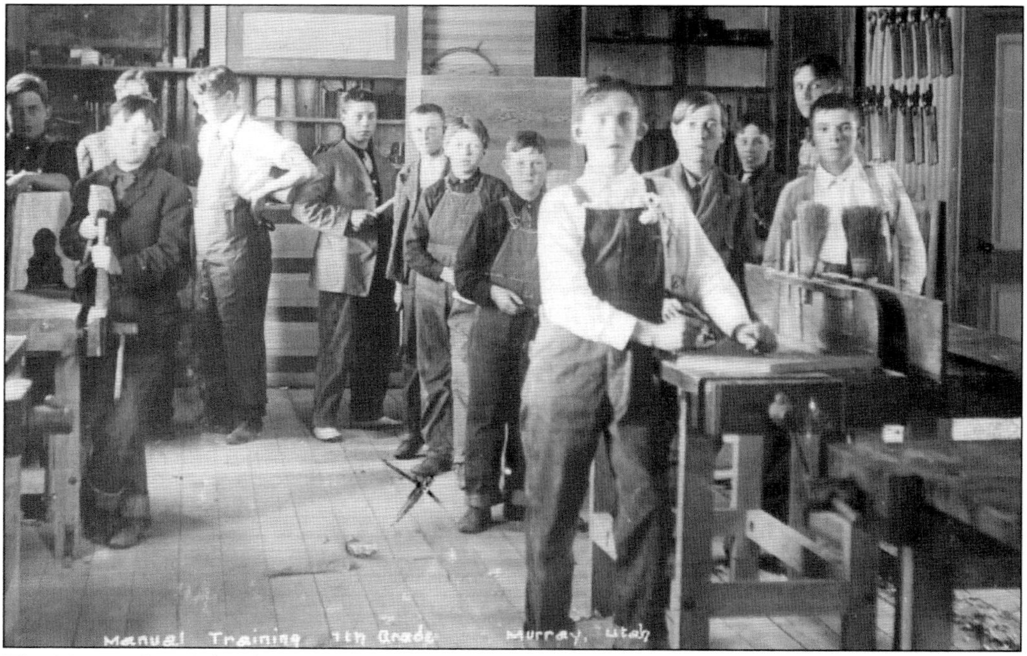

The Murray City School District provided eight years of schooling for its students. Subjects taught included arithmetic, reading, writing, spelling, language, geography, history, and civics. The district hired a manual-training supervisor who taught in the district's two shops, "equipped with a complete set of bench and tools second to none in the state," according to the *Murray Eagle*. This seventh-grade manual-training class was photographed at Arlington School in 1908. (MCM.)

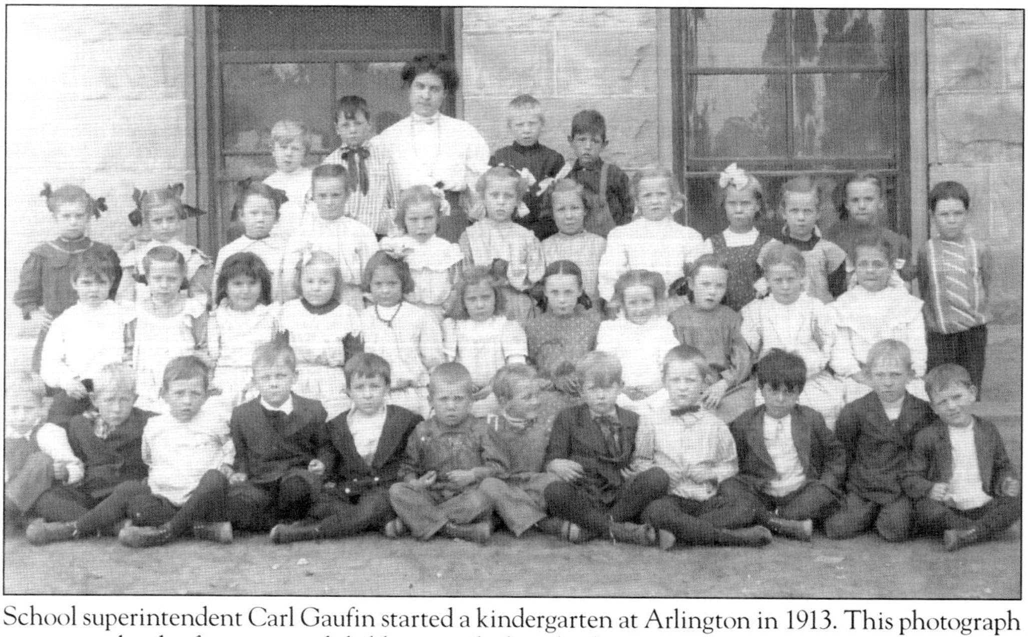

School superintendent Carl Gaufin started a kindergarten at Arlington in 1913. This photograph appears to be the first group of children taught by Charlotte Cottam Hatch. Married with small children, Hatch commuted to schools in Murray and Midvale from her home in Salt Lake City. In 1927, the Murray Board of Education took the dramatic step of passing a resolution making married women ineligible to teach in Murray. (MCM.)

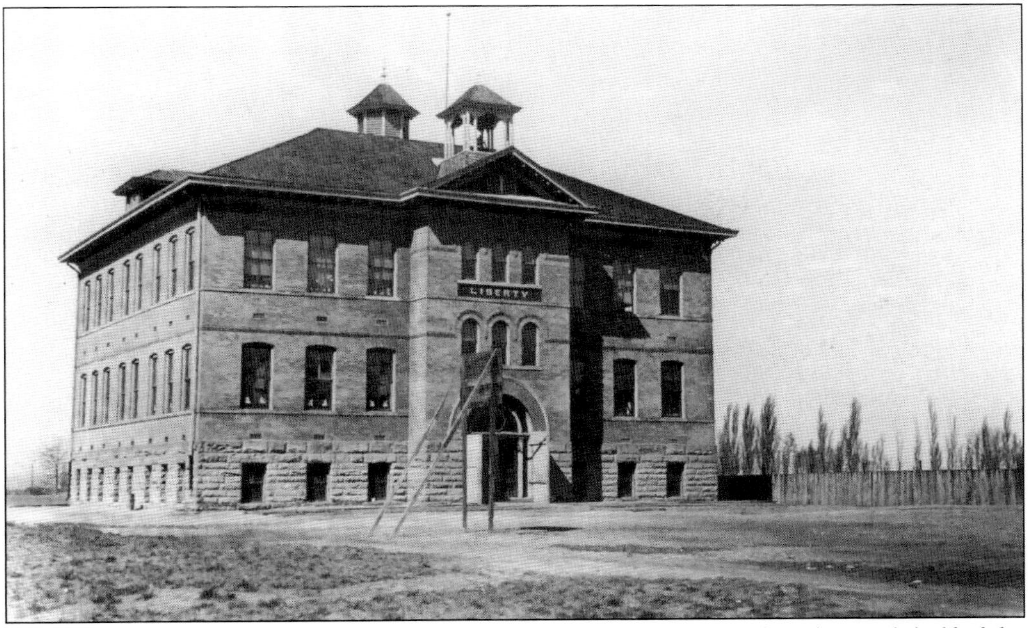

The Liberty School was built in 1905 to replace the Winchester School in the south half of the city. Teachers at Liberty School were paid more for their services than teachers at Arlington, primarily because of the poor road conditions between State Street and the school grounds. In the winter, the school district hired a wagon to drive the teachers from the streetcar line to the school. (MCM.)

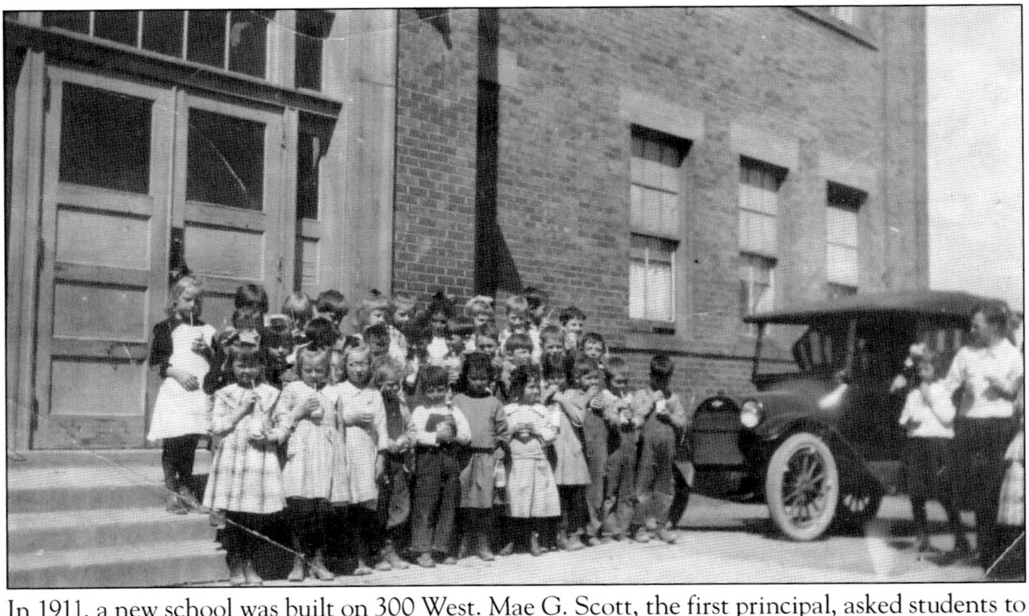

In 1911, a new school was built on 300 West. Mae G. Scott, the first principal, asked students to vote on a name. Bonnyview was chosen because the hilltop building provided a "beautiful view of the mountains and valley to the west," according to the students who submitted the winning entry. This photograph of students enjoying drinks on the steps of the Bonnyview School was taken in 1920. (MCM.)

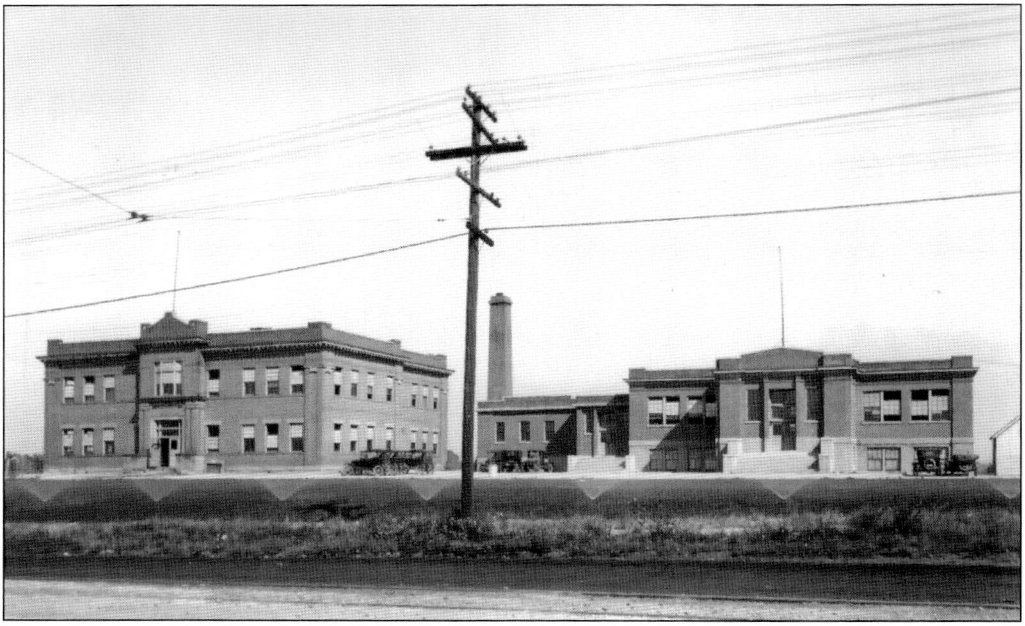

In 1911, Murray built a second school, originally called Hillcrest, at the corner of 5300 South and State Street (on the left). Within two years, plans were made to convert the building into a much-needed junior-senior high school. The campus was expanded to include a gymnasium in 1915 (on the right). The first commencement exercises were held in May 1917, with high school diplomas awarded to five graduates. (USHS.)

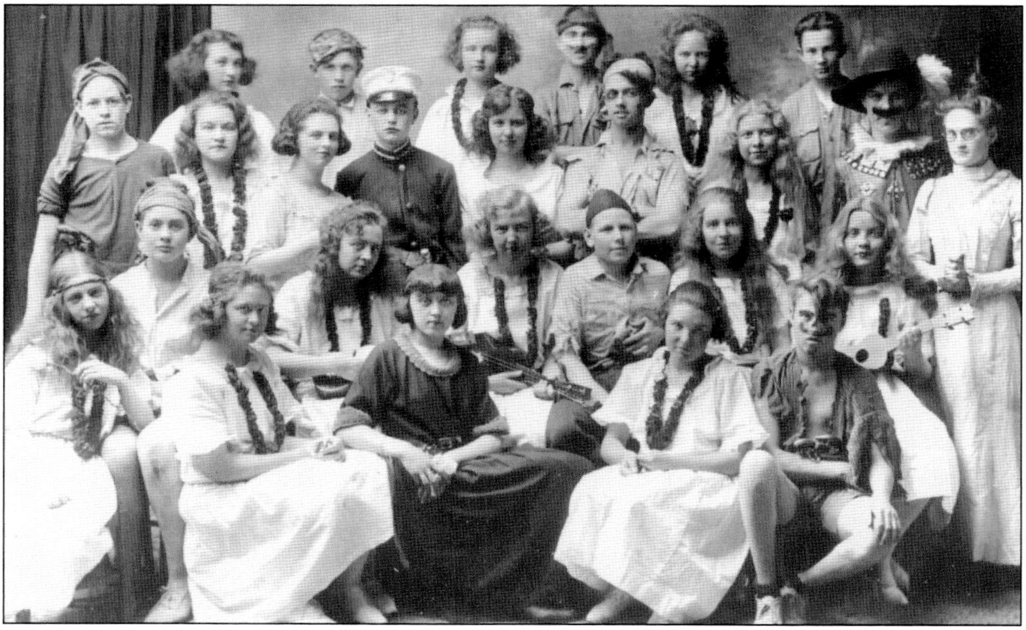

Murray High School expanded opportunities for students in art, music, and drama. One year, the senior chorus produced an operetta, *All at Sea*, while the junior chorus presented *Love Pirates of Hawaii* in 1922 (pictured). During this era, the school district and community presented monetary awards for "skill in public speaking, music, scholarship and activities, mental arithmetic, spelling and penmanship," as described by the *Murray Eagle*. (MCM.)

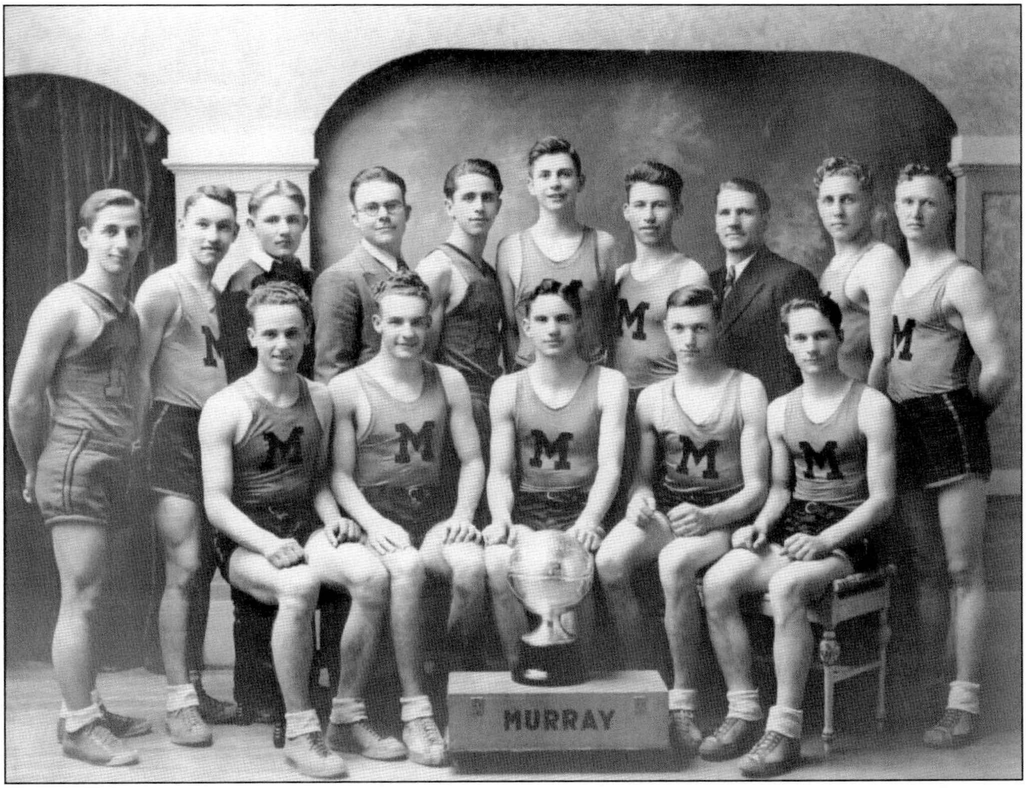

With a win over Bingham High School, Murray High School basketball players won the state championship in 1931. The team was awarded a silver trophy from the state athletic association but not the customary gold basketball watch fobs. The *Murray Eagle* requested that local businesses contribute to buy individual awards for the team members. (MCM.)

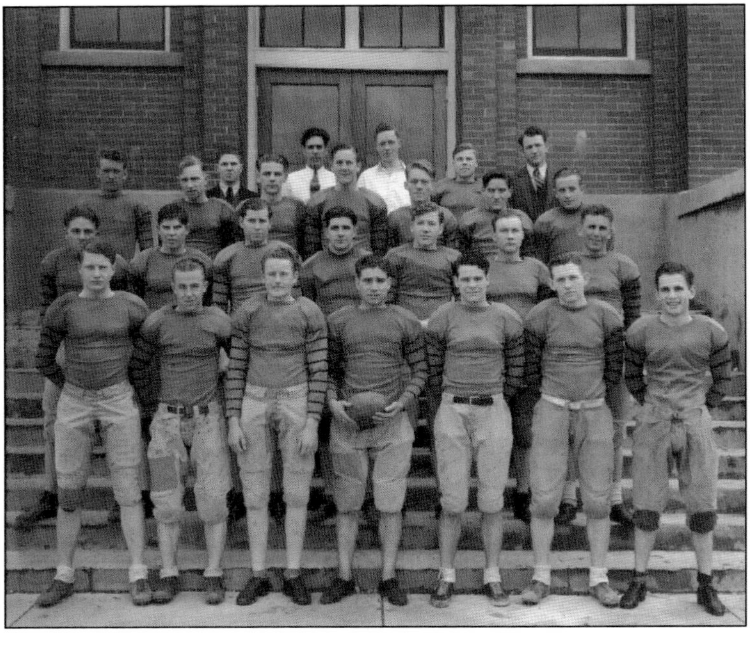

In the 1920s, a Salt Lake newspaper used "Smelterites" to describe Murray High and the nickname stuck. The school's first colors also came from the smelter, where the orange glow of the burning slag gave the night sky a purple hue. The colors were officially changed to orange and black in 1926. In this 1934 photograph, the Murray High School football team poses on the steps of the gymnasium. (USHS.)

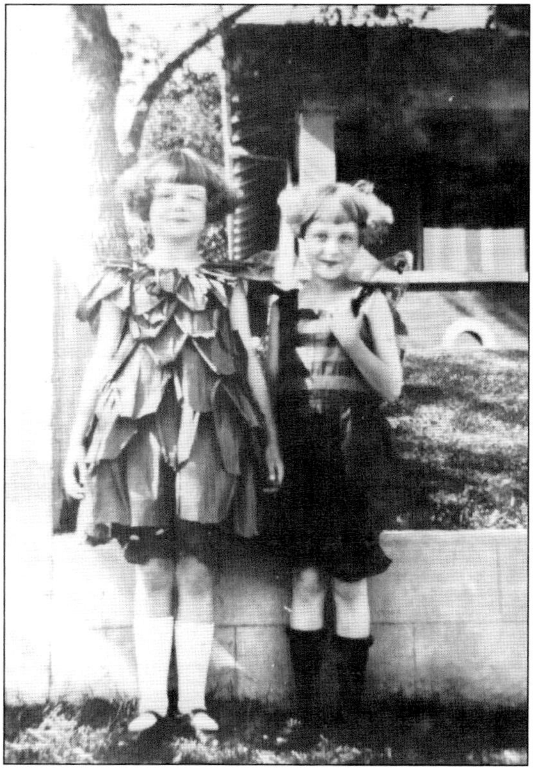

Beth Boggess (left) and Mary Jenkins pose in front of Beth's house in 1921. Boggess's father, Elmo Boggess, served as principal of Liberty and later Arlington Schools. Her mother, Mary Ann Larson Boggess, taught art in both schools. Jenkins was the daughter of George A. and Annetta Williams Jenkins. George was Murray's most prominent undertaker, and his legacy lives on in today's Jenkins-Soffe Mortuary. (MCM.)

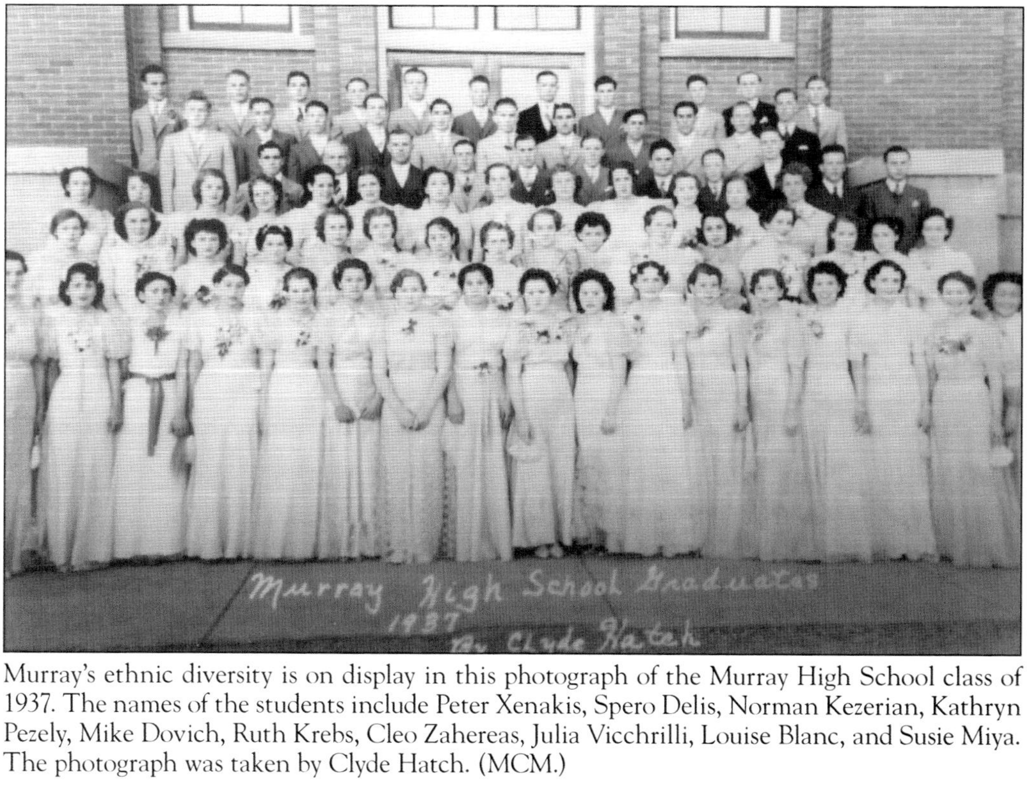

Murray's ethnic diversity is on display in this photograph of the Murray High School class of 1937. The names of the students include Peter Xenakis, Spero Delis, Norman Kezerian, Kathryn Pezely, Mike Dovich, Ruth Krebs, Cleo Zahereas, Julia Vicchrilli, Louise Blanc, and Susie Miya. The photograph was taken by Clyde Hatch. (MCM.)

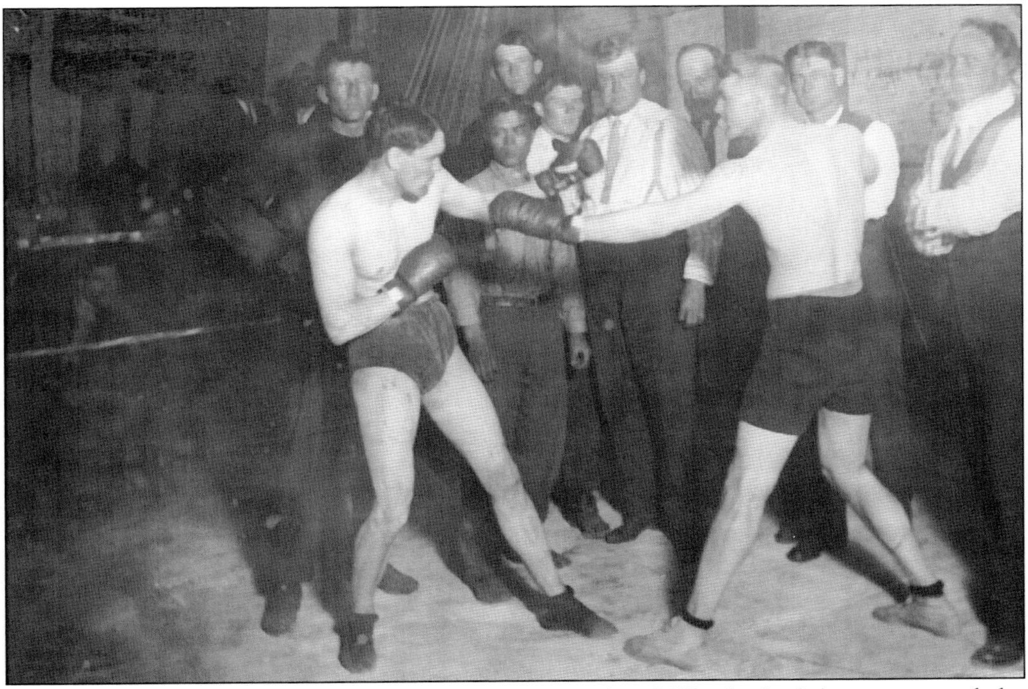

Boxing was a popular pastime in Murray. Ernest "Cyclone" Wright (right) was crowned the Welterweight Champion of the Western United States three years before this photograph was taken in 1913. Wright was a charter member of the city's volunteer fire department. World Heavyweight Champion Jack Dempsey built a home for his mother, Cecelia, on Murray's east side. Dempsey visited with children in Murray schools and practiced at local venues. (MCM.)

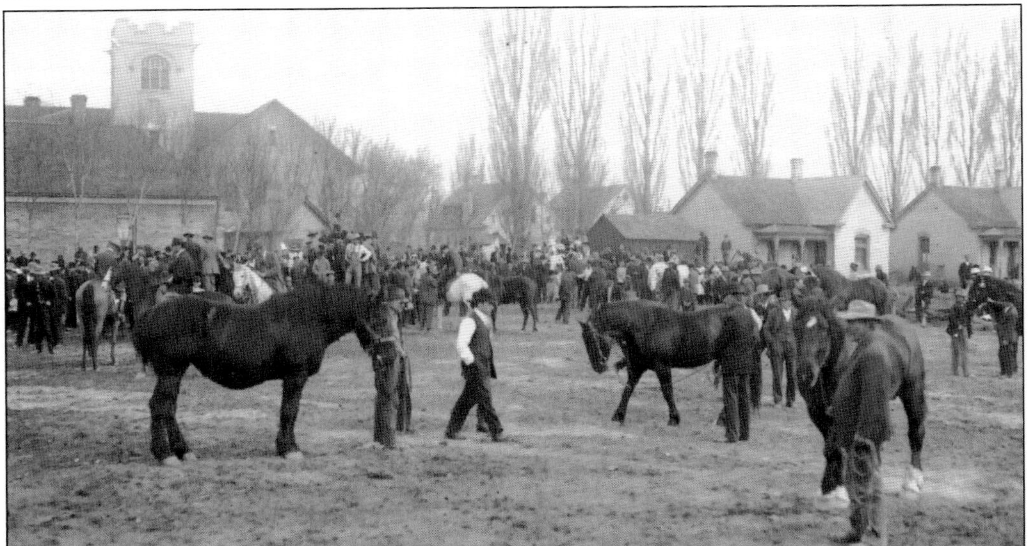

On April 3, 1911, the Murray Commercial Club promoted a thoroughbred horse show held on the fields behind the Arlington School. Breeders and horse fanciers from all over the state attended the show. This photograph of the event shows the rear of the Murray First Ward on Vine Street (background left) and the two barn-like duplexes on Jones Court (background right). All three buildings are still standing. (USHS.)

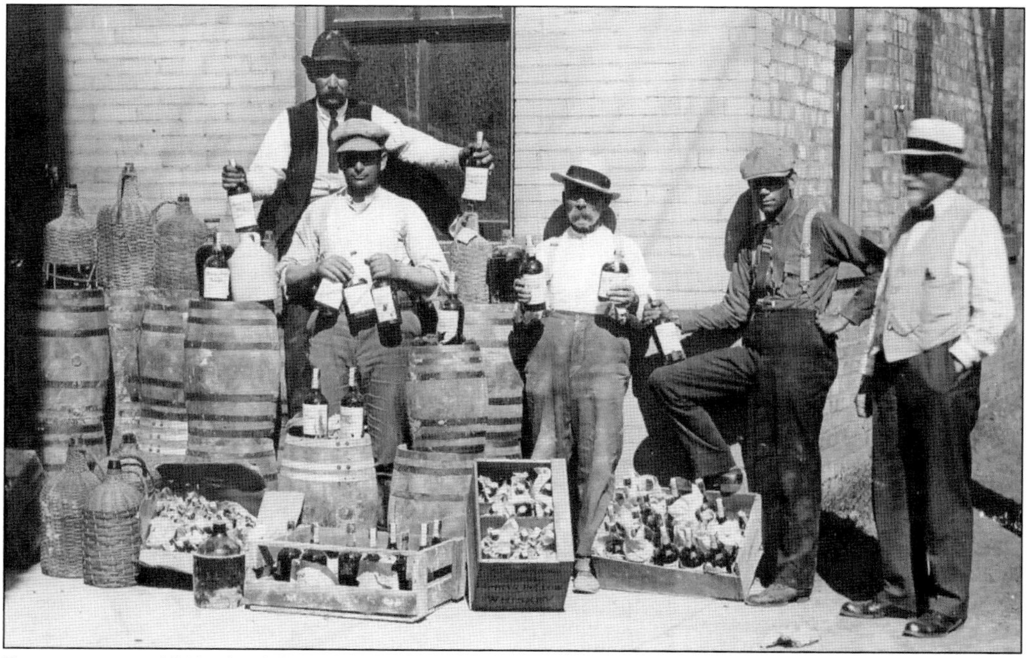

Beginning in 1911, the Murray City Council passed ordinances prohibiting the manufacture, sale, barter, or use of "intoxicating liquors" within the city limits. Taken in 1917 during a rare enforcement, this photograph features, from left to right, J.W. Caldwell (fire chief), Ed Larson (constable), two unidentified men, and Judge Birmingham, along with several cases and barrels of confiscated alcohol. (MCM.)

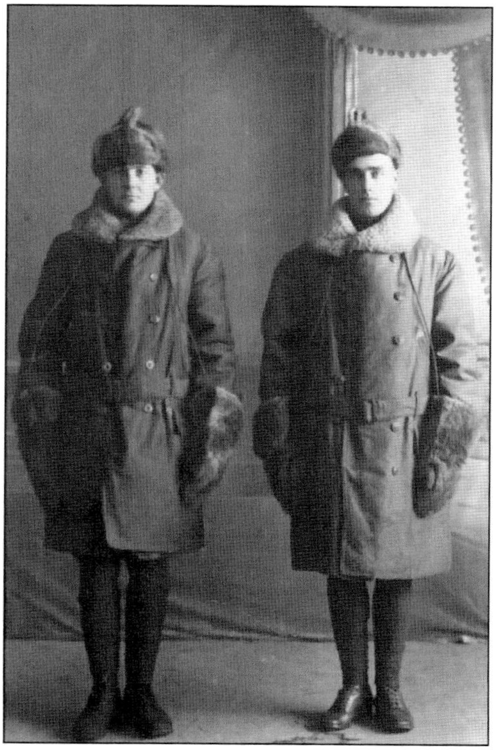

It is not known how many Murray residents were in the military during World War I, but it is likely that some of the 665 Utahans who died had ties to Murray. Art Bishop survived the war as a member of the 148th Field Artillery unit. Bishop (right) and William Davis are seen here dressed for the weather while on assignment in Russia near the end of the war. (MCM.)

The Waverly Building at 4910 South State Street is pictured here soon after it was constructed in 1904. It was the second location for the First National Bank. The north storefront was retail, and the upper floor housed professional and medical offices. Between 1924 and 1933, the corner storefront was occupied by George H. Lyon's drugstore. Murray Music, later Day Murray Music, has occupied the building since 1946. (MCM.)

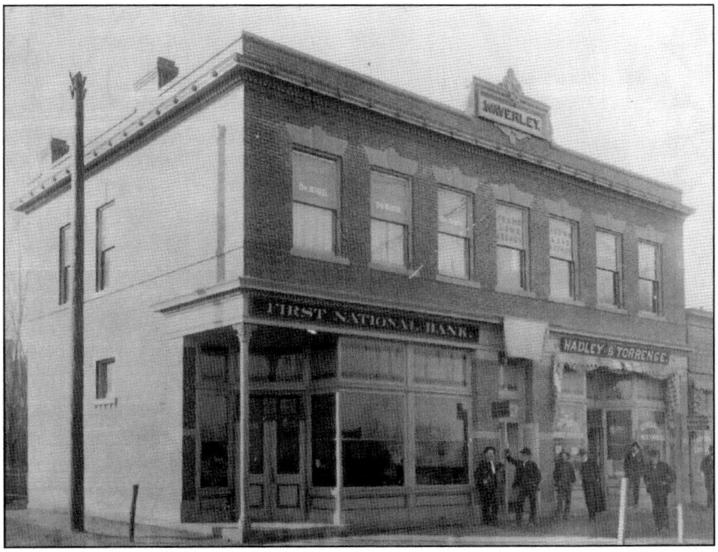

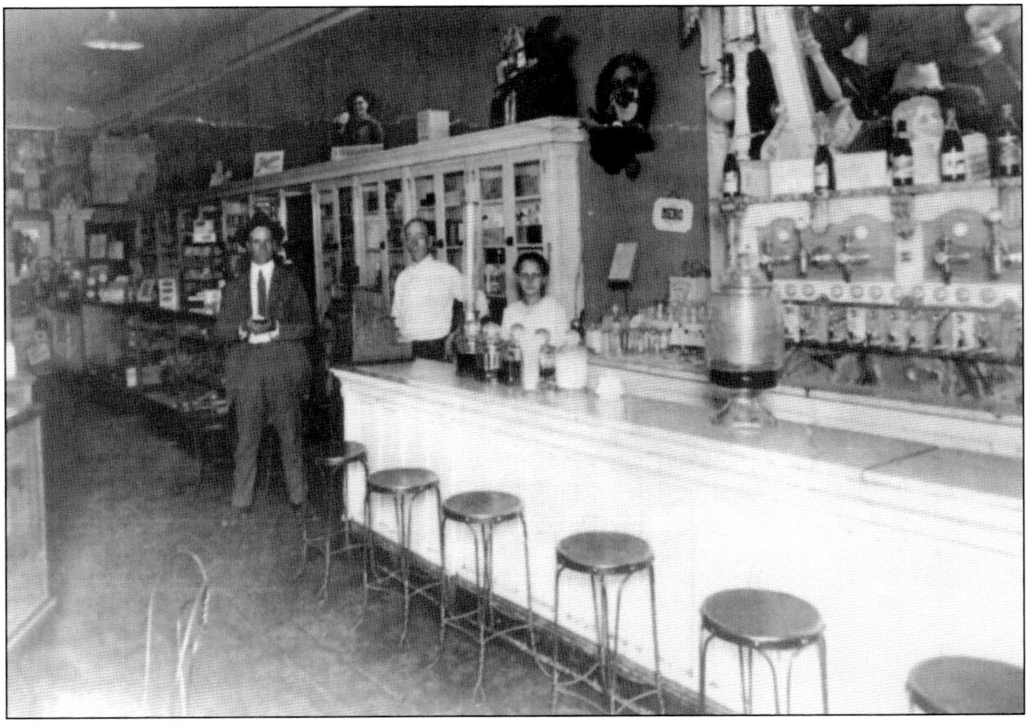

George H. Lyon learned pharmacology from Dr. Ferrebee and established his first drugstore in the opera house block. Each time George H. Lyon moved his drugstore to a larger location, he would install a soda fountain and counter. This photograph from about 1920 shows George (center) with his eldest child, Elmyra, and an unidentified customer, probably at the store at Third Avenue and State Street. (MCM.)

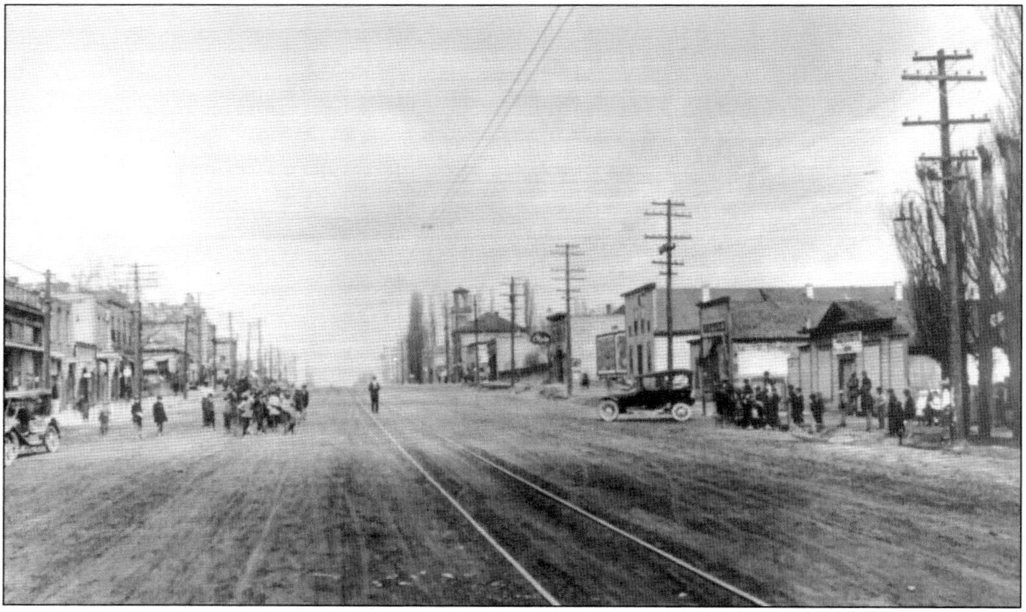

During the Roaring Twenties, automobile ownership rates increased dramatically. These two photographs are of the same accident on State Street in downtown Murray. After reportedly hitting a streetcar, the disabled automobile landed in front of the Trocadero Dance Hall (on the right above) and across the street from the Emporium (below). The Trocadero, later called the Alcazar, was an octagonal building with an iron roof and a spring-mounted dance floor. A complaint of permitting "lewd dancing in the dark" brought the owners before the city council at least once. Two doors north of the Trocadero, the Iris Theater was Murray's most successful early purveyor of motion pictures. (Both, MCM.)

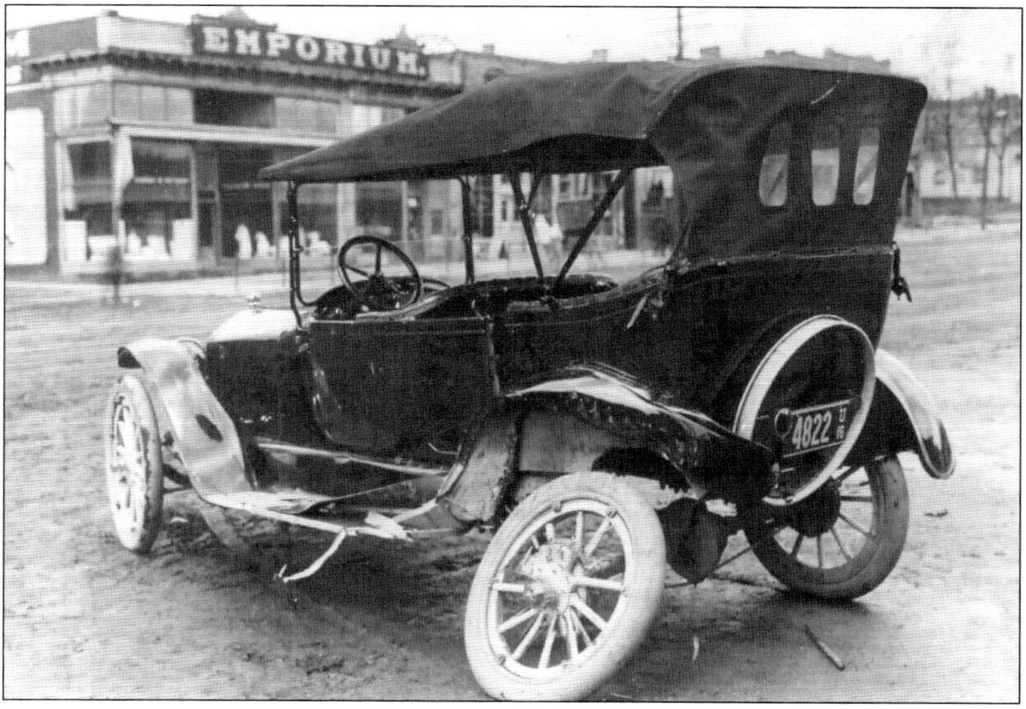

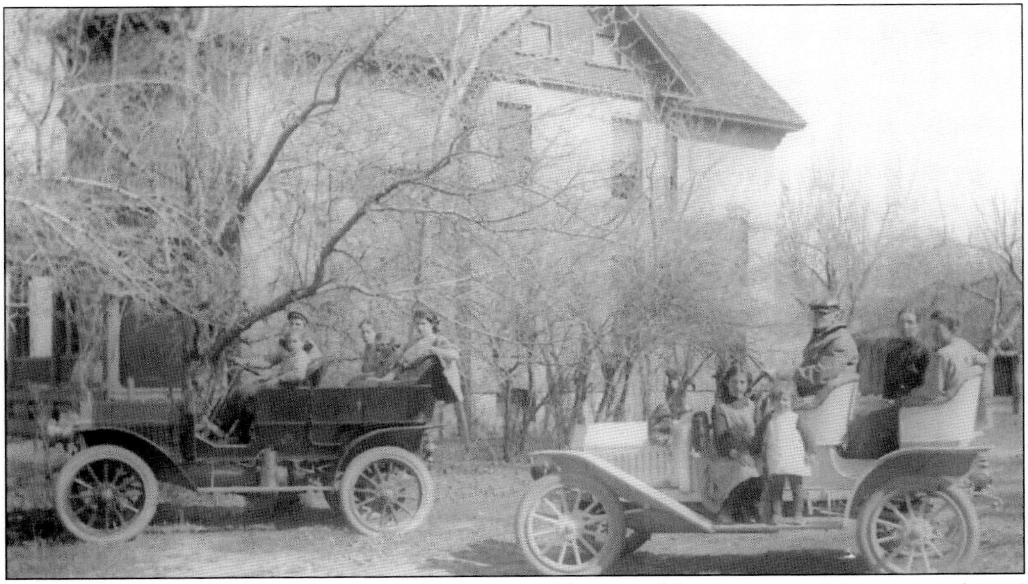

Automobiles connected Murray to outlying areas. The grand home pictured here around 1915 is located in a neighborhood annexed by Murray City in 2003. The house was built in 1895 for Wesley K. and Frances Huffaker Walton. The family had a successful ranching business in Woodruff, Utah, and lived on the Huffaker farm during the summer until they took up permanent residence in 1908. (MCM.)

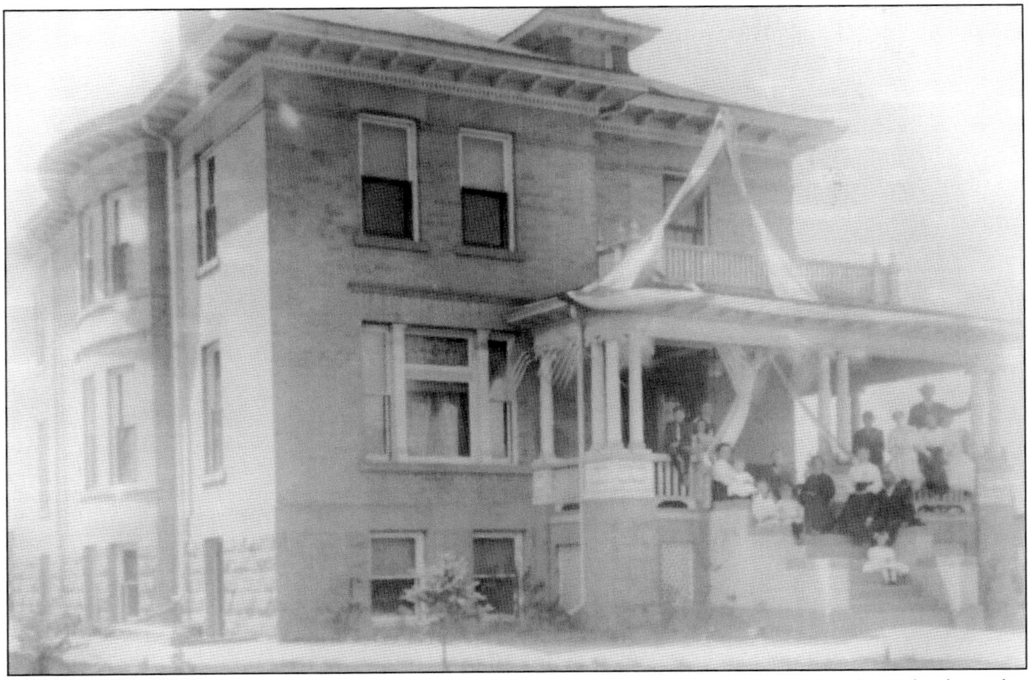

Built around 1899, the home of John P. and Elizabeth Gordon Cahoon was described in the *Salt Lake Tribune* as "easily the finest home in the county outside of Salt Lake City." In this photograph taken on the Fourth of July in 1904, family and friends enjoy the holiday from their porch facing Poplar Street in Murray. In 1987, Bill and Susan Wright restored the home as the Murray Mansion Reception Center. (MCM.)

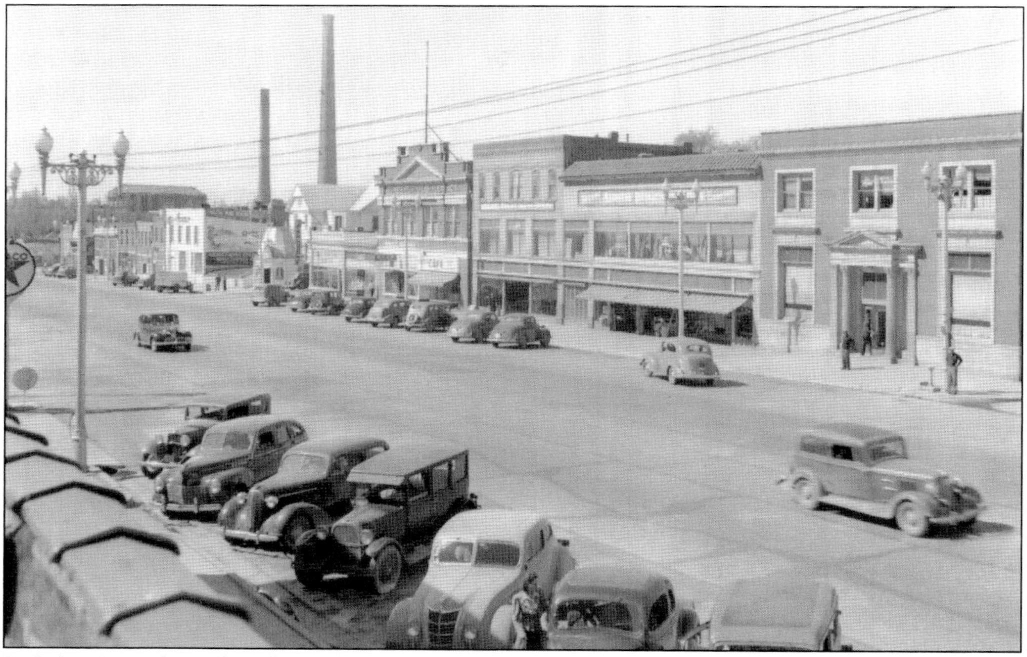

In July 1940, the *Salt Lake Tribune* photographed scenes of State Street in Murray. The most prominent buildings in the above photograph with a view facing southwest are the Fraternal Hall, Madsen's Hardware, and the First National Bank Building. Murray's first female physician, Dr. Mildred Nelson, began her practice in 1929 in an upstairs office in the bank building. The below image with a view facing northeast on State Street includes the Safeway grocery, Grand Central Drugs, three-story Harker Building and apartments, Murray Mercantile, Hoffman Building, and Piggly-Wiggly. The "White Way" street lighting installed by Murray City is also on display in these 1940 photographs. (Both, Salt Lake Tribune Collection at the USHS.)

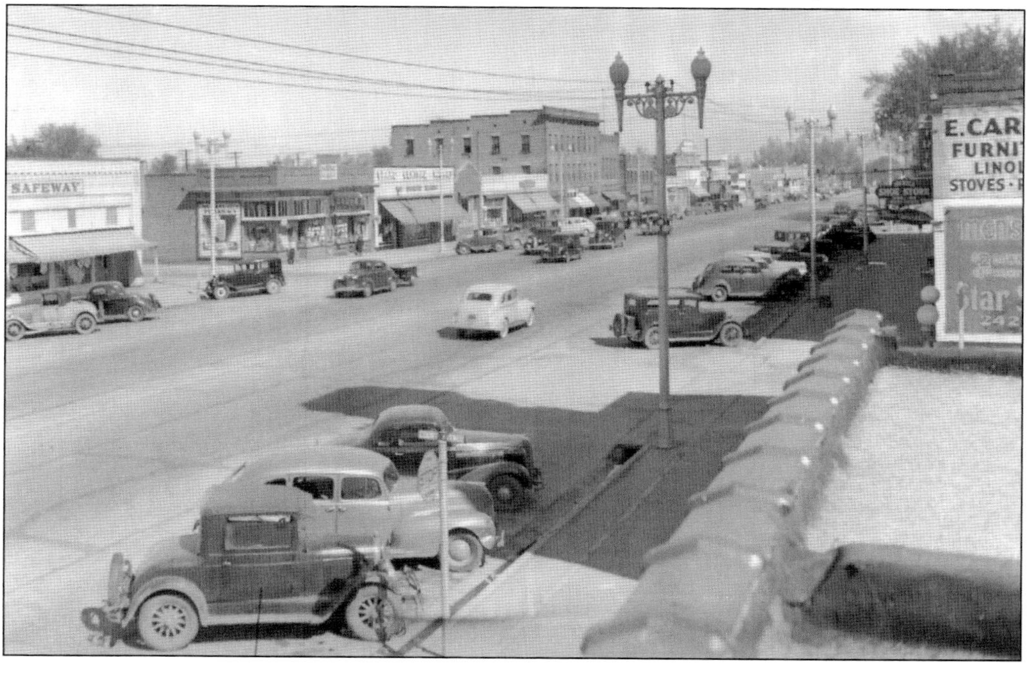

The Duvall family owned the east side of State Street to Heckel's Shoe Shop. Tony Duvall had worked in the old Iris Theater and in 1930 built the new Iris Theater with retail storefronts and apartments on the second floor at 4861 South State Street (pictured in 1937). During the Great Depression, Duvall would let needy children in for free after the movie had started. (USHS.)

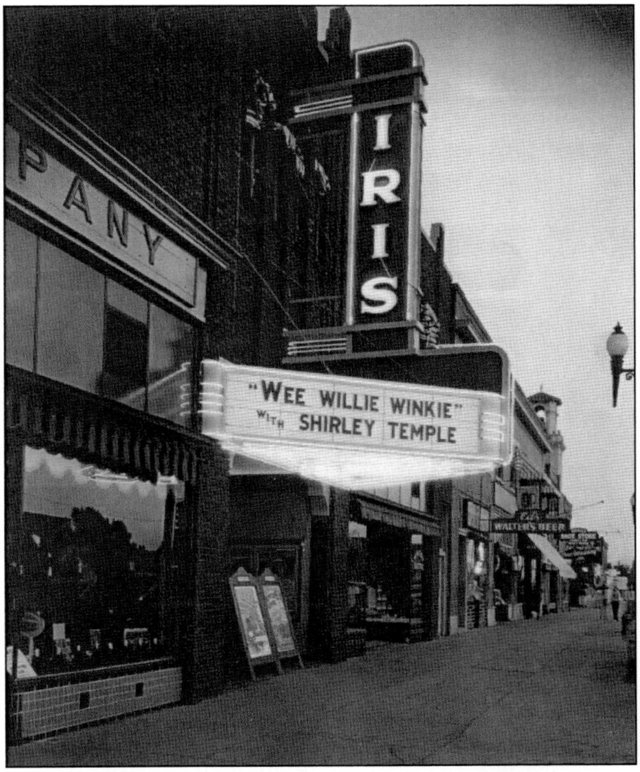

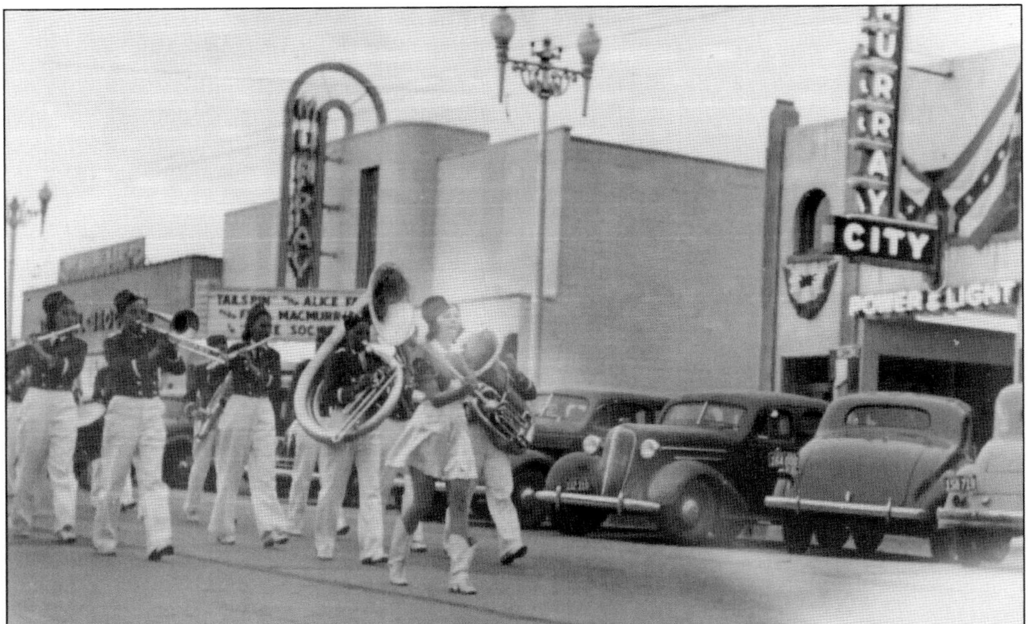

Tony Duvall, with partner Joe Lawrence, built the Murray Theater at 4961 South State Street (left). In the 1940s, the Iris would close during the summer while movies were shown in the larger (and cooler) Murray Theater. In this image of the MHS band in a parade around 1940, the old Iris Theater had been converted to the Murray City Power Department offices (right). (MCM.)

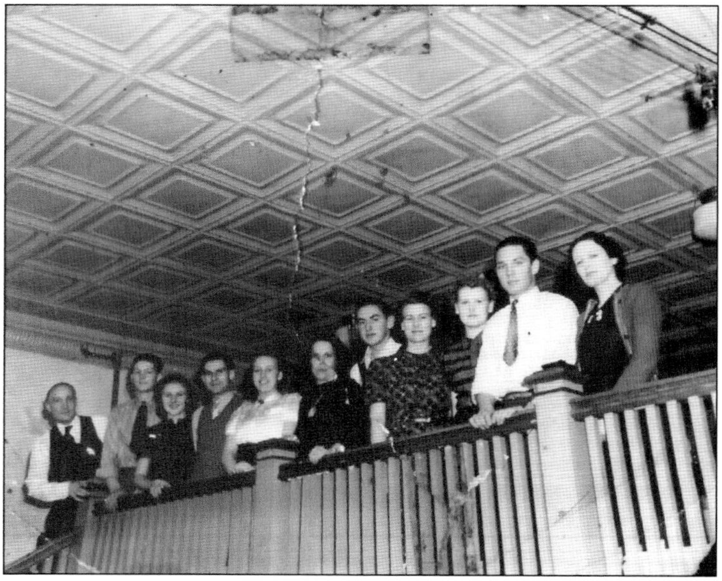

In 1930, J.C. Penney's dry goods moved into the north storefront of the new Iris building. Many Murray shoppers still remember the overhead conveyor system at Penney's, which moved cash and receipts between the sales floor and a central cashier in the mezzanine. In this photograph from the 1930s, employees hold a party for head cashier Alberta Morris Midgley. (MCM.)

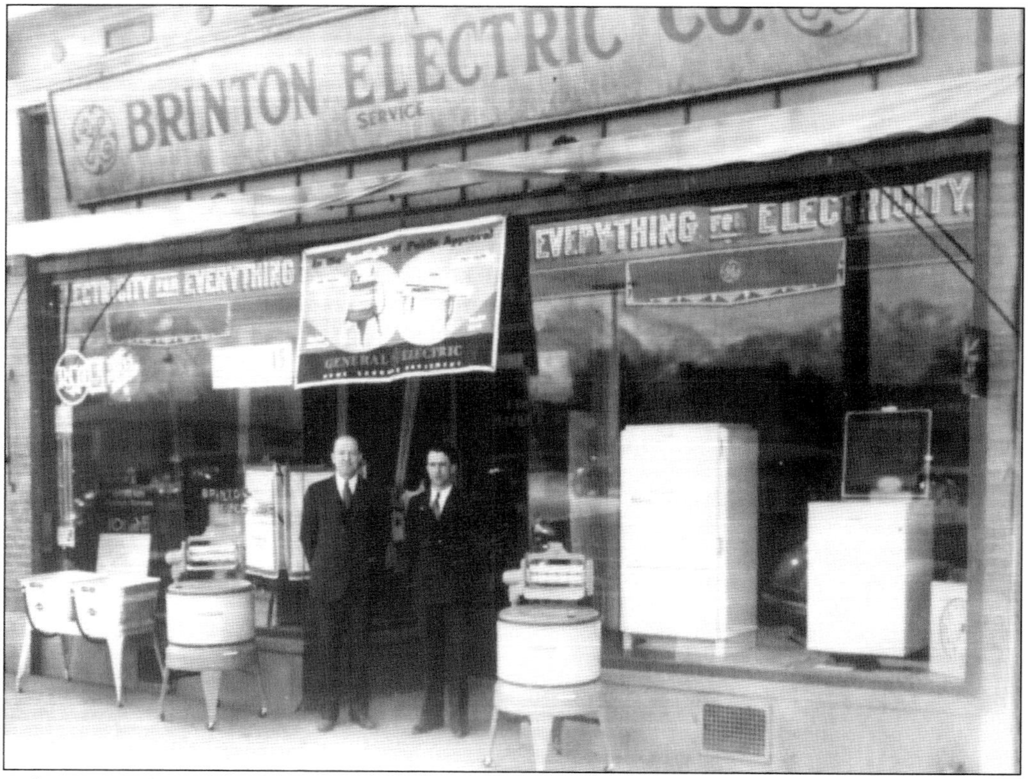

A former employee of Progress Power, Branson Brinton founded the Brinton Electric Company at 4792 South State Street. Brinton (left) is pictured here with William Winger around 1925. The *Murray Eagle* noted in 1934 that "housewives have found it desirous to own refrigerators, radios, ranges, washers, toasters, waffle irons, percolators, and other electric appliances around the house." Many Murray residents bought these appliances from Brinton Electric. (MCM.)

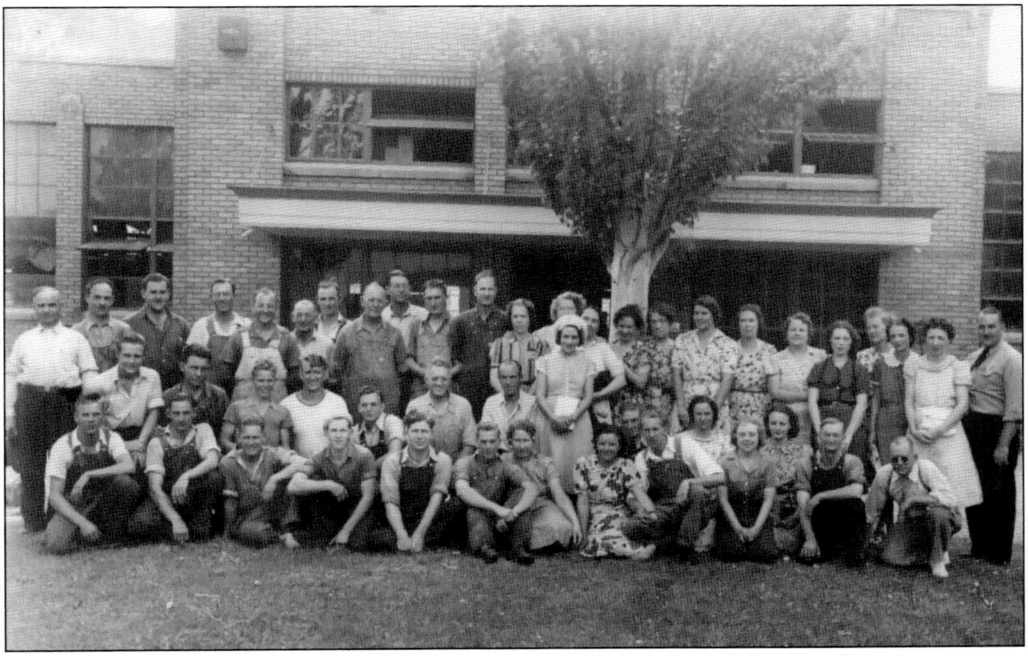

The Utah Woolen Mills built a blanket factory at 4400 South State Street in 1928. An article in the *Murray Eagle* reported that the company chose Murray for its central location, advantageous power rates, and ready workforce. The employees of the factory pose in front of the building about 1935. The building was later used by LDS Church Welfare Services (MCM.)

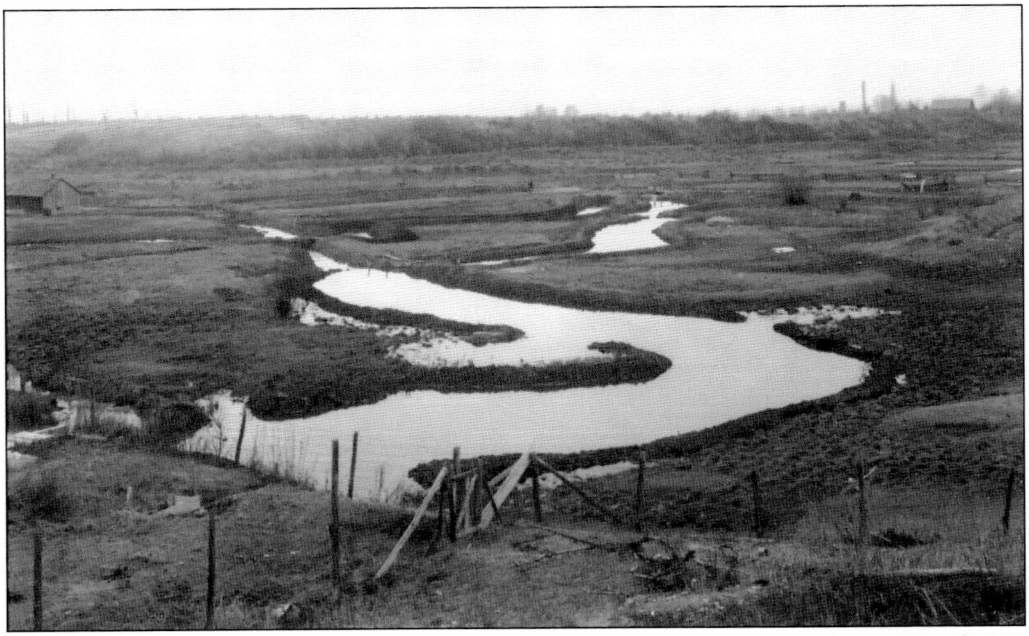

H.N. Welch advertised the location of his trout farm and fish hatchery as the corner of 4800 South and 1300 East in Murray, although the area has never been within the corporate limits. Welch advertised "market trout, fish fry, eggs, and supplies" in the local directories. This view looking southwest from the trout farm toward Murray was taken in December 1917. The larger smokestack is visible under construction in the upper right. (USHS.)

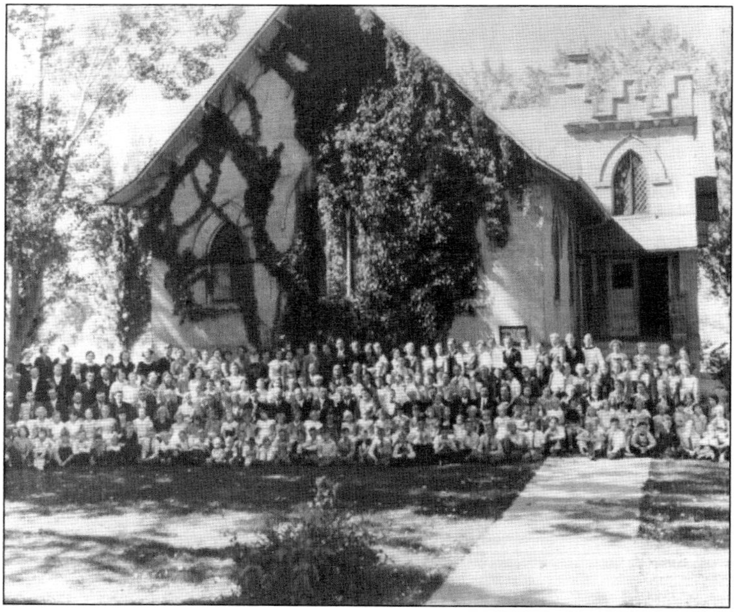

The LDS Church divided its congregation at the turn of the 20th century: Grant Ward at the south end of the city (1900), Murray First Ward near downtown (1906), and Murray Second Ward west of the railroad tracks (1906). This photograph of the entire Second Ward was taken by A.J. Peters, a professional photographer in Murray, around 1930. The building still stands on 300 West. (MCM.)

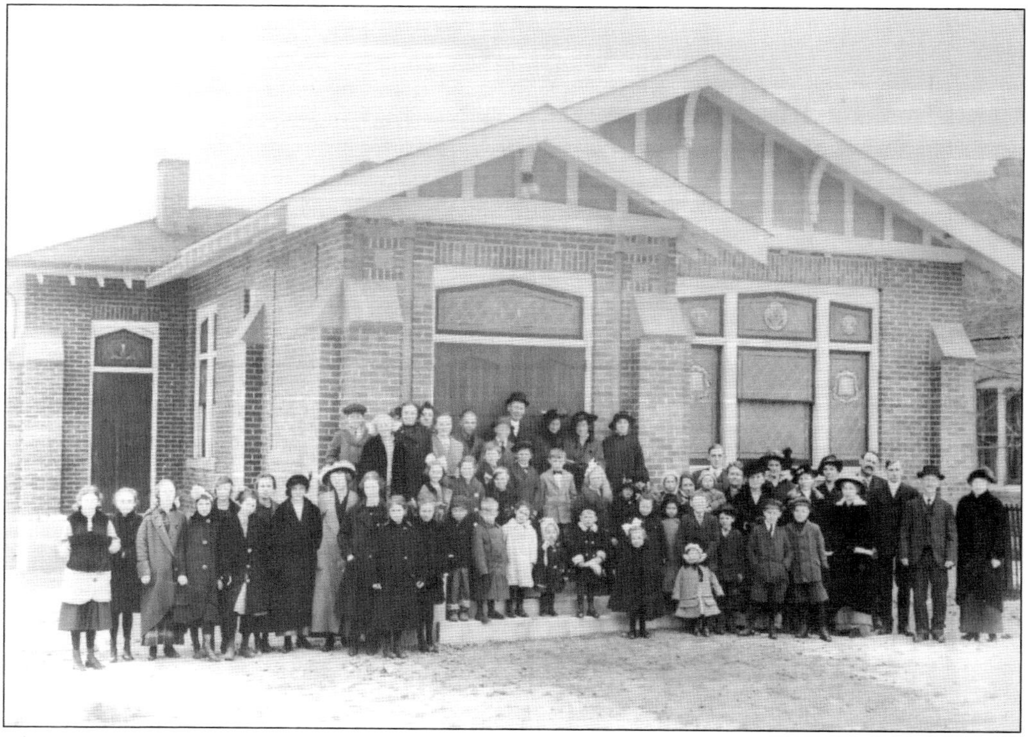

The Methodist Church established a congregation and a denominational school in Murray in 1884. The church met in a frame building near the railroad tracks until the congregation built a brick meetinghouse at 167 East 4800 South in 1911. This photograph of the membership was likely taken shortly after the construction was completed. The building later housed the Christ Lutheran Church and the Murray Bible Church. (USHS.)

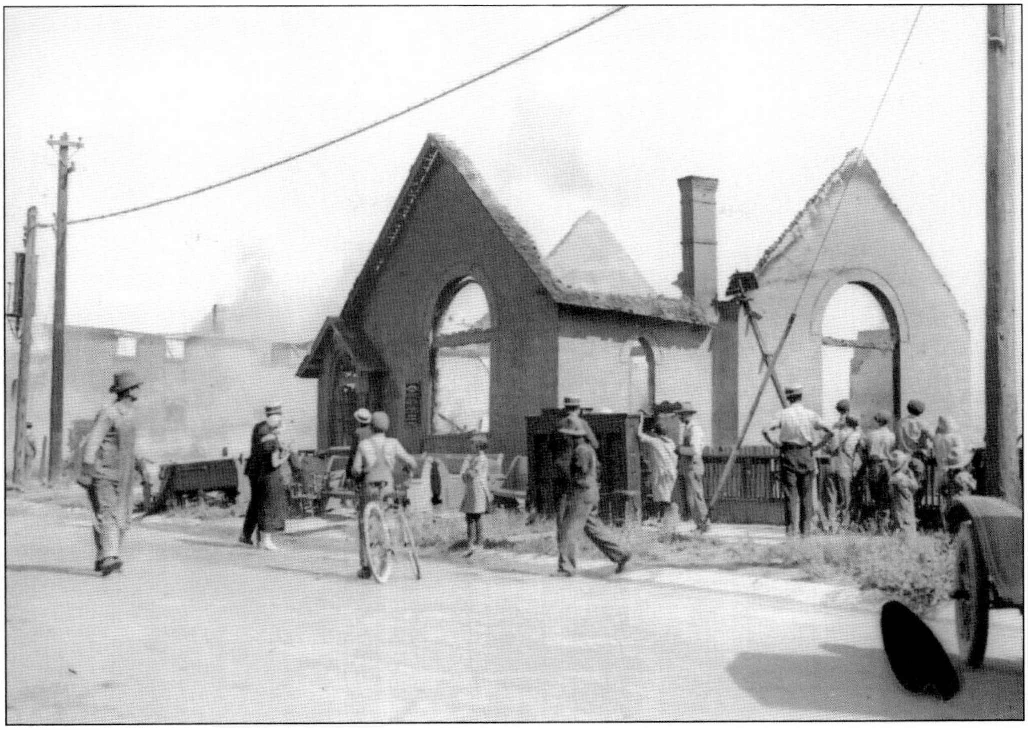

On August 10, 1924, a fire that began in the *Murray Eagle* print shop spread to the Murray Baptist Church (built in 1902–1903). The congregation met in homes, halls, and the empty city jail until a new meetinghouse was completed in 1926 on the same site on 4800 South. The 1926 building was moved to Poplar Street in 1987. (University of Utah, Marriott Library Special Collections.)

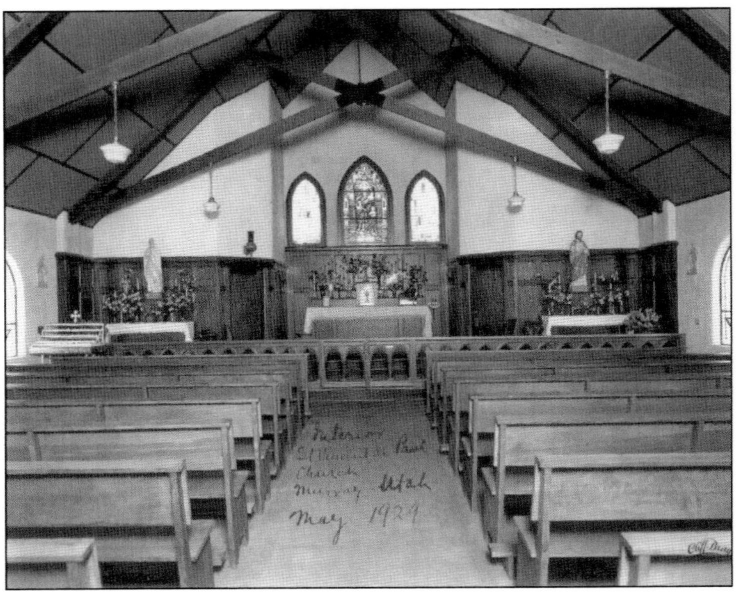

The Catholic Church's St. Vincent de Paul in Murray was made an official parish in 1925. On May 30, 1927, the chapel at 4893 South Wasatch Street was dedicated. The worship space was photographed in May 1929. Today, the building is home to the St. Jude (Maronite) Catholic Church. (MCM.)

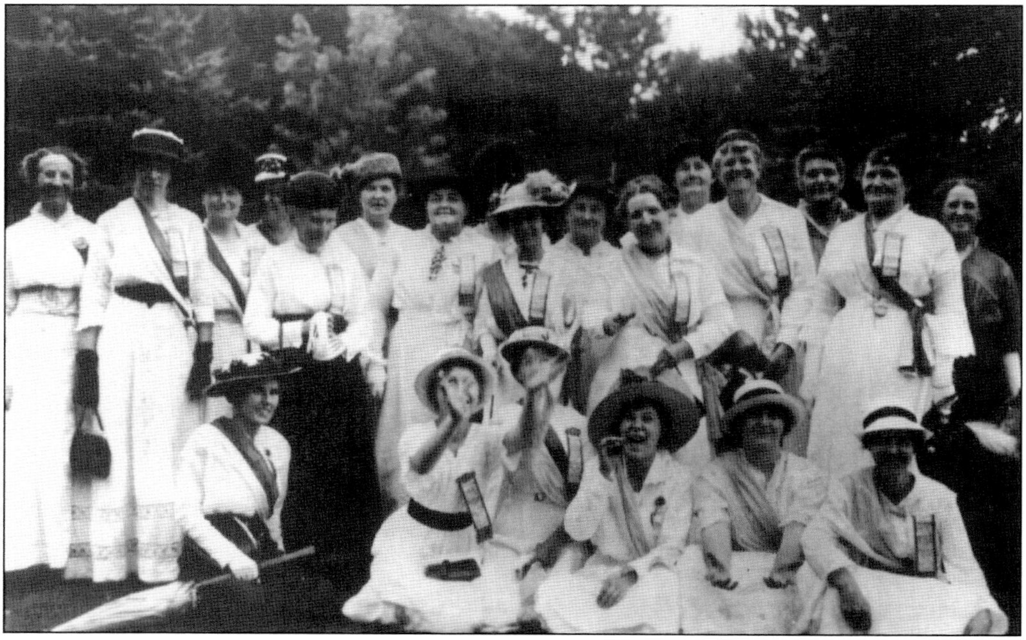

Pictured here in 1921, the Murray Women's Club was organized in 1905. Members worked on projects such as women's suffrage, sidewalks near city schools, campaigns for pure milk, and the city library. During World War I, the club discontinued activities while its members worked for the Red Cross. The organization still exists more than a century after its founding. (MCM.)

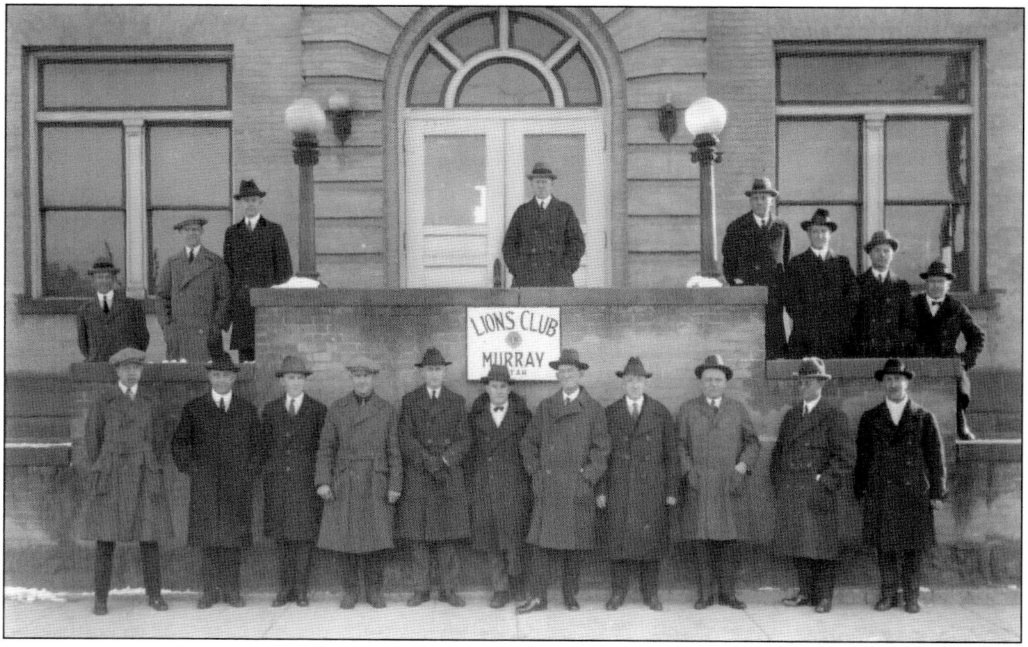

When the Murray Lions Club was organized in 1923, it was only the third club in Utah. This photograph of members on the steps of city hall was probably taken at one of the club's first meetings. The Murray Lions helped establish the Community Unemployed Relief Store during the Depression years. One of the club's longest traditions has been the Fourth of July breakfast at Murray's Fun Days celebration. (MCM.)

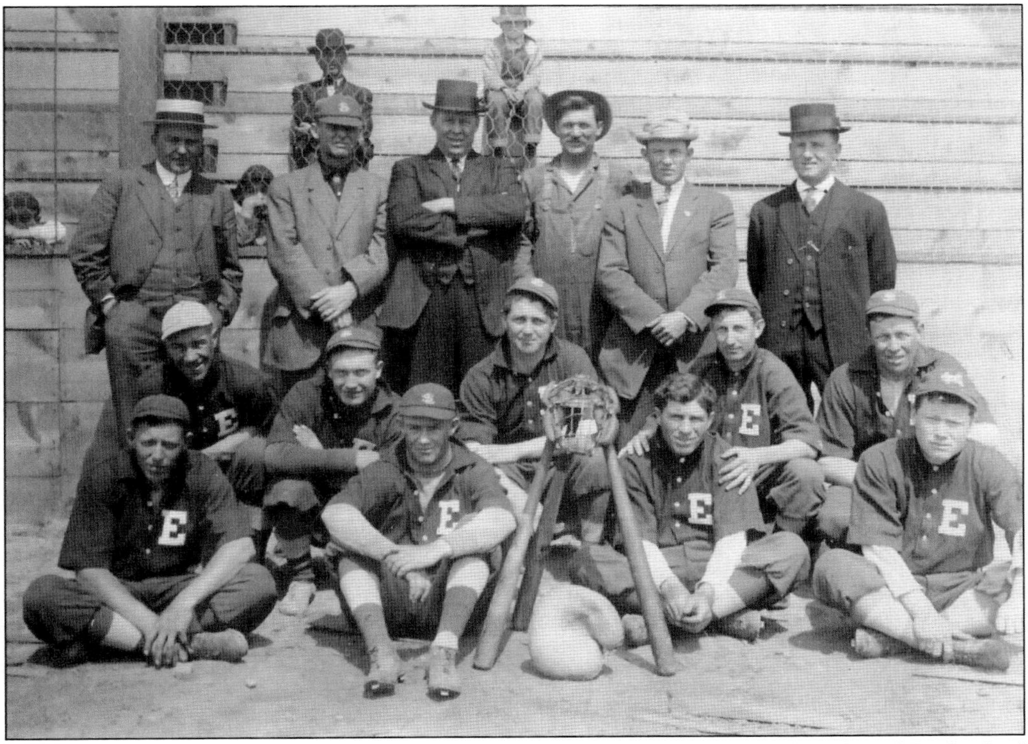

Like many fraternal organizations in the early 1900s, Murray's Fraternal Order of Eagles had its own baseball team (pictured here in an undated photograph). Other early baseball teams in Murray included the volunteer fire department team, the telephone company team, and a team of downtown businessmen. (MCM.)

The family of Arthur and Lovenia Harker Townsend had strong ties to Murray. Arthur founded the Murray Mercantile and built the adjacent Harker Building on State Street. He was Murray's mayor in 1930–1931. His middle son, Delbert, served as Murray's fire chief for 14 years. The family lived on Poplar Street behind the mercantile. Pictured here around 1910 are, from left to right, Lovenia, Delbert, Ruby, Leo, William, and Arthur. (MCM.)

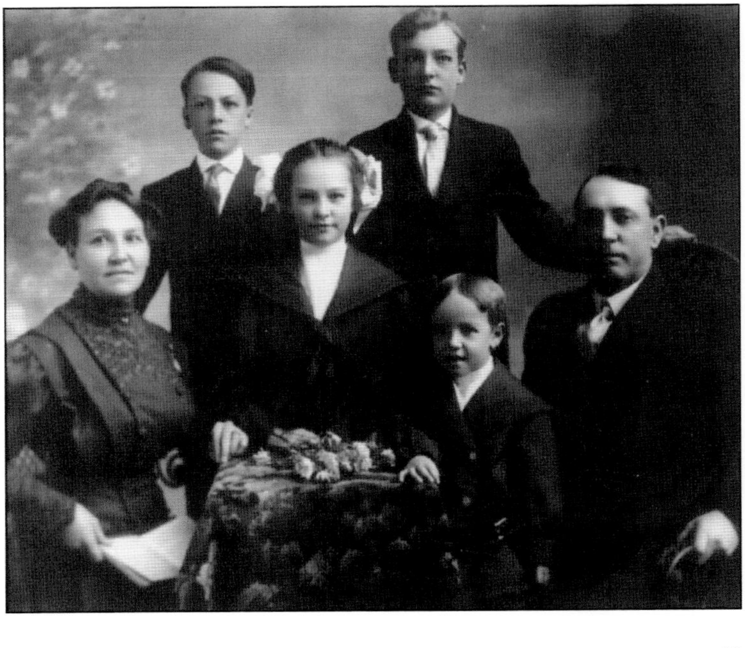

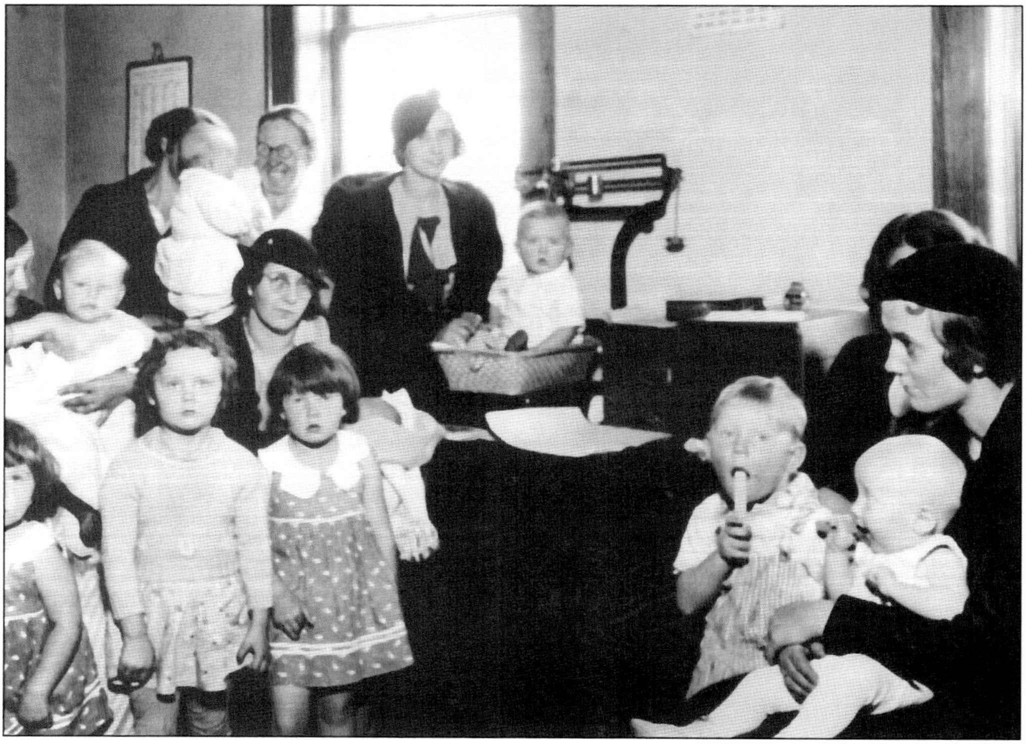

Alice Godfrey Silver (in glasses at rear) organized the Murray Free Baby Clinic. For 35 years, she worked with Murray doctors in several locations to provide checkups and care for infants and toddlers. Silver also worked with Amanda Bagley and others to open the Cottonwood Maternity Hospital, where most of Murray's babies were born between 1924 and 1962. (MCM.)

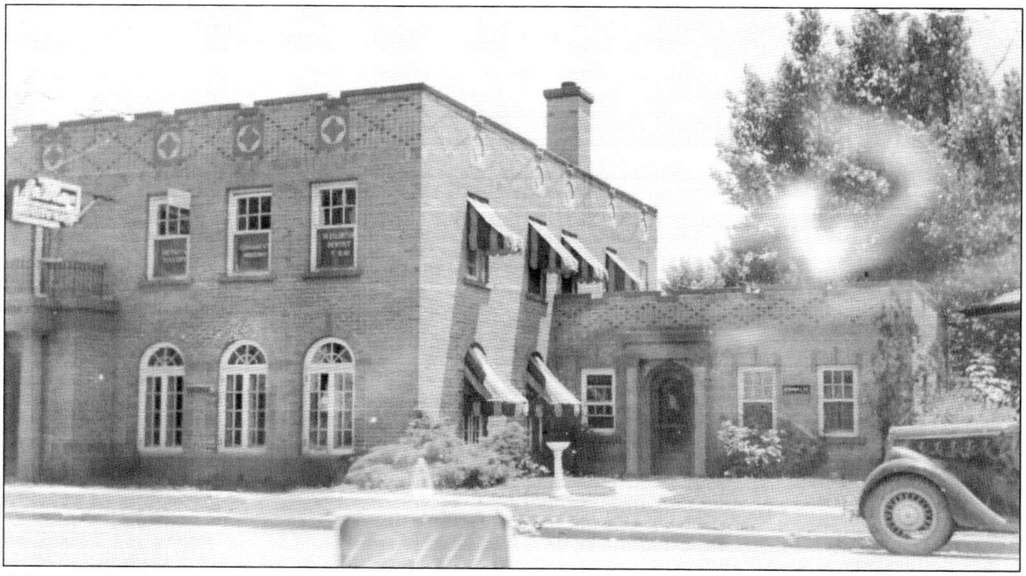

After medical training, Dr. Herond Sheranian returned to Murray in 1921. He had offices in the Harker Building before establishing the Murray Clinic Hospital in 1927 (seen here in 1936). The building was designed by Murray architect Lenord C. Nielson, the architect of numerous public buildings and private residences in Murray. (SLCA.)

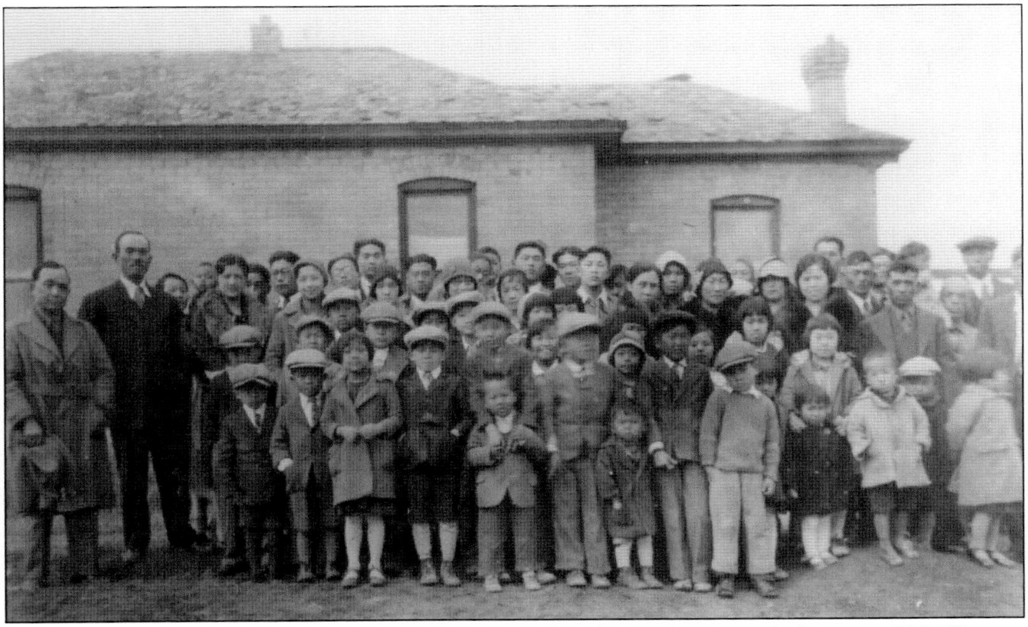

The Tadehara family came to Murray in 1921. They had a large truck farm on 700 West at approximately 6300 South. In 1927, the family provided a building for use by the Japanese *doshikai*, a community organization of about 15 families. The doshikai provided a Saturday school of Japanese language and culture for the children. (MCM.)

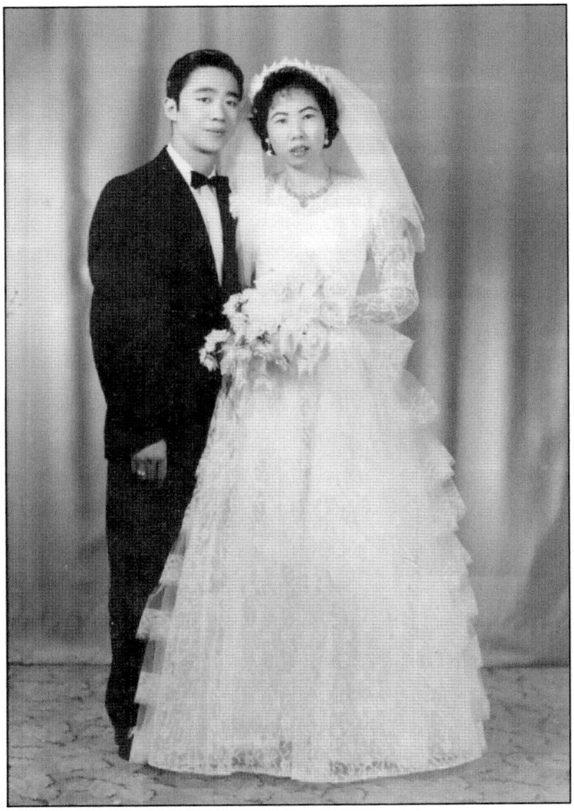

The ASARCO smelter closed intermittently from the beginning of the Great Depression through the 1940s, causing both longtime and more recent families to leave. This wedding photograph of an unknown Asian couple in the 1940s was found in a vacant home on Fifth Avenue and represents Murray's many temporary residents during this period. (MCM.)

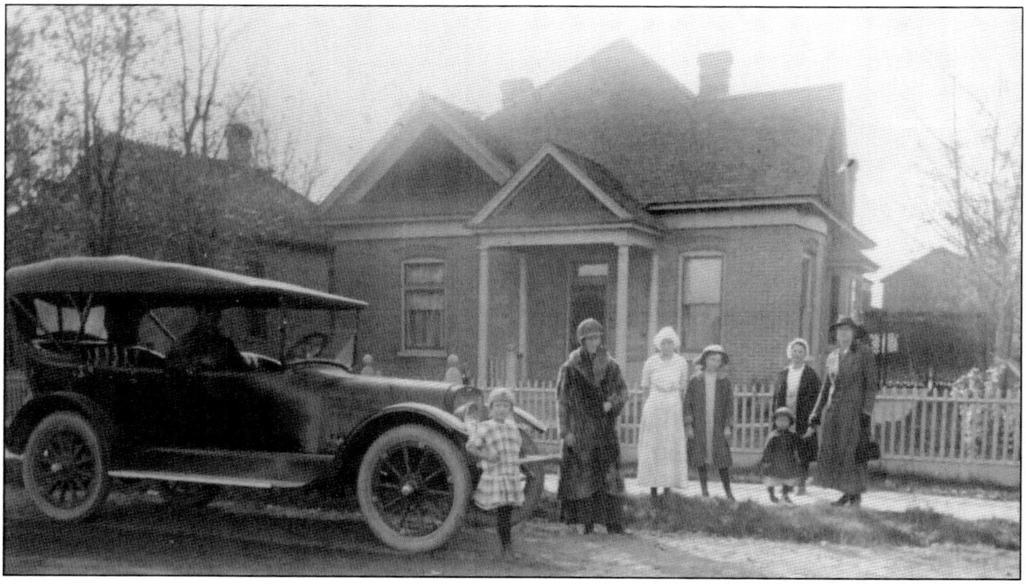

As a young married couple, George and Lottie Watts built a home in Murray in 1905, but they also owned a sheep ranch in Opal, Wyoming, which employed 10 to 20 ranch hands. George was a wool merchant. This photograph of the family with their first car, an Overland, was taken in front of the family home on 4800 South. (MCM.)

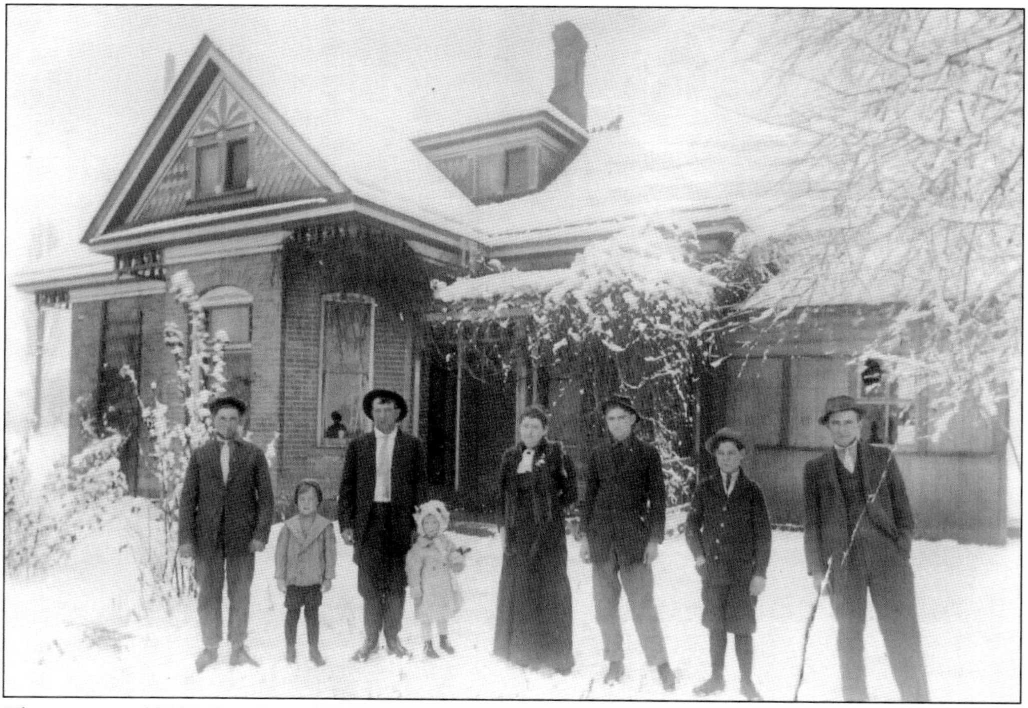

The corner of 5900 South and State Street was known as Simper's Corner. In 1896, Ernest Simper married Katie Bird from Bird's Corner at 5900 South and 300 West. They lived in a brick house on State Street (pictured here about 1915) that was later sold to Ernest's sister Rosella, the wife of Michael McMillan Jr. The McMillans owned most of the property around 5900 South and 300 East. (MCM.)

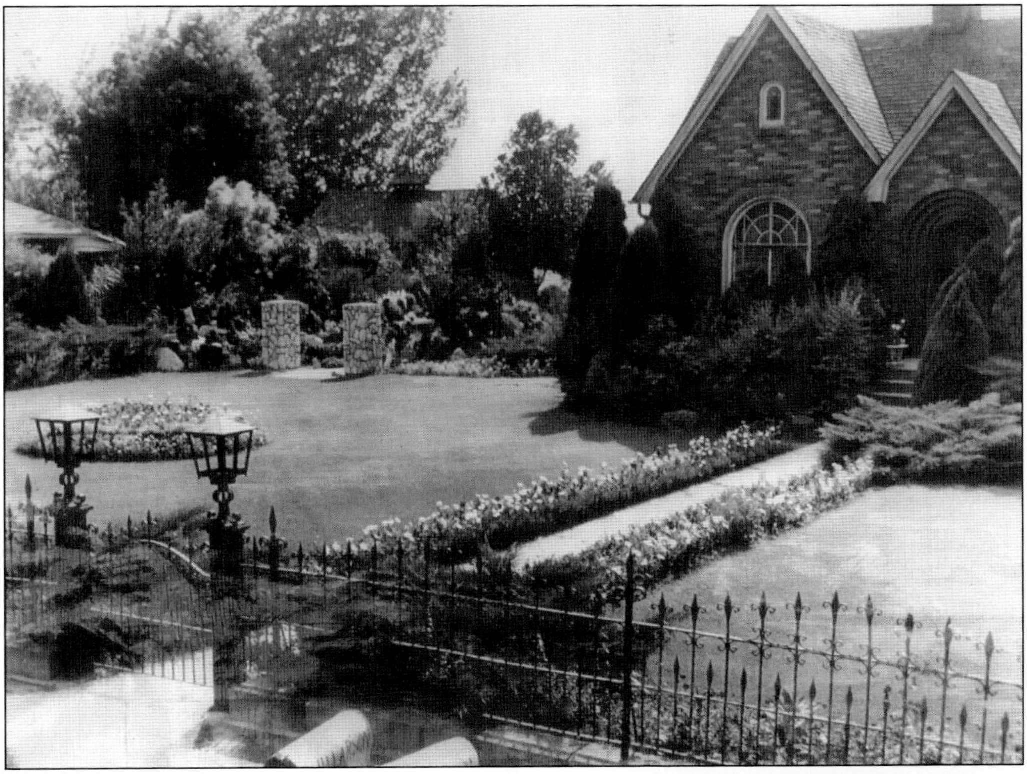

The home of David and Elva McGuire Bowen was the centerpiece of their business, Bowen Flower Gardens, at 6460 South State Street (pictured here in an undated photograph). The Murray Park War Memorial Rose Garden is an example of their legacy in the community. The Bowen property was demolished when Interstate 215 was connected to Interstate 15. (MCM.)

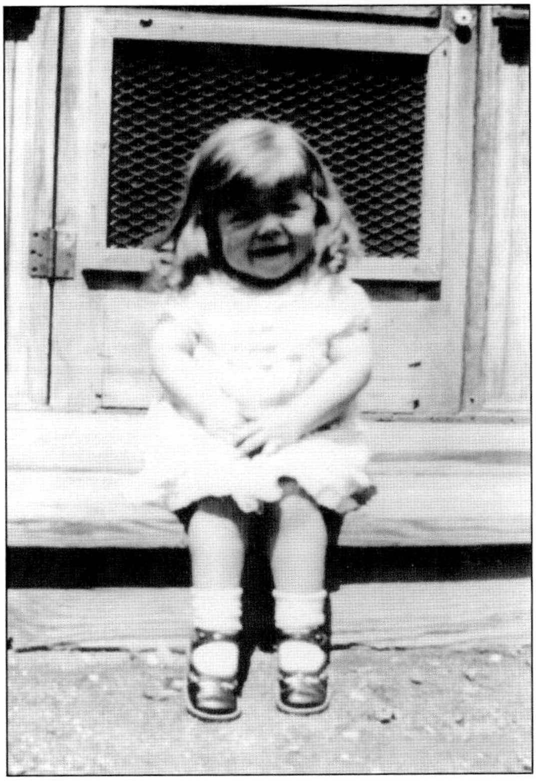

Around 1937, three-year-old Colleen Joy Warner Mix was photographed sitting on her front stoop. Colleen's father worked for the smelter, and their rented home was located across the street from Murray Park. By the 1930s, the smelter slag heap had spread almost to the banks of the Little Cottonwood Creek and the backyards of the remaining houses on State Street. The Warners purchased a nicer home in 1941. (MCM.)

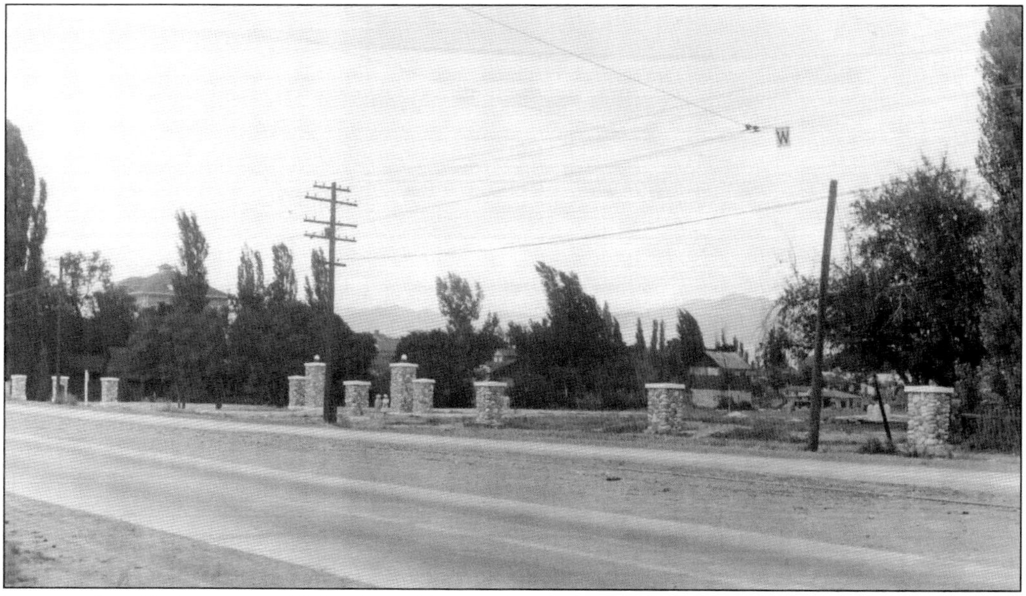

Murray City Park was established in 1924 on the east side of State Street; the west entrance is pictured here around 1930. The original landscape design was executed by the Utah Nursery Company, owned by Albert and Bertha Vorse. Their daughter Barbara Vorse Fealy, in college at the time, became Utah's first female landscape architect. (MCM.)

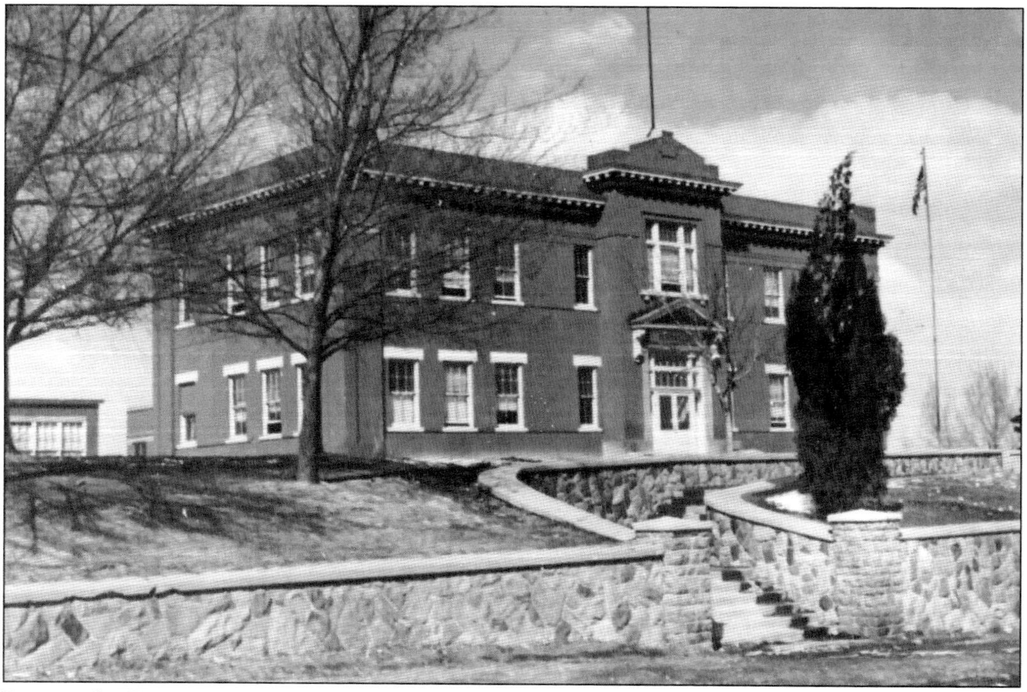

During the Depression years in the 1930s, Murray City officials made use of several federal work programs to boost employment. Projects included stone bleachers for the softball field in Murray Park, a new Arlington School building, and a stone retaining wall for Bonnyview Elementary (pictured here). The wall and steps are the only remainders of Bonnyview, which was demolished in 2005. (MCM.)

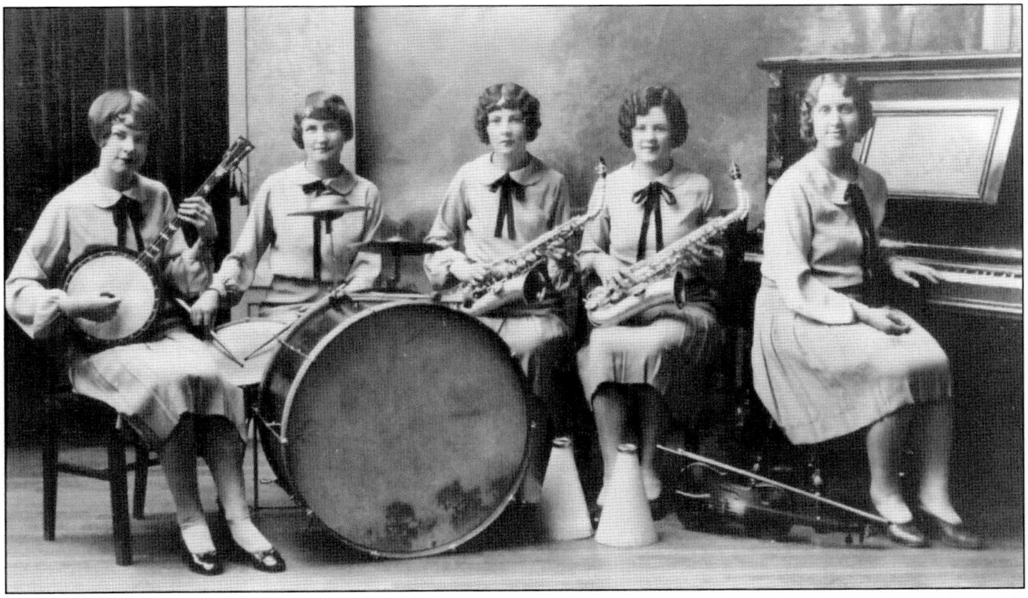

The Melody Maids all-girl orchestra was organized in 1929 and in demand throughout the Salt Lake Valley. The group was paid $20 for dances and other events during the four years members played together. Pictured here are, from left to right, Marjorie Carlson, Beatrice Simper, Vivian Carlson, Norma Olson, and June Ballard. (MCM.)

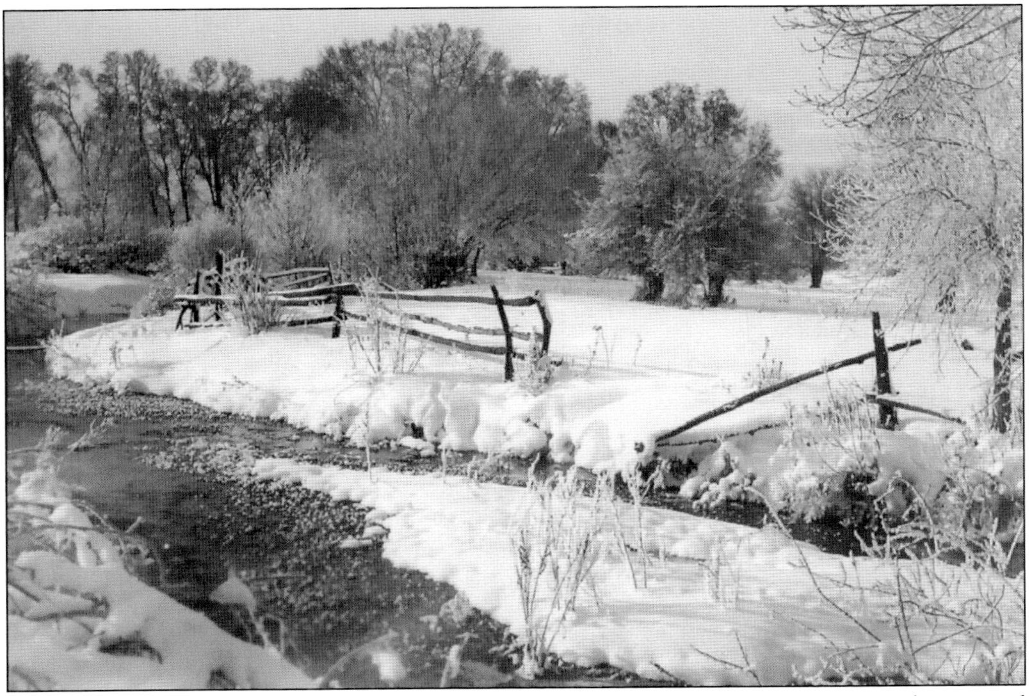

Pictured here in 1941, Godfrey's Grove on Little Cottonwood Creek below 5300 South was used for picnics by the pioneers. The grove was called Liberty Glen when it was chosen for the first LDS summer camp for girls. Between 1912 and 1915, small groups would take the streetcar from Salt Lake City to spend a week swimming in the creek, cooking outdoors, and studying the local flora and fauna. (MCM.)

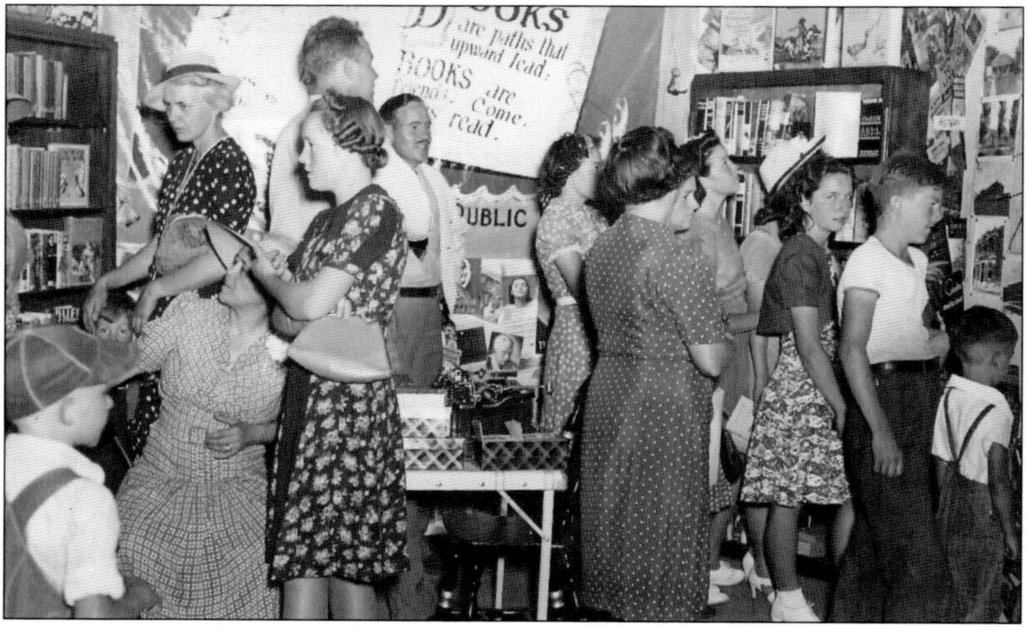

On September 2, 1939, the Salt Lake County Fair opened on land adjoining the north side of Murray Park. According to the *Murray Eagle*, Murray was chosen for its central location, easy access, and "appropriate country atmosphere." This would be the site of the county fairgrounds for the next six decades. In this photograph, the Murray City Library sponsors a book booth at the first fair, in 1939. (MCM.)

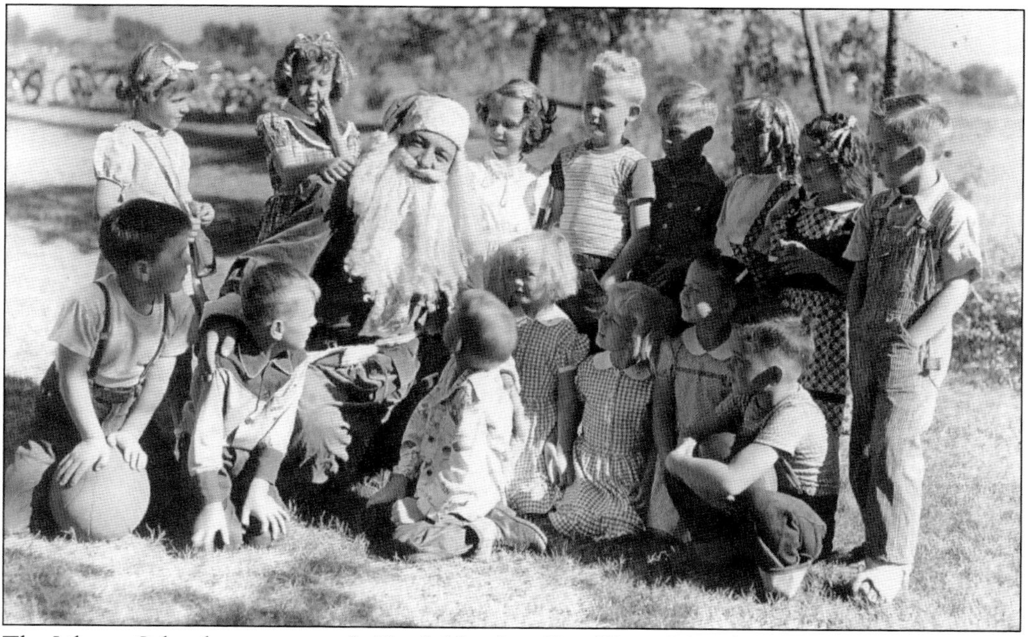

The Liberty School was surrounded by fields when Ken "Santa" Sanders Jr. entertained children on the front lawn (photographed here around 1940 judging by the ringlets). Within a decade, this area in southwest Murray would experience a postwar subdivision boom, and the school population would triple. Liberty Elementary was expanded twice, in 1957 and again in 1964. The original building was demolished in 1988. (MCM.)

Four

The Suburban Center of Salt Lake County

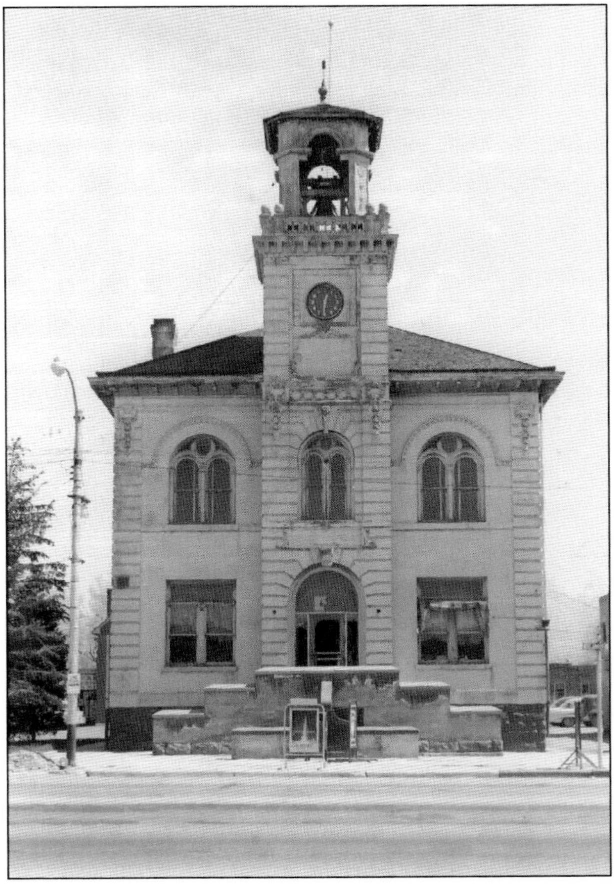

The first Murray City Hall was a part of the community until its demolition in 1958. Within these walls, Murray City officials managed a population that jumped from 5,740 in 1940 to 16,806 in 1960. This 1950s photograph shows the public "comfort station" built under the front steps in 1931. (MCM.)

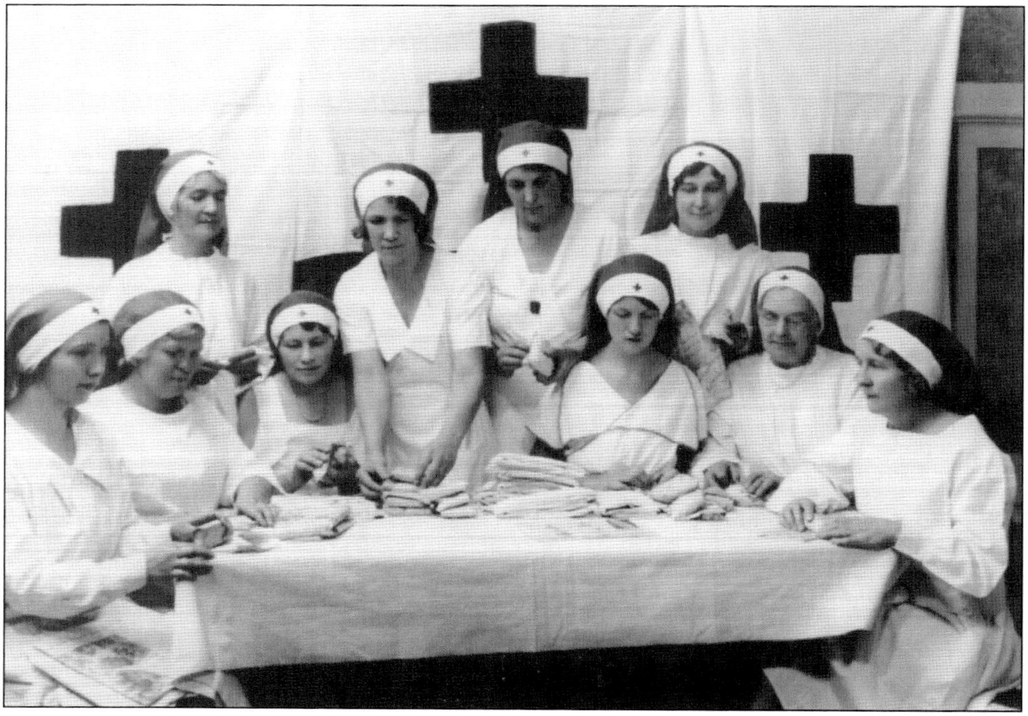

In the years leading up to World War II, Murray braced for change. This photograph taken in 1935 shows women of the American Red Cross chapter in Murray learning to roll bandages. The ASARCO smelter, which closed between May and October during the Depression years, was able to employ 100 men to make lead bullets for the war. (MCM.)

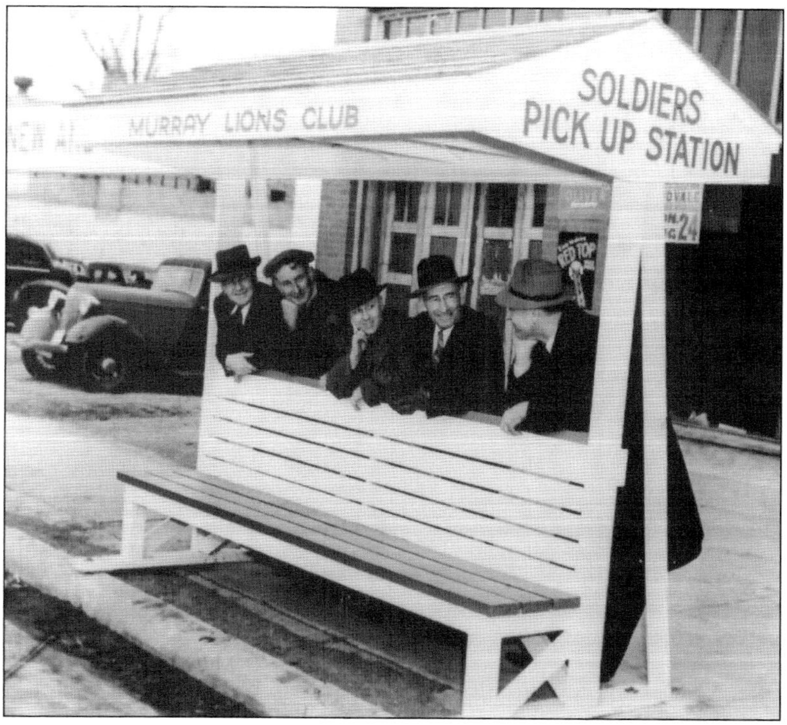

Two weeks after the bombing of Pearl Harbor in December 1941, Murray's civic leaders began organizing committees to help the war effort. On the home front, Murray residents endured food rationing, collected rubber and scrap metal, bought war bonds, and planted victory gardens. Pictured here around 1942 is a special bus stop for soldiers sponsored by the Murray Lions Club. (MCM.)

William Fillmore Smith was married with small children and a meat cutter in the family business when he joined the US Navy. Smith is pictured here with two buddies around 1944. To signify the end of the war, on December 19, 1945, Murray City sent certificates to a roster of several hundred men and women veterans of World War II. (MCM.)

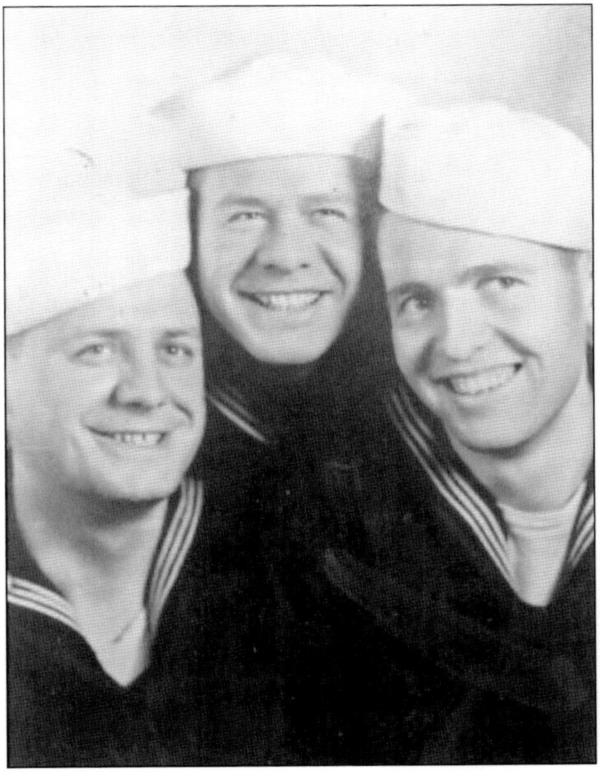

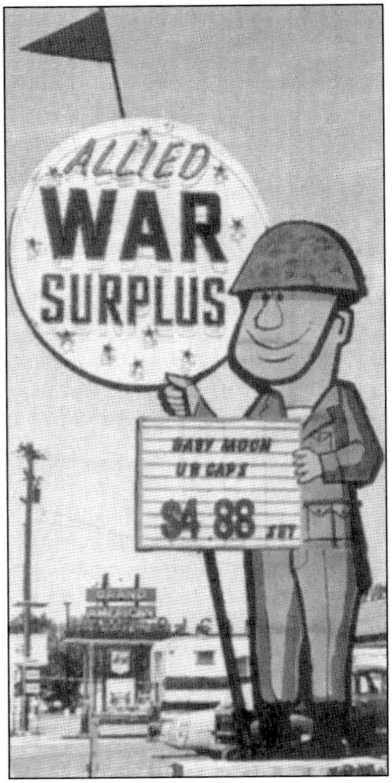

The Allied Development Company was organized in November 1946 to sell war surplus. The first store at 6400 South State Street (Lovenhdahl's Corner) was in a converted livery stable with a war plane in the parking lot. The attire of the man on the sign was changed to civilian clothes when Allied's expanded into a discount store in the 1950s. (MCM.)

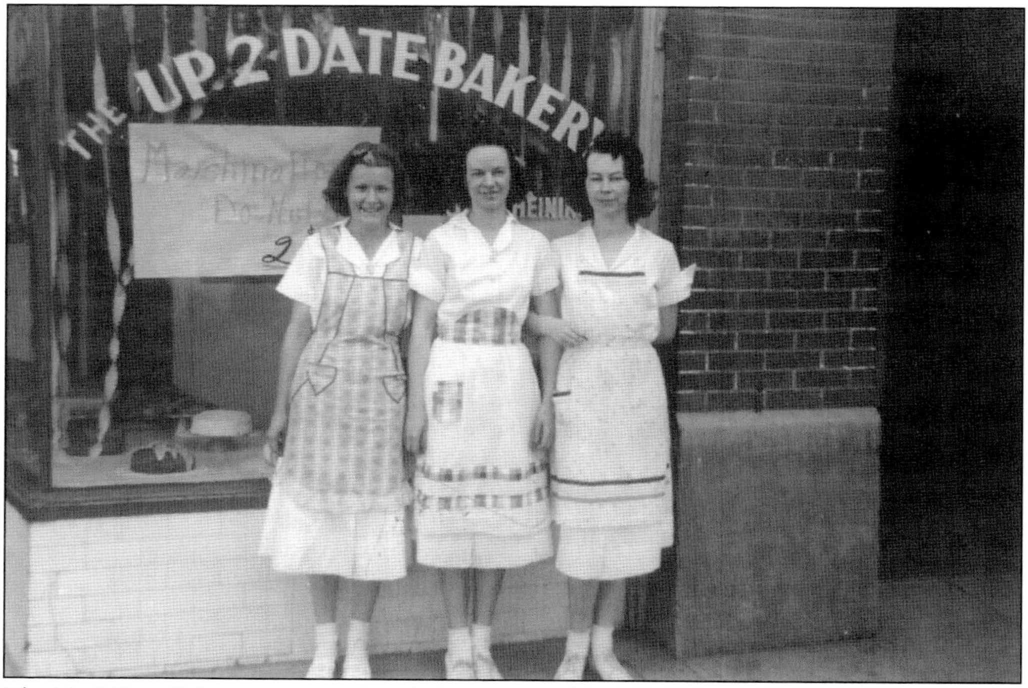

The Up 2 Date Bakery was one of two bakeries owned by Dutch immigrants Frank and Johanna Kaper. Their nephew John Van Heiningen took over in 1929. This photograph of the bakery in the Hoffman Building was taken in the 1940s. Pictured here are, from left to right, Jean Walters and her cousins Josephine and Fern Walters. (MCM.)

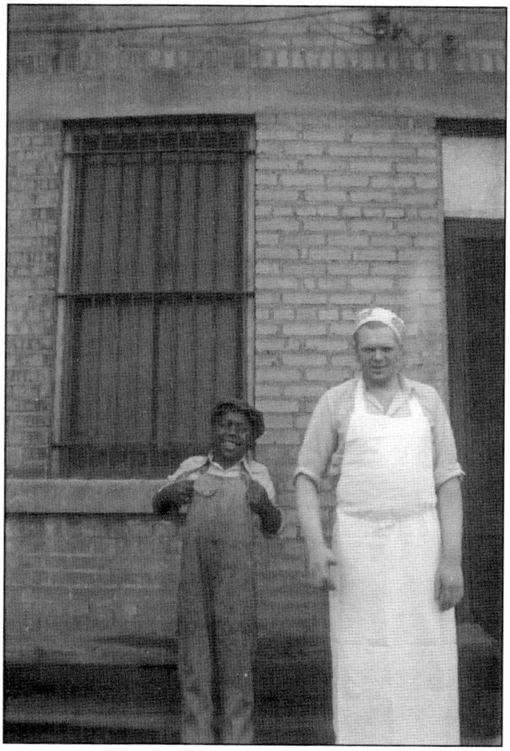

At the rear of the Up 2 Date Bakery, baker Bill Groepas (right) is pictured with Gene Bankhead. Bankhead's parents, Nathan and Henrietta Bankhead, raised eight children on Poplar Street. When his grandparents George and Sina Bankhead lived in Murray, their daughter, Carrie was the only black child in the school district. Gene's great-grandparents Nathan and Miriam were freed slaves who came to Utah in 1848 and 1851 respectively. (MCM.)

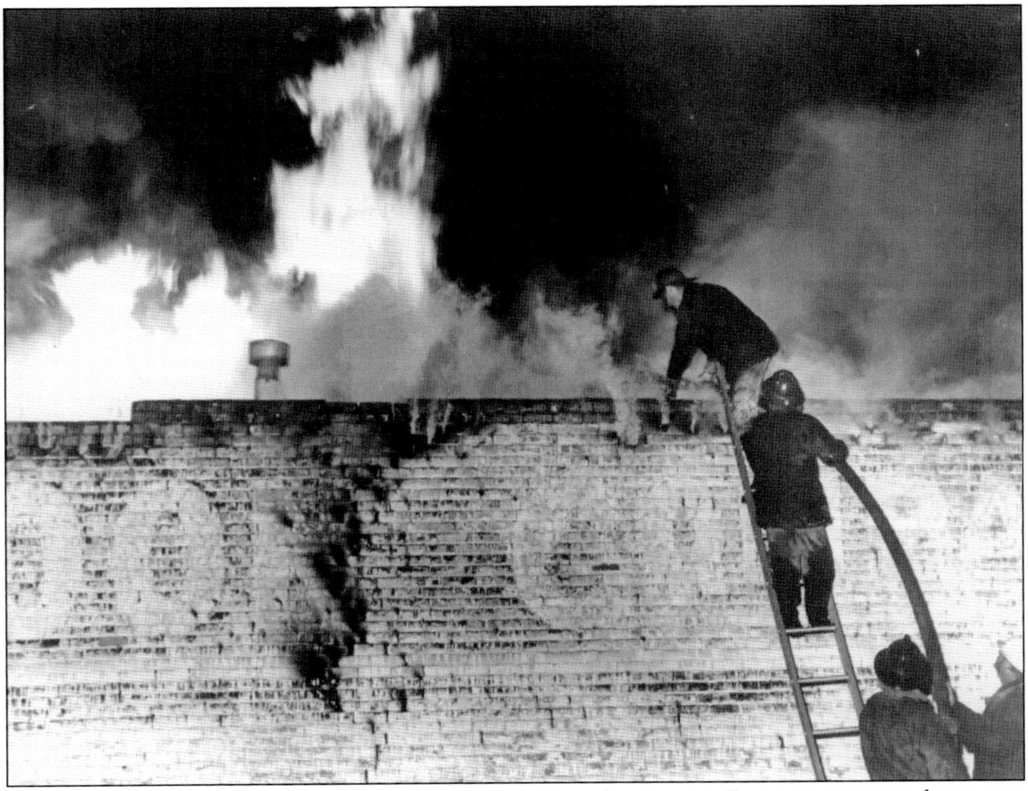

Murray's volunteer fire department tried in vain to save the Granite Furniture store at the corner of 4800 South and State Street. Arsonists were suspected of setting two fires at the same location in one week in 1961 (above). A few Murray residents remember the roller-skating rink that was on the top floor of the furniture store. Like many older buildings in Murray's commercial business district, it was not replaced, and the corner remains a parking lot. In contrast, an old building that had been used for both a lodge hall and a city jail found a new use as the Jack Bush Tire Service, a sales and repair shop, in the late 1950s (below). This building on Second Avenue eventually succumbed to the wrecking ball in the 1980s (Both, MCM.)

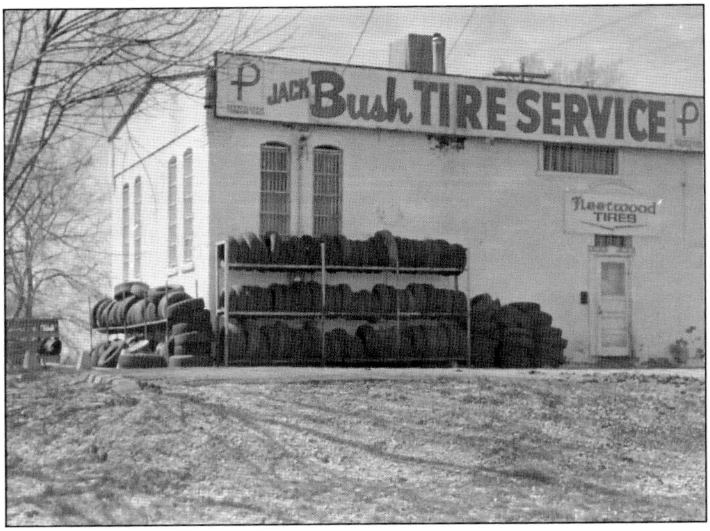

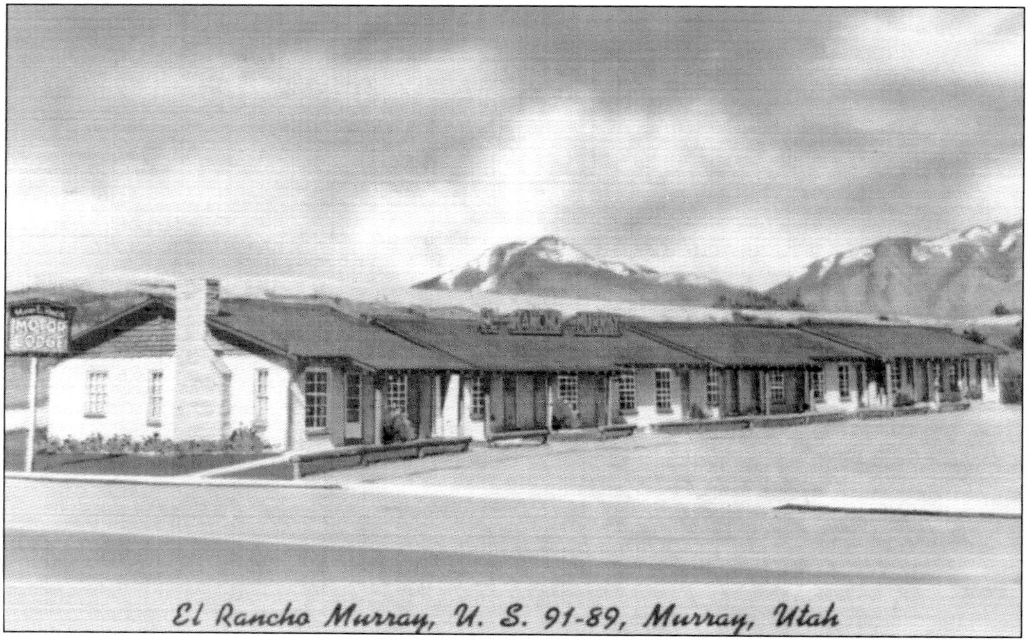

The El Rancho Motor Lodge at 5203 South State Street in Murray was built in 1946 and catered to out-of-state tourists traveling US Highway 89-91 (State Street). According to this postcard mailed to Connecticut in 1948, the motel had the following amenities: "roomy, elegantly furnished, fire-proof, fully carpeted, tiled showers, steam heat, radios, and free fishing" in the adjacent pond. The motel was razed in the 1990s. (Author's collection.)

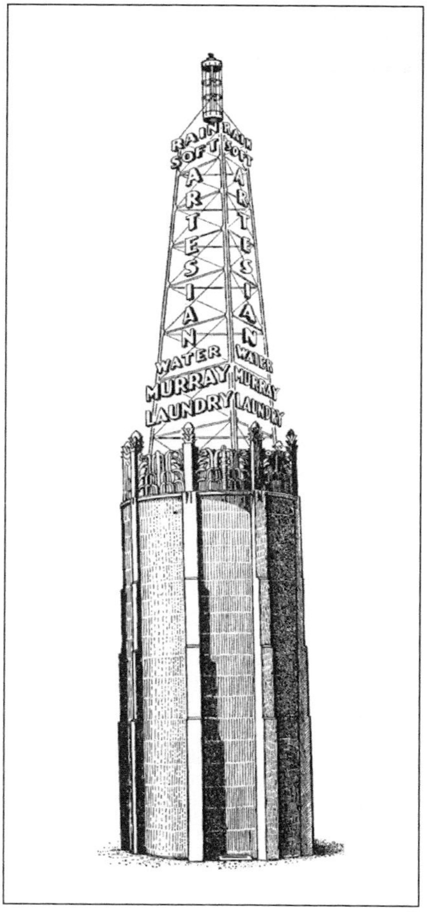

The Murray Laundry was established in 1910 at 4200 South State Street near the Big Cottonwood Creek. With nine artesian wells on the property, the company expanded in the 1920s. The laundry's water tank with its illuminated sign tower was built in 1930–1931. Although the laundry buildings have disappeared, the Art Deco landmark still stands. This drawing was used to advertise the business in the 1940s and 1950s. (MCM.)

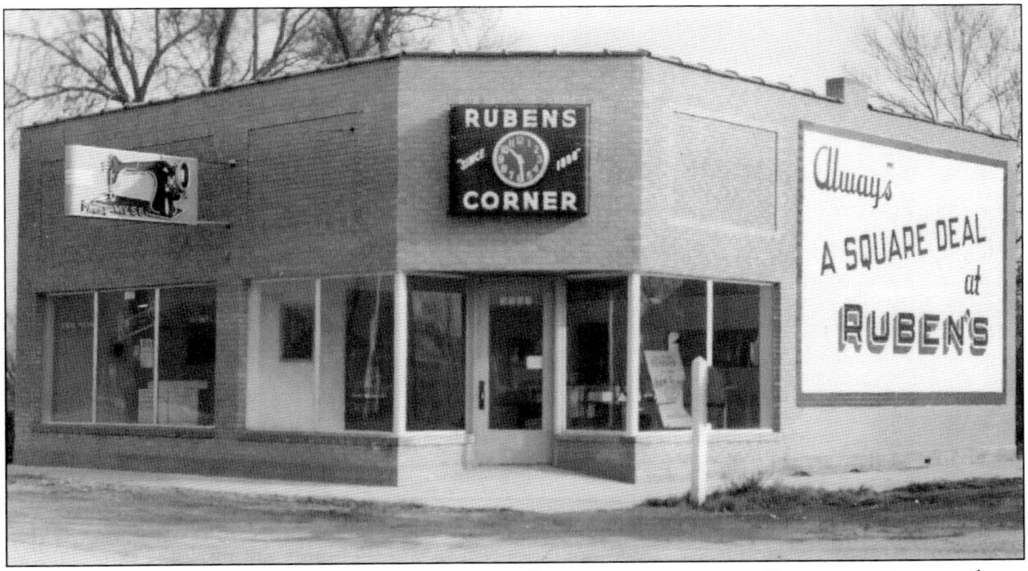

East Prussian immigrant Arthur Ruben Sr. earned a one-way passage to Boston repairing sails on the ship. He married Violet Gray, whose family owned property at 5600 South and State Street. At Ruben's corner, Arthur used his sewing skills to establish a sewing machine shop in 1888. The shop was updated by Arthur Ruben Jr. in 1960, when this photograph was taken. (MCM.)

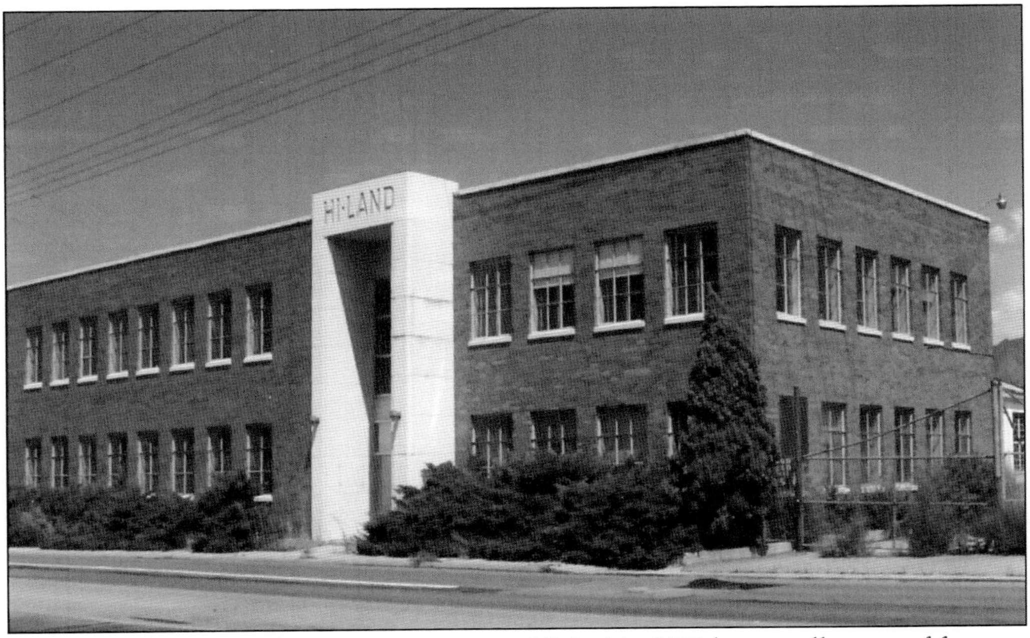

The Hi-Land Dairymen's Association was established in 1939 by a small group of farmers, including some of Murray's east side dairymen. By the 1950s, the company's central processing plant at 700 East and Vine Street was one of Murray's largest employers. This 1960s photograph shows the Hi-Land Dairy administration building. The sprawling complex was demolished in 1992. (MCM.)

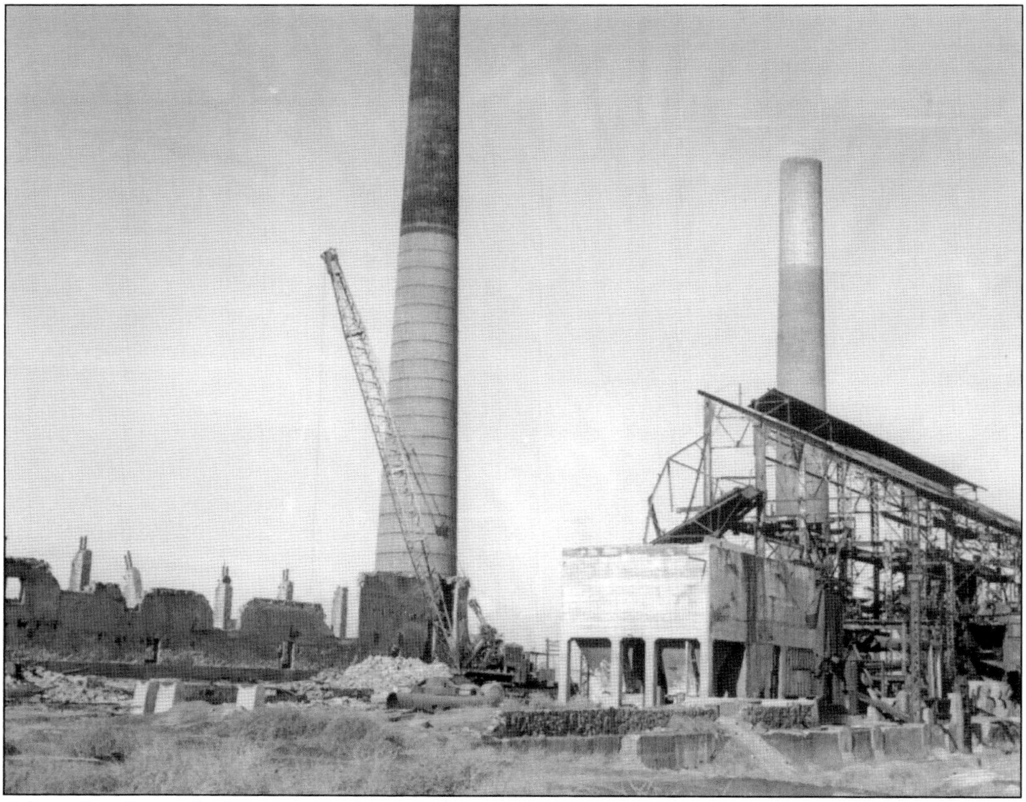

After a brief period of intense production during World War II, the smelter in Murray permanently closed in November 1950. ASARCO moved much of the equipment to its Garfield plant. This photograph from about 1954 illustrates the partial dismantling of the buildings. The stacks remained intact, and the uncontaminated buildings were used by the subsequent owner, Otto Buehner's concrete block company, until the late 1990s. (MCM.)

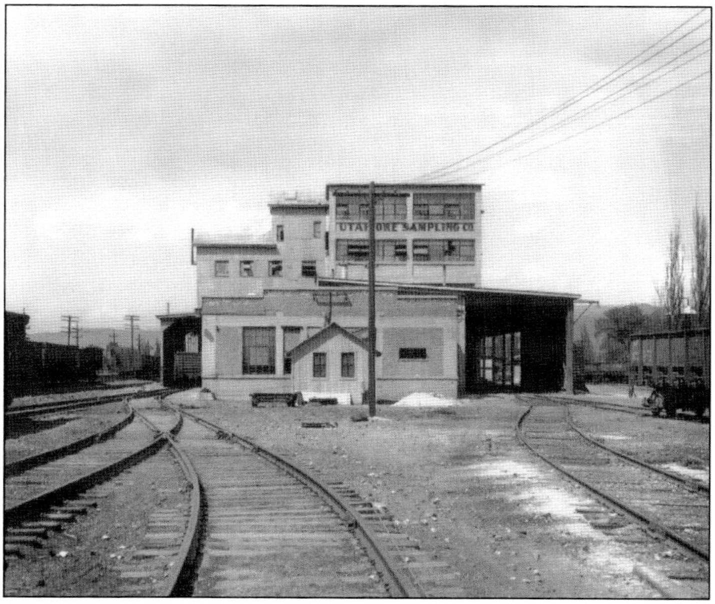

Around 1909, the Taylor & Brunton sampling mill was sold to the Utah Ore Sampling Company. During the 1920s, the company expanded the facility several times. This photograph taken in 1944 shows the thaw shed (built 1927, foreground) and the four-story concrete Mill D (built 1928, background). Today, the Utah Ore Sampling Mill complex is the only remaining building in Murray with ties to the smelting process. (USHS.)

The Italian community of immigrants in Murray had a support system that allowed them to leave the smelter and acquire land for truck farms. For example, the Mash and Deniro families had adjacent vegetable farms on east 4800 South (pictured here in the 1940s). Other Italian surnames associated with farms include Marcovicchio (700 West), Serre, Sardella, (Murray Park area), Delliskave, DiPietro, Motta, Leva, Cecalla, and Remoselli (900 East to 1600 East). (MCM.)

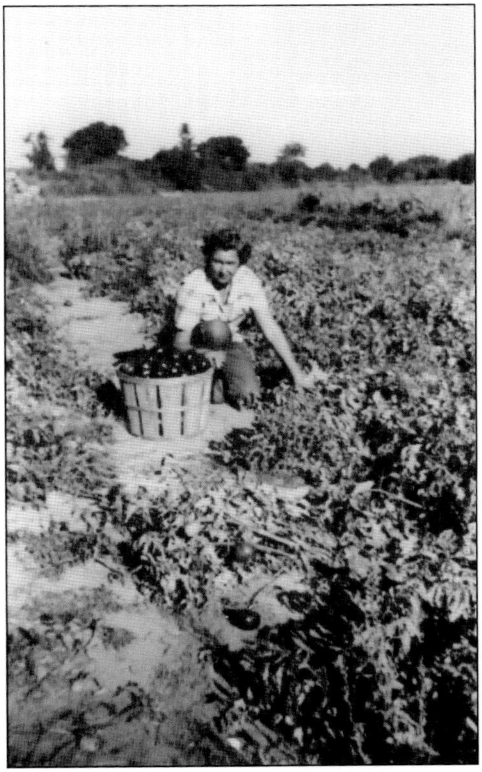

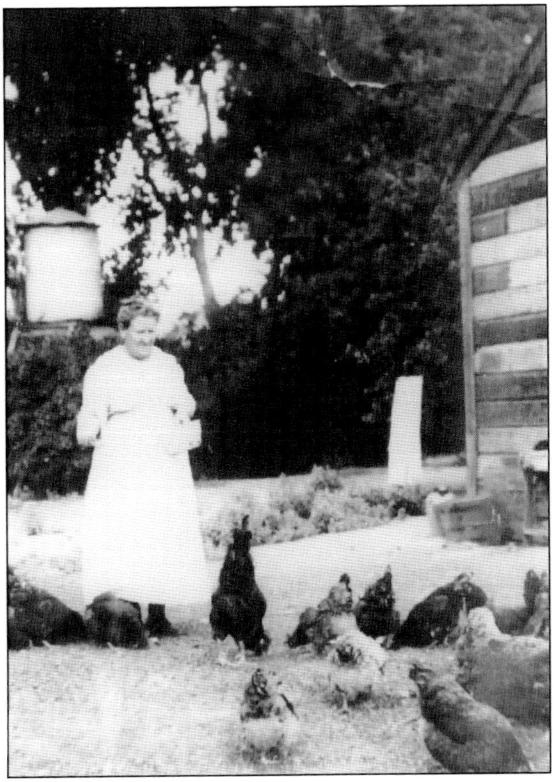

In the first half of the 20th century, many Murray residents raised poultry either for cash or family consumption. In this photograph from the 1940s, Magdalena "Maggie" Berger Riley tends her chickens on a small farm, probably on Wilson Avenue or Riley Lane. Her son John was an electrician who worked at the ore-sampling mill. (MCM.)

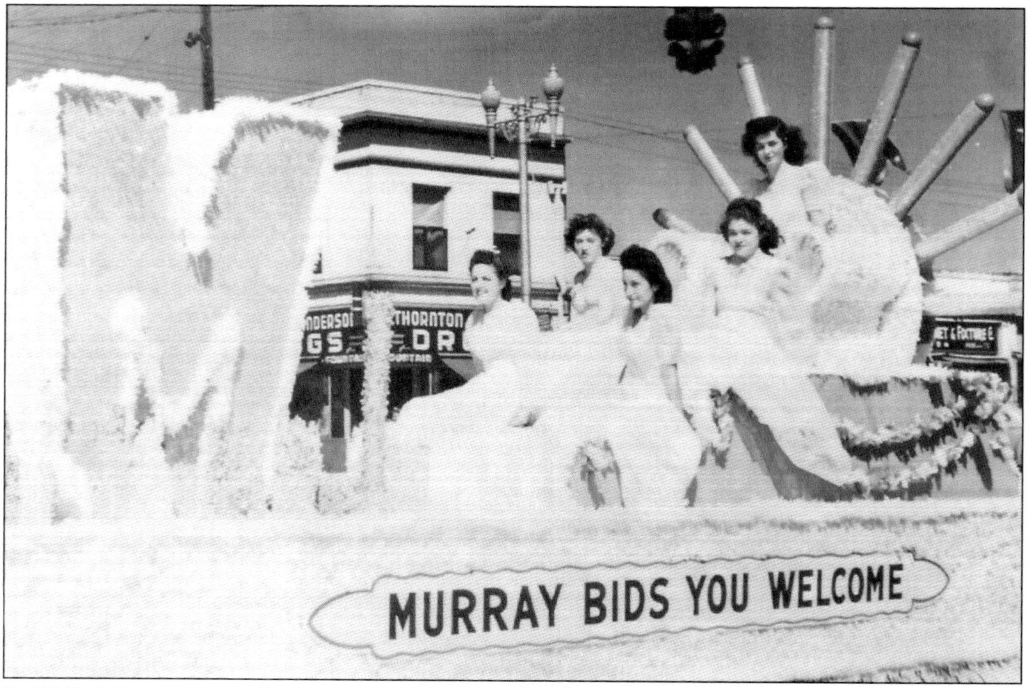

In 1941, Murray City's float in its annual Fourth of July parade featured a welcoming theme. This photograph was taken at the intersection of State Street and 4800 South, where the city's first traffic light was installed in 1929. Pictured are, from left to right, Virginia Lu Jensen, Faye Morgan, Marian Stauffer, Mary Vicchrilli, and Selina Price. (MCM.)

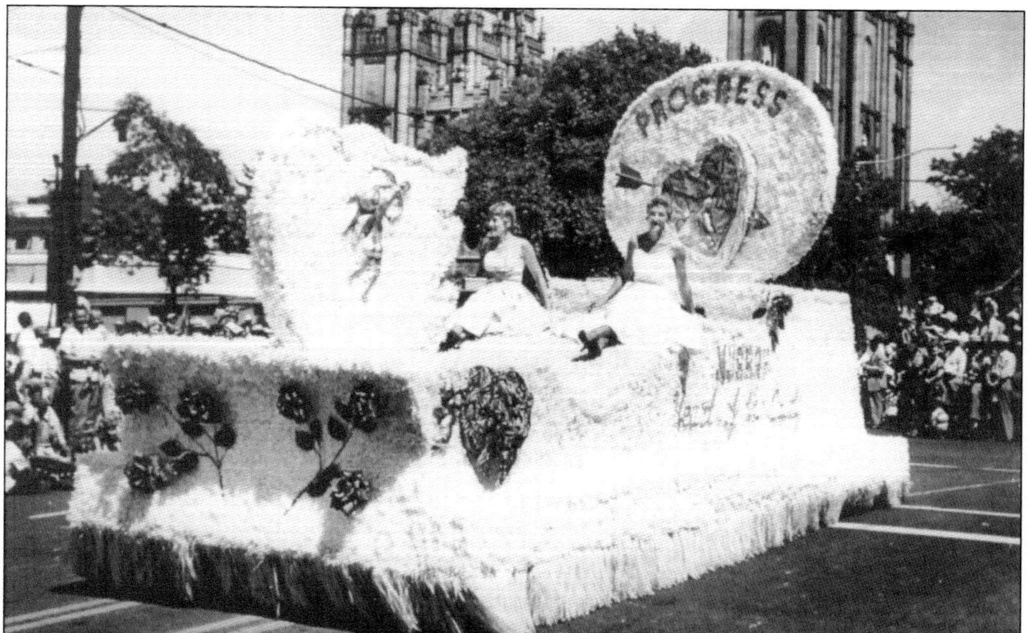

Sherry Johnson (left) and Joanne Johnson ride a Murray City float as it passes the Salt Lake Temple in the annual Days of '47 parade on July 24, 1954, through Salt Lake City. The float conveys Murray's progressive spirit as well as its location as the "Heart of Salt Lake County." (MCM.)

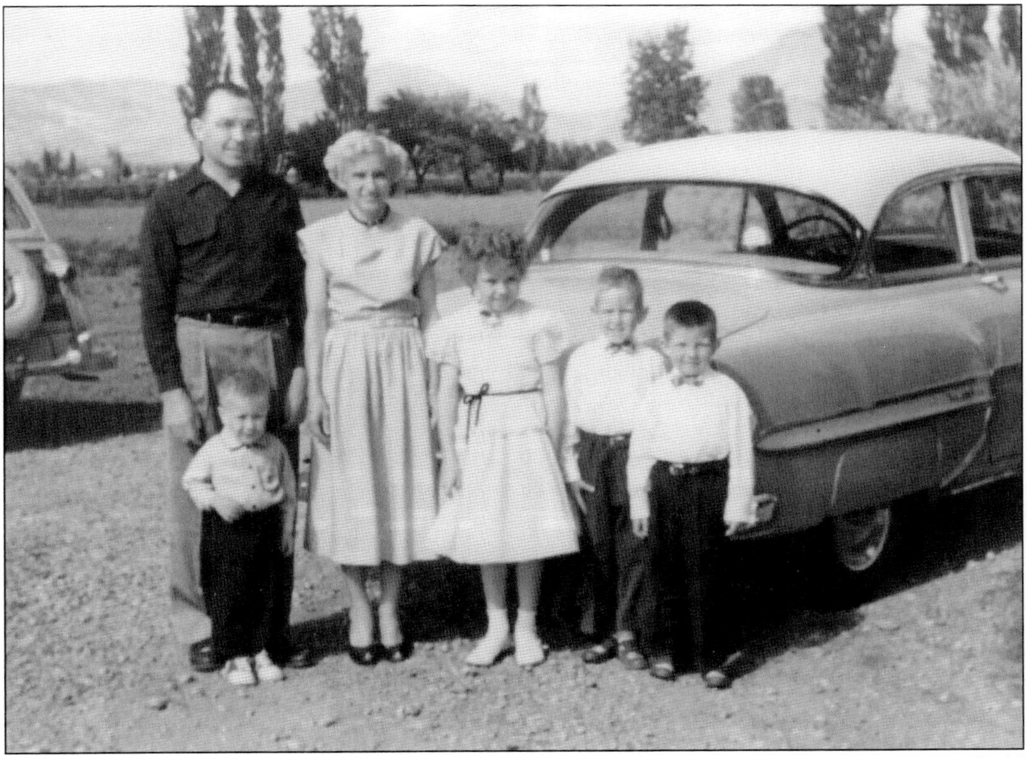

Born in Murray, Beatrice Goff moved to Salt Lake City after her marriage to Gordon A. Heinhold in 1942. The family enjoyed car rides to visit her parents at Goff Lane, near 700 West and 6300 South (pictured here with the family car in the 1950s). A branch of the family established the Goff Mortuary in Midvale. (MCM.)

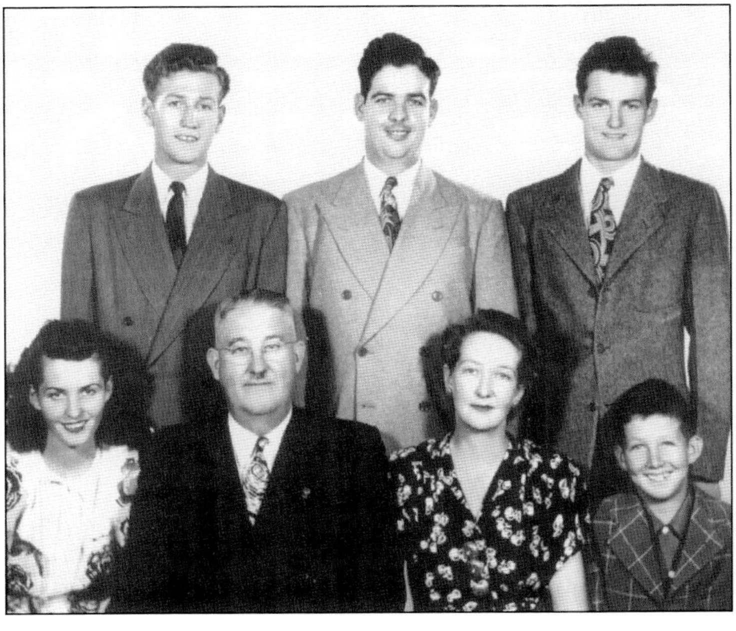

Three generations of Jensens represent upward mobility. Niels Jensen lived on Cherry Street and worked at the flour mill. His son James Leo was a local banker who lived downtown on Wasatch Street. James Leo and Grace Jensen are shown here with their children around 1945. Boyd Jensen (upper right) was an executive for the Lagoon Amusement Park and commuted from a modern ranch house on Hillside Drive. (MCM.)

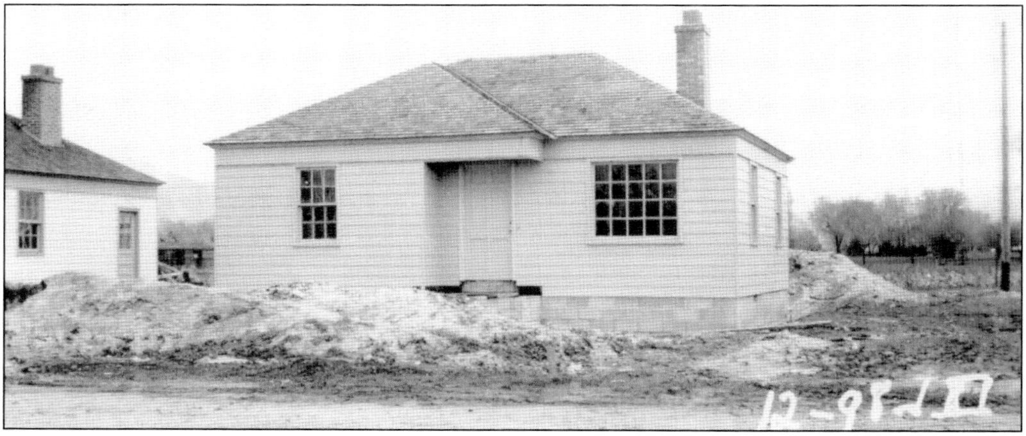

Photographs taken by the Salt Lake County tax assessors record the period of postwar growth. This home on Box Elder Street, built in 1944, was in a rare wartime subdivision. When interviewed for the *Murray Eagle*, the builder "declared that Murray was ideal for the project having a sewer line, city water and power and being located in a good area of convenient proximity to State Street and the Murray business section." (SLCA.)

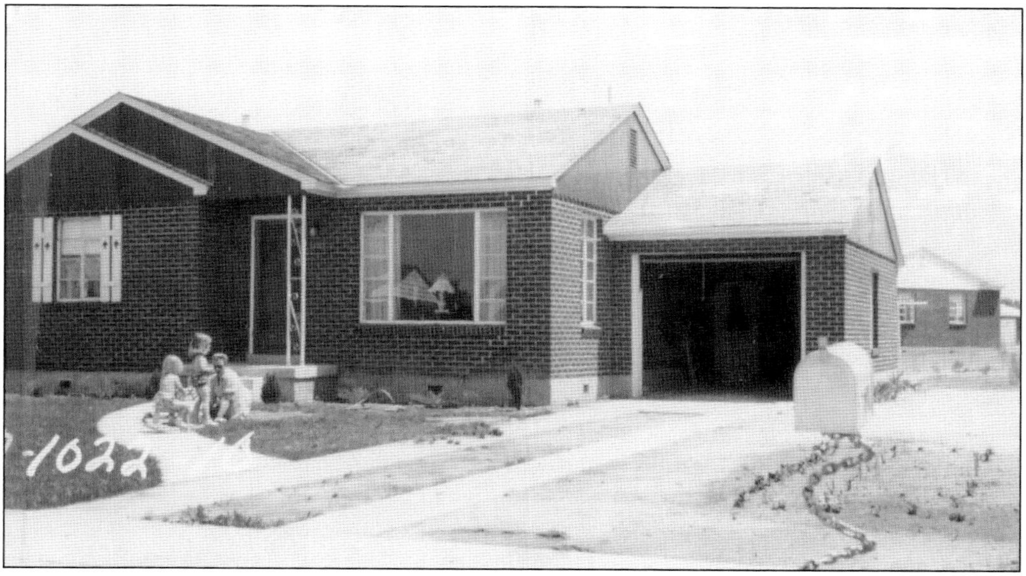

During the 1950s, the *Murray Eagle* noted month after month of record-breaking building permits in the city. This home was built in 1950 in Murray Heights, a subdivision of sturdy brick homes with attached garages. The neighborhood was designed with sidewalks connecting a trio of cul-de-sacs so children could visit friends without encountering automobile traffic. (SLCA.)

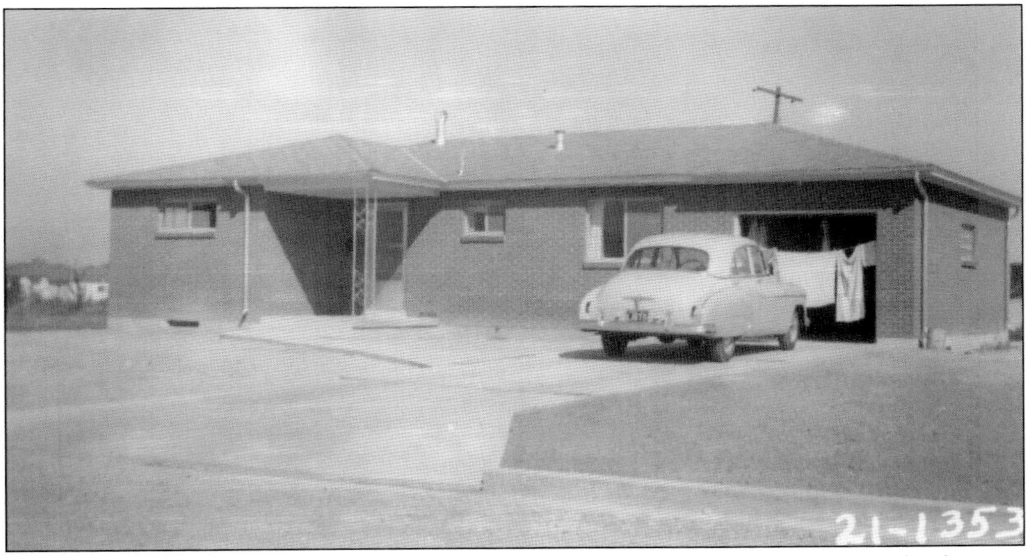

The South Cottonwood Heights subdivision was created by seven Murray couples with adjoining parcels of land on the ridge above Godfrey's Grove. This brick rambler was built in 1955 on Avalon Drive. While this subdivision looked back to the original name of the settlement, other Murray subdivisions of the 1950s embraced the atomic age with street names like Nova, Moon Ridge, Starlite, and the unforgettable Spacerama Drive. (MCM.)

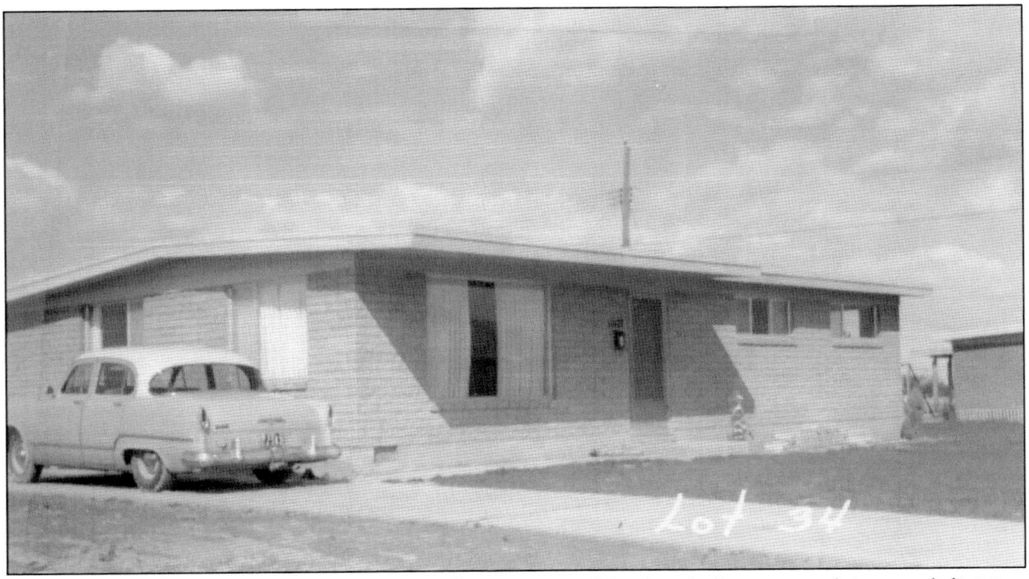

The pioneer-era name was also honored in the creation of the South Cottonwood Acres subdivision in unincorporated Salt Lake County (later annexed into Murray). Built in 1956, this home on 1080 East was among 200 flat-roof ranch houses in the neighborhood. The population increased so quickly in the area that the Granite School District built two new schools—Twin Peaks Elementary (1965) and Cottonwood High School (1970). (MCM.)

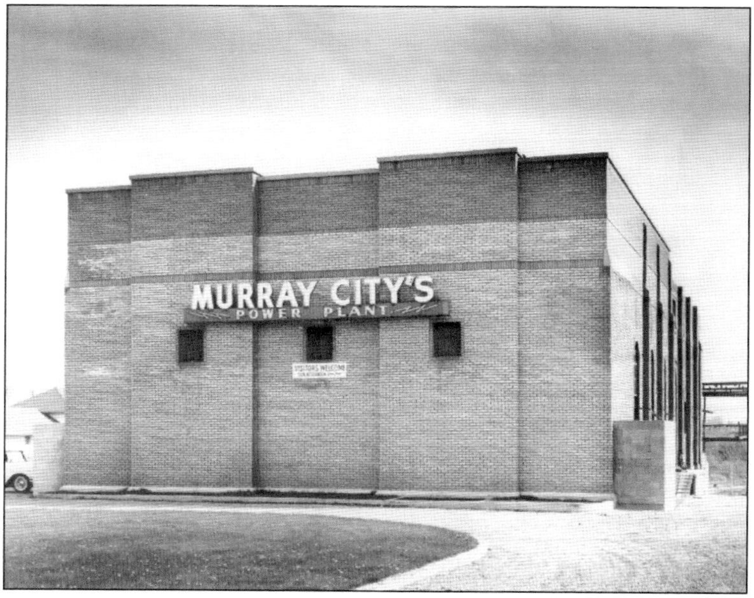

In December 1945, the *Murray Eagle* reported Murray City officials, anticipating postwar growth, announced a plan to expand the diesel power plant, acknowledging the "electric light and power system is entirely inadequate to take care of the present and future needs of the city." The plant size was doubled in 1947–1948 and the neon sign installed in 1953 (pictured here in the mid-1950s). (MCM.)

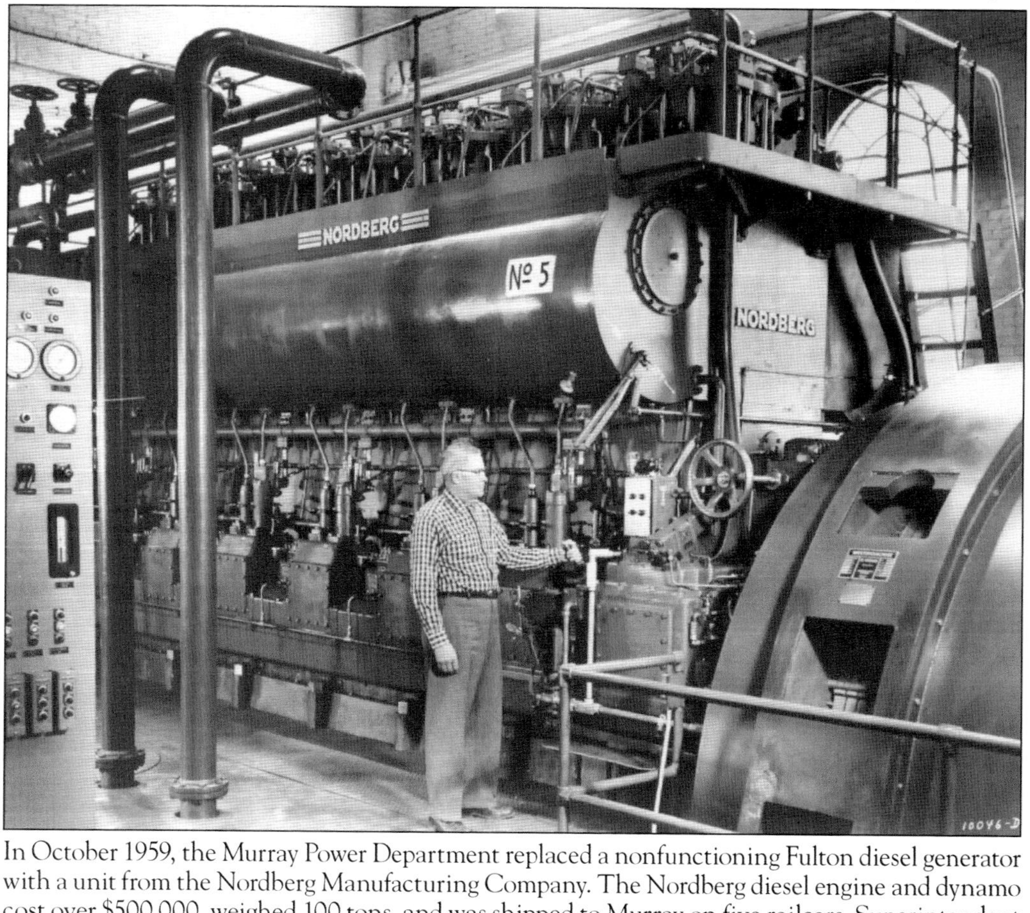

In October 1959, the Murray Power Department replaced a nonfunctioning Fulton diesel generator with a unit from the Nordberg Manufacturing Company. The Nordberg diesel engine and dynamo cost over $500,000, weighed 100 tons, and was shipped to Murray on five railcars. Superintendent Bill Riding is seen here inspecting the new unit around 1959. (MCM.)

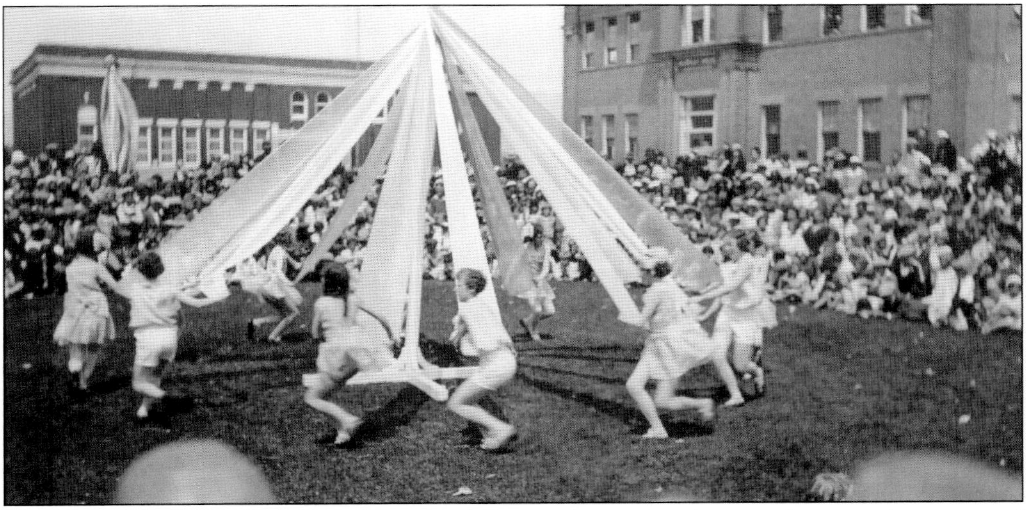

The annual May Day celebration began at Arlington but was such a popular event it was moved to Murray High. This photograph of maypole dancers was taken after the auditorium was built in 1930 (left background). By the early 1950s, the student body had outgrown the campus. The junior and senior high schools were separated, and the upper grades moved to a new building across the street in 1953–1954. (MCM.)

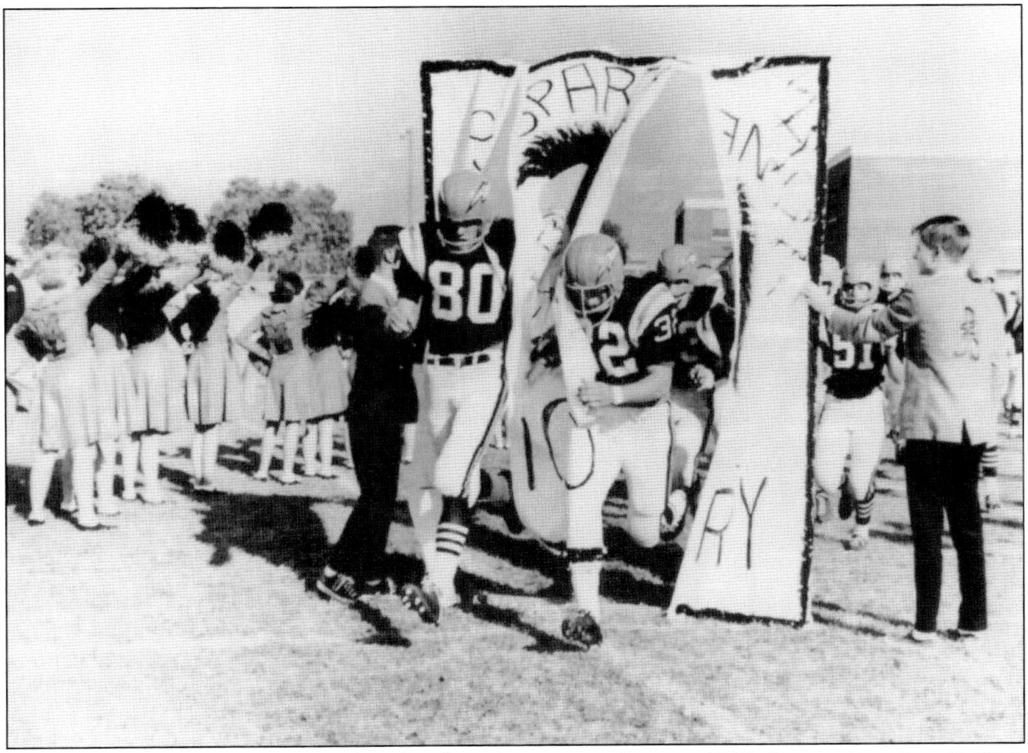

This photograph of Murray High School students was taken in 1966 during the school's 50th anniversary homecoming celebration. With the closure of the smelter and anticipation of the new high school on the west side of State Street (right background), the student body elected to become the Spartans. The 93 members of the graduating class of 1952 were the last to graduate from the Smelterite School. (MCM.)

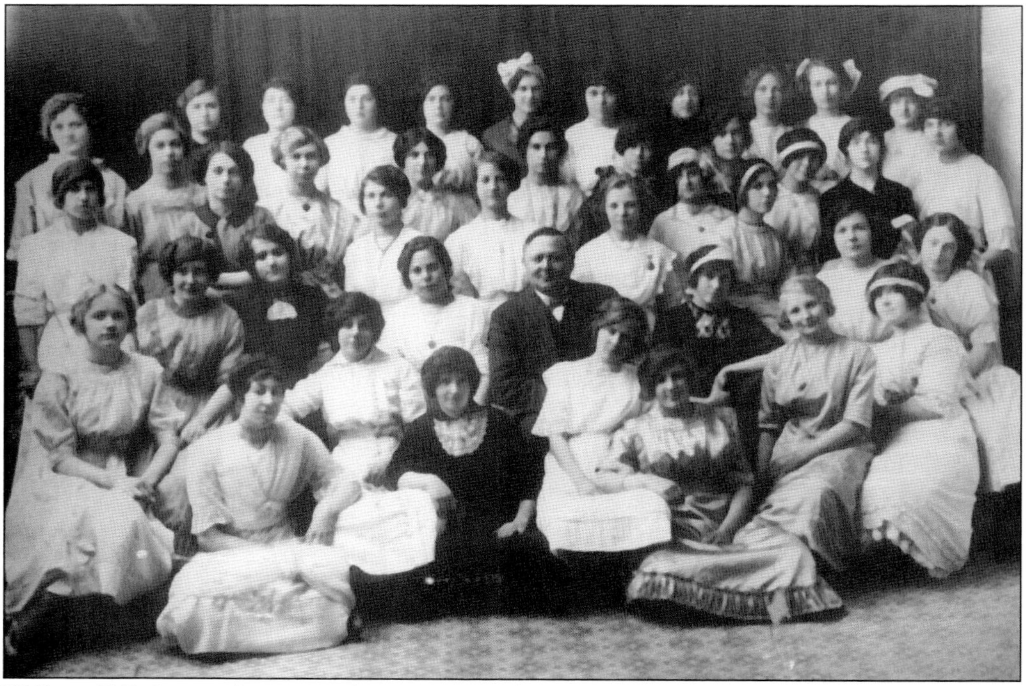

William F. Robinson began teaching music in the Murray School District in 1907. During the early years of his career, he would walk from one district school to another. Seen above about 1918 in the center of the high school girls' chorus, Robinson taught band and choir. In 1912, he organized the first orchestra by selling musical instruments and providing 20 free lessons to each student buyer. Robinson was known as "Murray's Music Man" and the "Father of Christmas Caroling" in the Murray community. He made arrangements of English carols he had sung as a boy, and each December, Robinson taught the carols at each school. Pictured below in 1959 at age 87 with the Arlington student body, Robinson retired in 1939, but he came back to conduct carols at Christmas. (Both, MCM.)

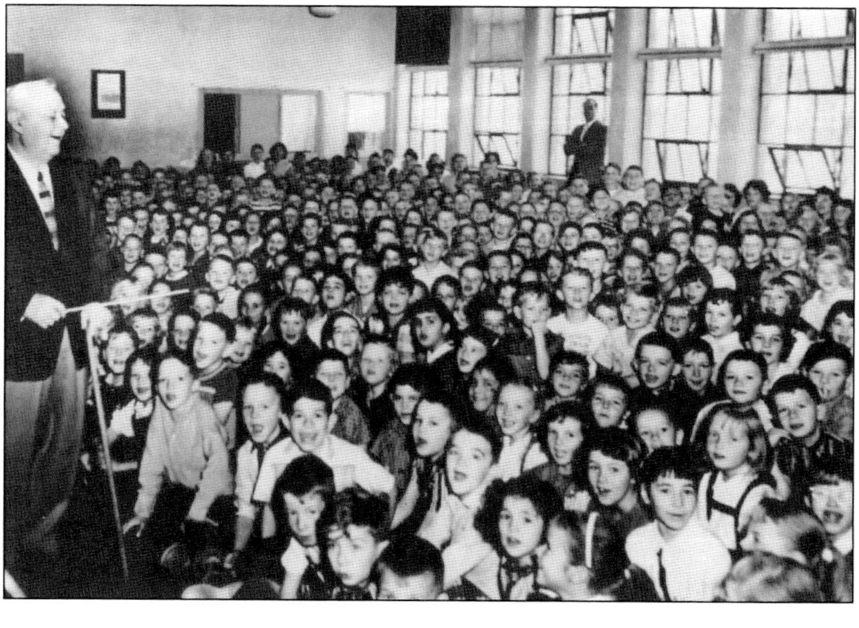

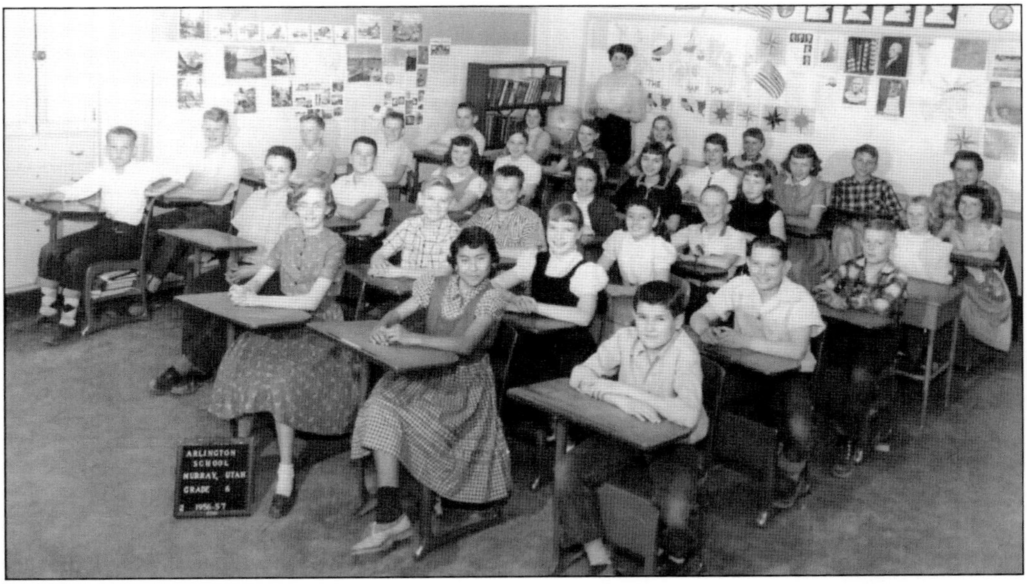

Every desk was filled when a sixth-grade class at Arlington posed for this photograph in 1956–1957. In addition to the new high school, the Murray School District constructed five new elementary schools and a new junior high in just over a decade—McMillan (1954), Grant (1959), Longview (1962), Viewmont (1964) Parkside (1967), and Riverview Junior High (1961). (MCM.)

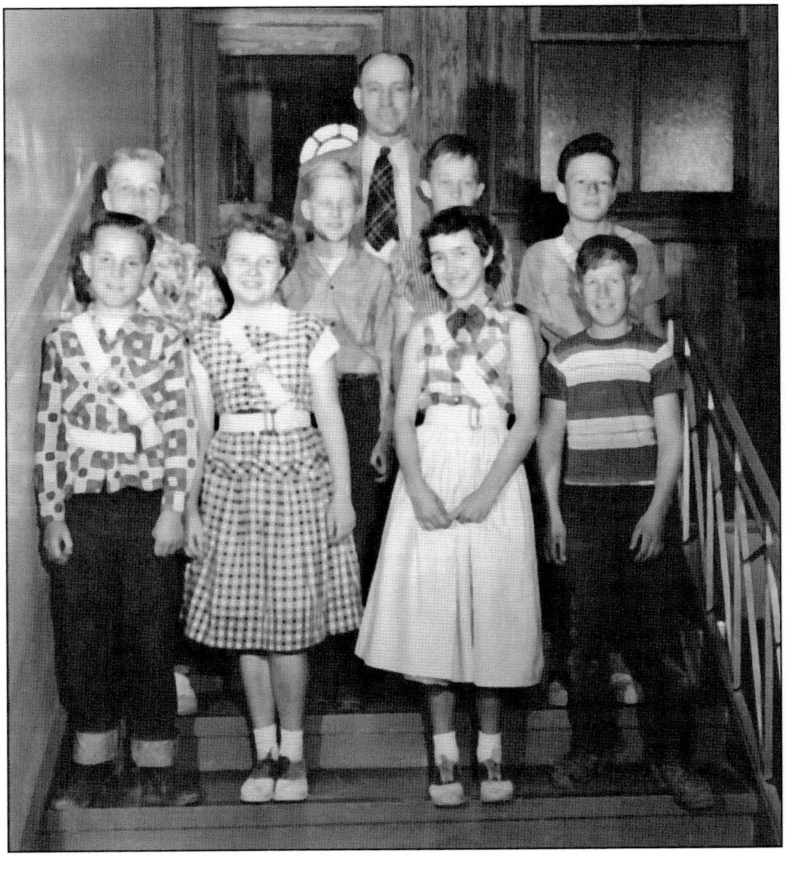

A member of Murray's 1931 championship basketball team, Webb Snarr had a 41-year career in Murray elementary schools. He served as principal at three—Liberty, Grant, and Bonnyview. Principal Snarr is pictured here with the Liberty School safety patrol on the stairs leading to the principal's office in the late 1950s. (MCM.)

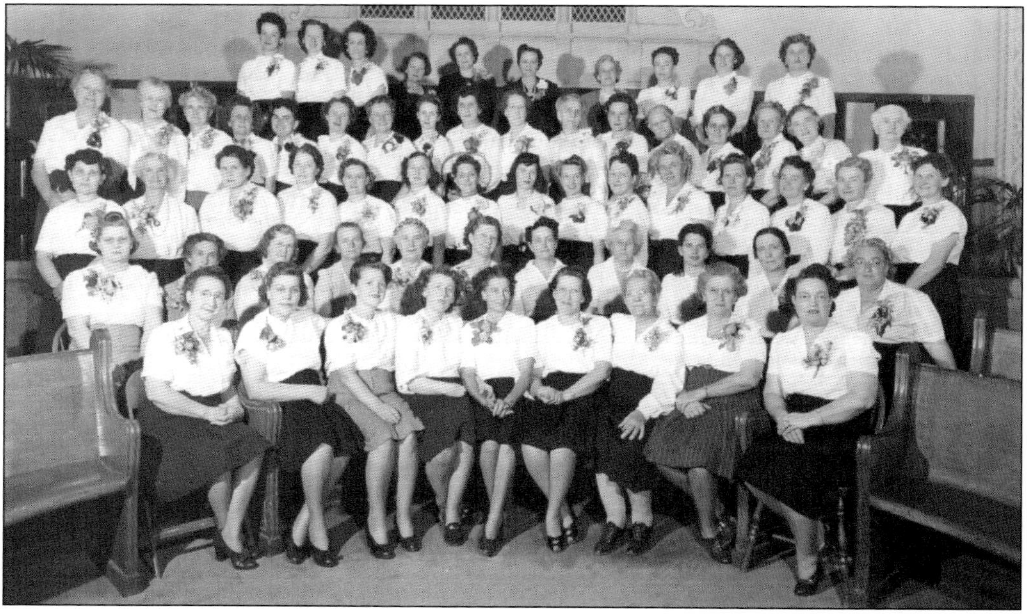

The LDS Church experienced phenomenal growth in Murray in the postwar period. Between 1945 and 1965, twenty new wards were created within its boundaries. The church provided valuable social support for the thousands of young families living in Murray's brand-new subdivisions, giving them the chance to interact with the more established residents. This photograph is of the Murray Stake Singing Mothers in 1947. (MCM.)

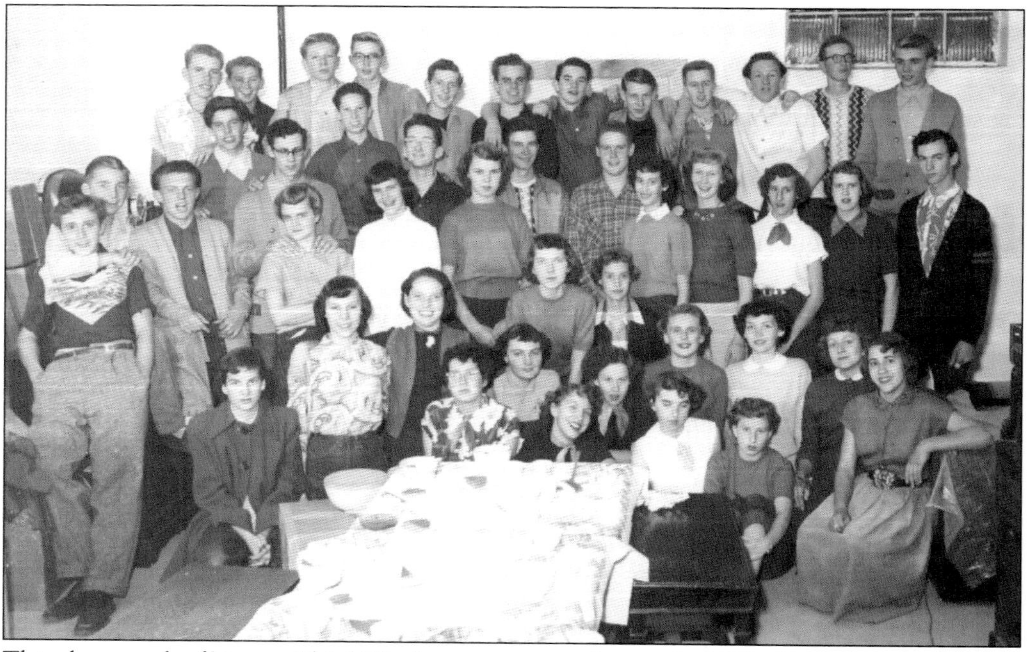

This photograph of Murray Third Ward teenagers was taken in the 1950s during a service project/party. Like most LDS youth, this group of teens was led by pillars of the Murray community. Arlette Day (not shown), owner of Murray Music, advised the young ladies. The young men's leader was Vaughan Soffe (not shown), who owned the Jenkins-Soffe Mortuary and was mayor in the 1970s. (MCM.)

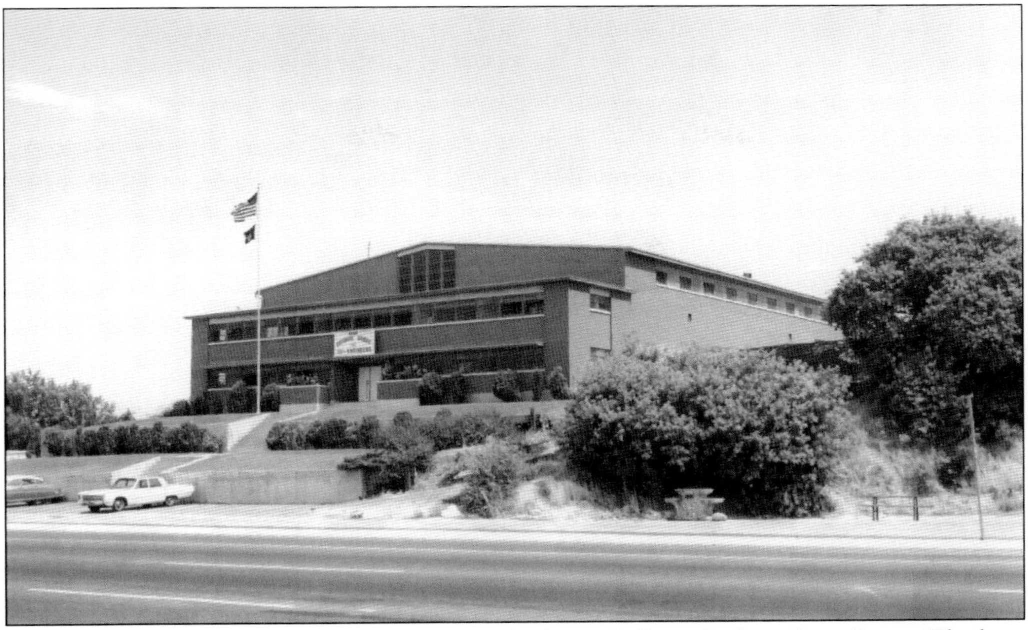

In 1955, the Utah National Guard Armory was built on a hill overlooking State Street. The long history of the hill includes the site of the first pioneer dugouts. The American Hill Smelter and a brothel occupied the hill in the late 19th century. The armory was used as exhibition space for the county fair. In the 1990s, the building was demolished and the hill leveled for commercial development. (MCM.)

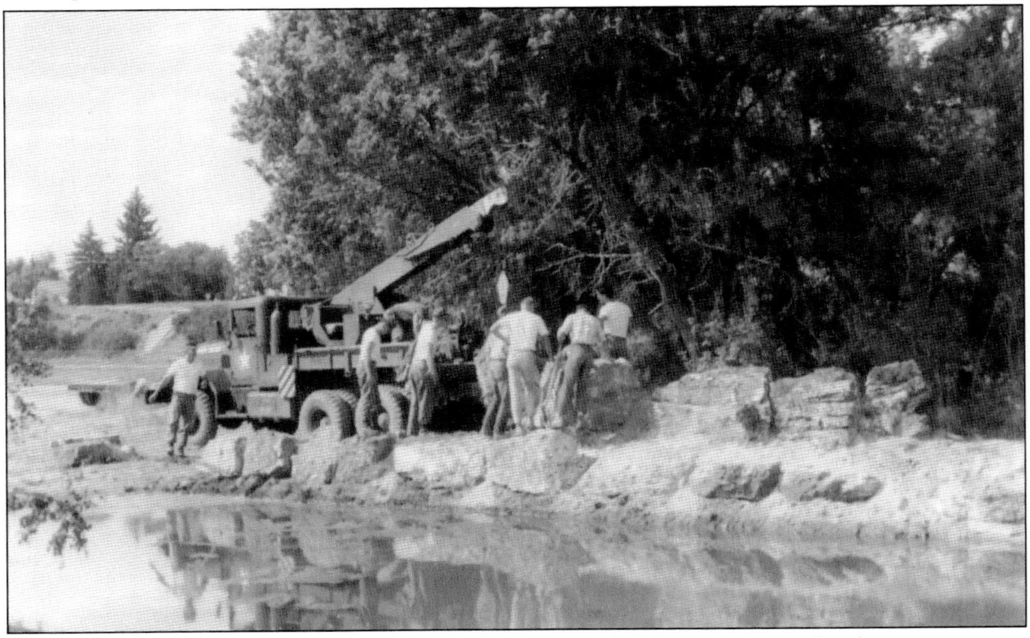

Engineering units from the Utah National Guard provided the manpower for the construction of a waterfall in Murray Park's Arboretum and Botanical Gardens in 1965. The National Guard also donated the field artillery guns mounted in the park's war memorial and an F-84 fighter plane converted to a playground slide, which was a favorite venue in the park until it was deemed a hazard in the 1990s. (MCM.)

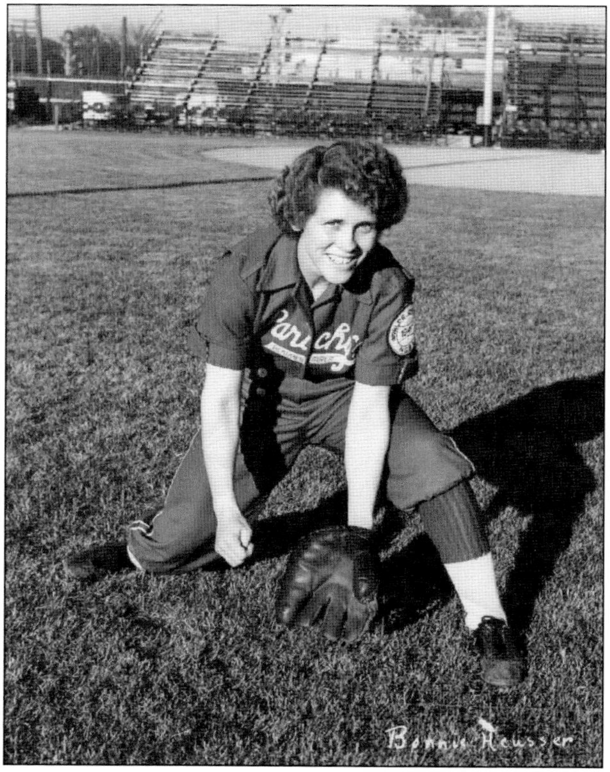

Bonnie Heusser (pictured here in 1948) was a member of a Murray baseball dynasty. Her German grandfather James and his three brothers played on a local team that won a state championship in 1912. Her uncle Ed played professionally for the St. Louis Cardinals. Bonnie played in the National Girls Baseball League for the Bloomer Girls in Chicago and for the Utah Shamrocks softball team. (MCM.)

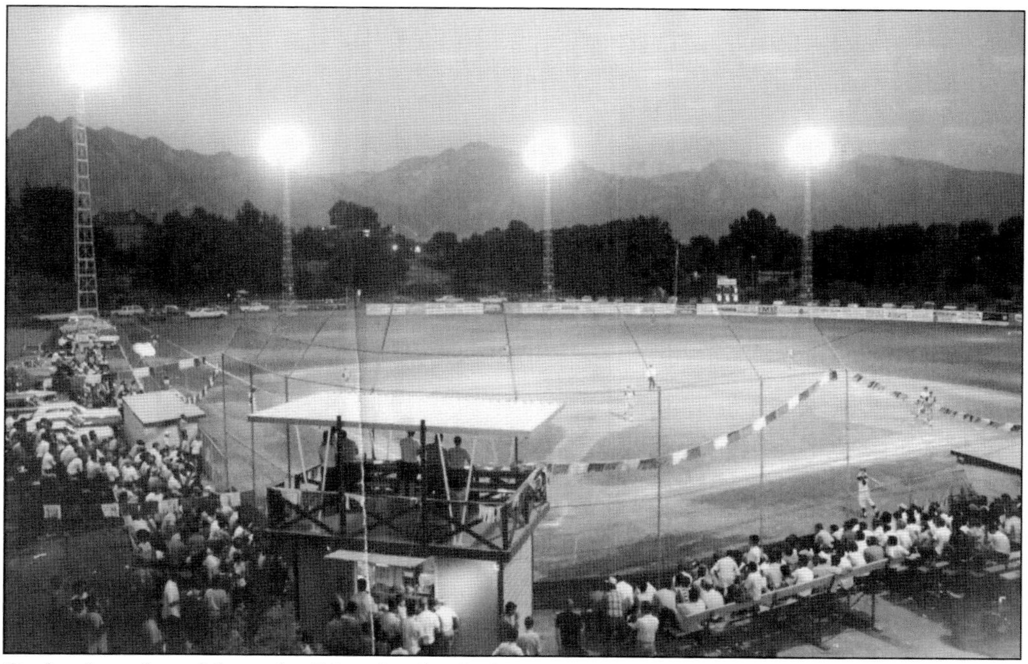

On land purchased from the Pilati family, the Murray City Park Baseball Field was completed in 1960. Ken Price, a local baseball enthusiast, helped finance the building of the dugouts, grandstand, and scoreboard. Pictured here at the rededication in June 1969, the ballpark was renamed Ken Price Field in his honor. It was one of first lighted fields in Salt Lake County. (MCM.)

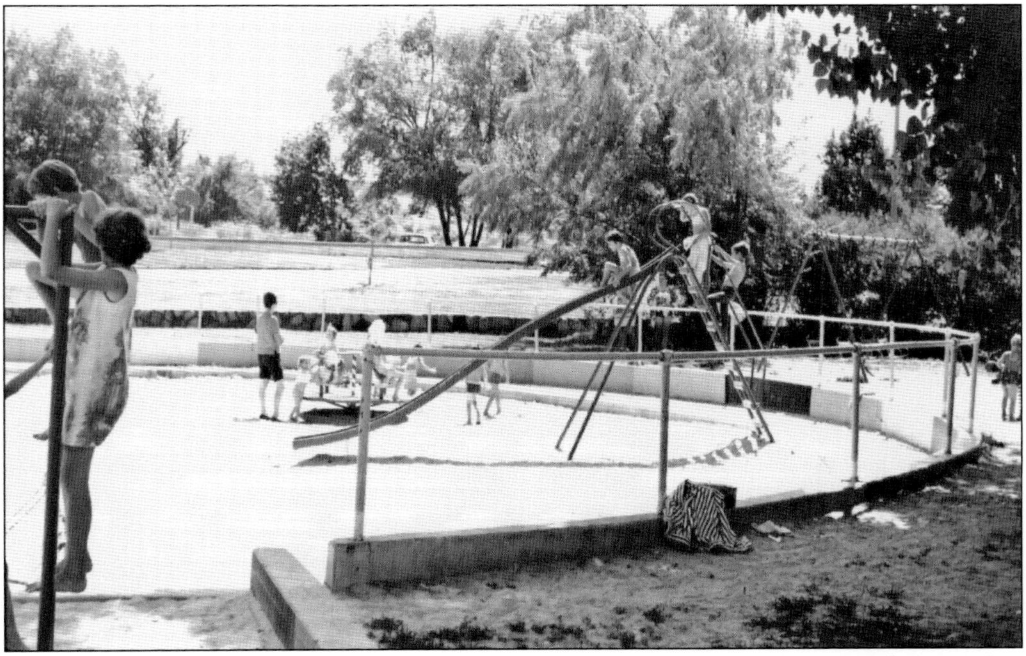

Although the Murray City Park was at the center of the community (playground pictured in 1967), the Murray City Parks system began adding neighborhood parks in the 1950s and 1960s. These include Valley Center Park, hidden in a subdivision (1952); Southwood Park, on the east side (1956); and Grant Park, with its four baseball diamonds (1965). (MCM.)

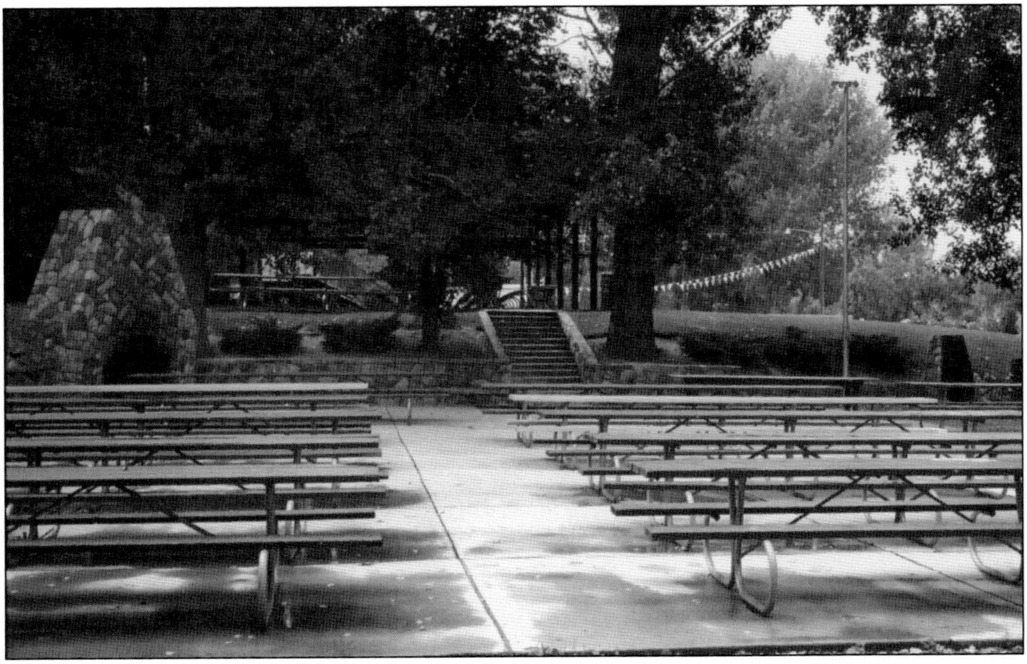

Nearly every community group in Murray has contributed to the beautification of the Murray City Park. The Rotary Club donated the money to build a picnic pavilion in 1962 (pictured). The Women's Club, Volunteer Fire Department, Fraternal Order of Eagles, American Legion, and Sons of Utah Pioneers are among the groups that have provided monuments in the park. (MCM.)

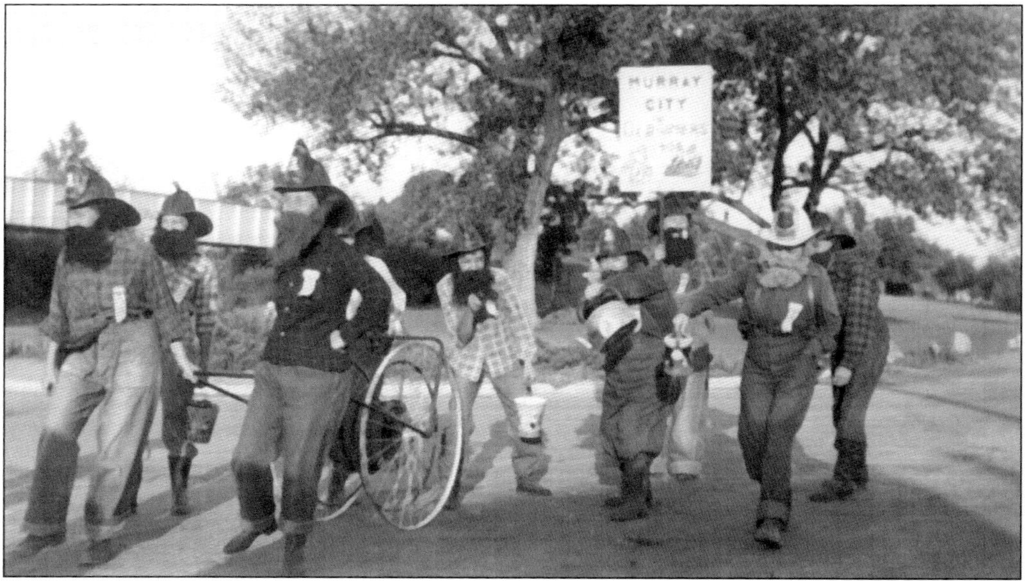

The year 1947 marked the centennial celebration of the Mormon pioneers' entrance into the Salt Lake Valley. Every local community in Utah participated. At a firemen's convention held in Price, Utah, the Murray Fire Department Women's auxiliary provided a reenactment of the city's first official volunteer fire brigade (complete with beards). (MCM.)

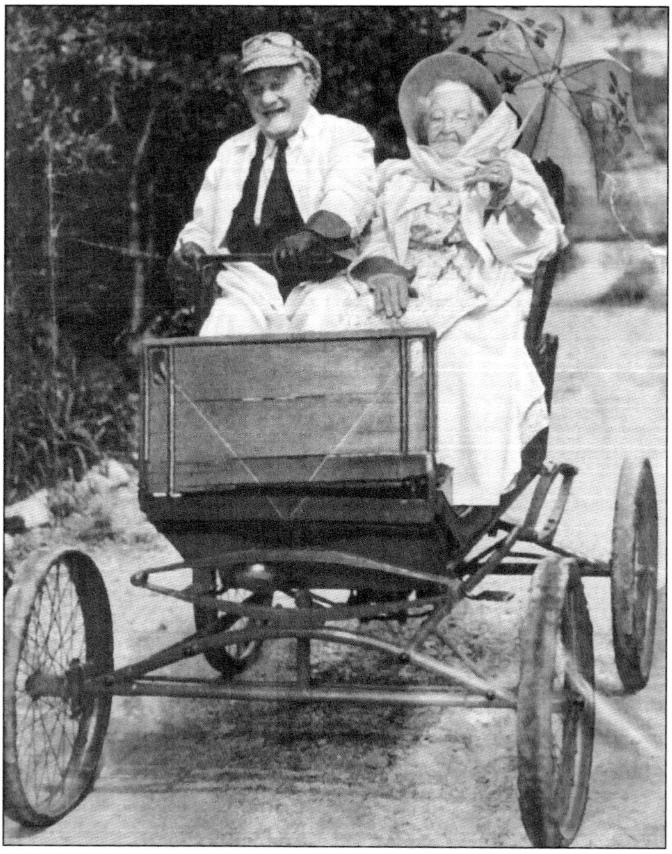

Ann Catherine Jarvis Milne was born in England in 1849 and walked across the plains at the age of 11. She raised a family in St. George, but in her later years was a celebrated resident of Murray. In this photograph, F. James Silvers drives Milne in a Days of '47 parade at the age of 102 or 103. She died two weeks before her 108th birthday. (MCM.)

Five

The Million Dollar Mile

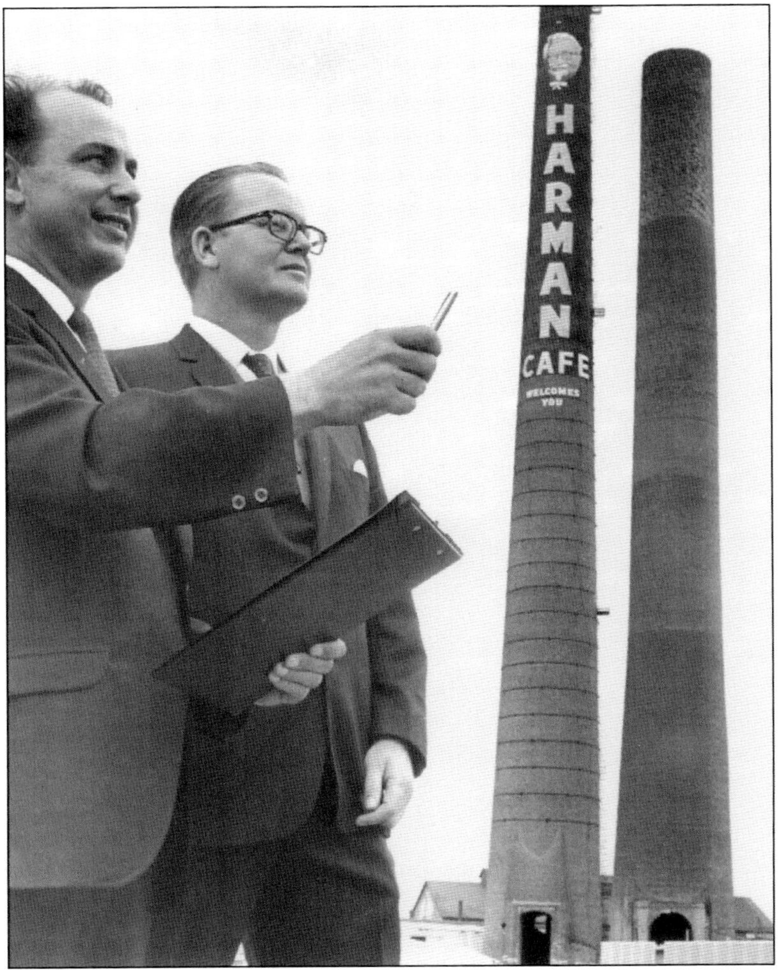

After its retirement from smelting, the taller ASARCO smokestack became a billboard for Pete Harman, whose South Salt Lake café was the world's first Kentucky Fried Chicken franchise. Colonel Sanders's smiling face was painted by the Keate brothers, professional painters from Murray. The stacks are pictured here with Mayor William E. Dunn (left) and Ralph Montgomery in the 1960s. (MCM.)

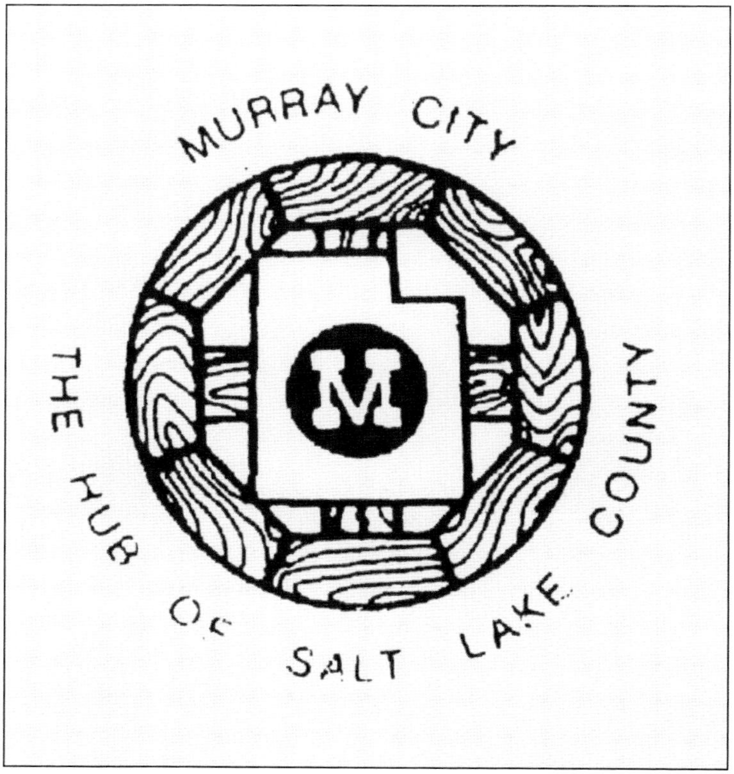

At the height of the suburban building boom, Murray City adapted the motto "Hub of Salt Lake County." Although not precisely the geographic center of the Salt Lake Valley, Murray had emerged as a regional retail center and a bedroom community. Many Murray residents commuted to work in downtown Salt Lake City as well as to major employers such as Kennecott Copper in the southwest corner of the valley. (MCM.)

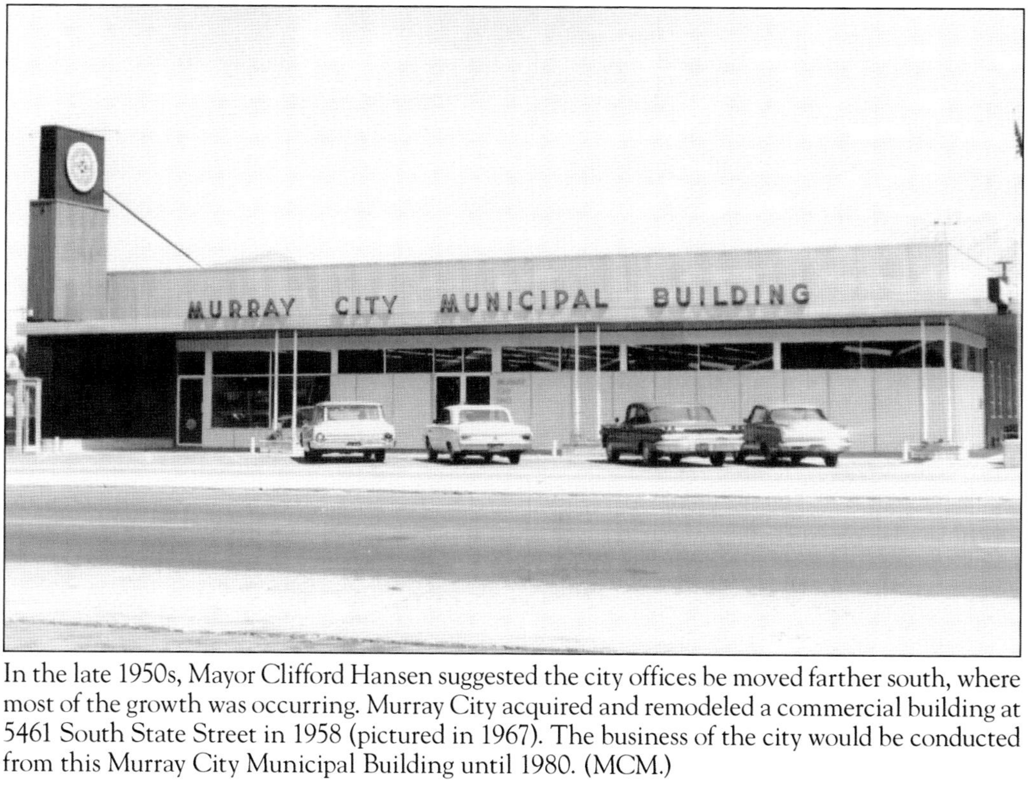

In the late 1950s, Mayor Clifford Hansen suggested the city offices be moved farther south, where most of the growth was occurring. Murray City acquired and remodeled a commercial building at 5461 South State Street in 1958 (pictured in 1967). The business of the city would be conducted from this Murray City Municipal Building until 1980. (MCM.)

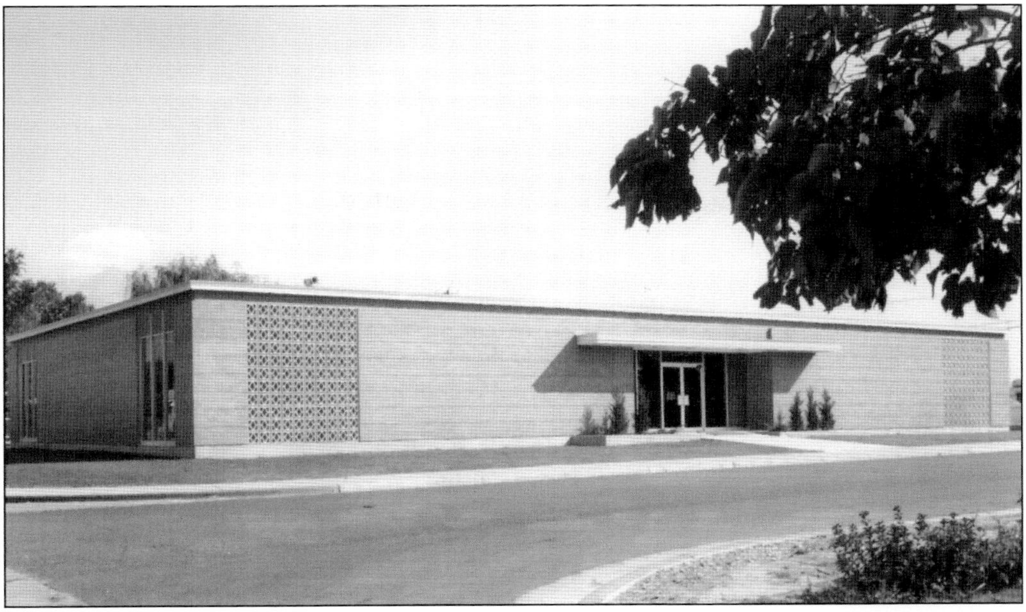

On December 11, 1965, Mayor Ray Greenwood presided over the opening of the new Main Library at 73 West 6100 South (above, about 1965). Approximately 15,000 books, costing $610,000, had been ordered for the library. The construction included an adjoining new fire station for the city. In 1965, the fire department had a combination of both paid and volunteer members, with the first full-time firefighters added to the city payroll the previous year. The mayor and fire department officials pose in front of Station No. 2 (below, about 1965). The older Carnegie library on Vine Street was retained and remodeled in 1970–1971. (Both, MCM.)

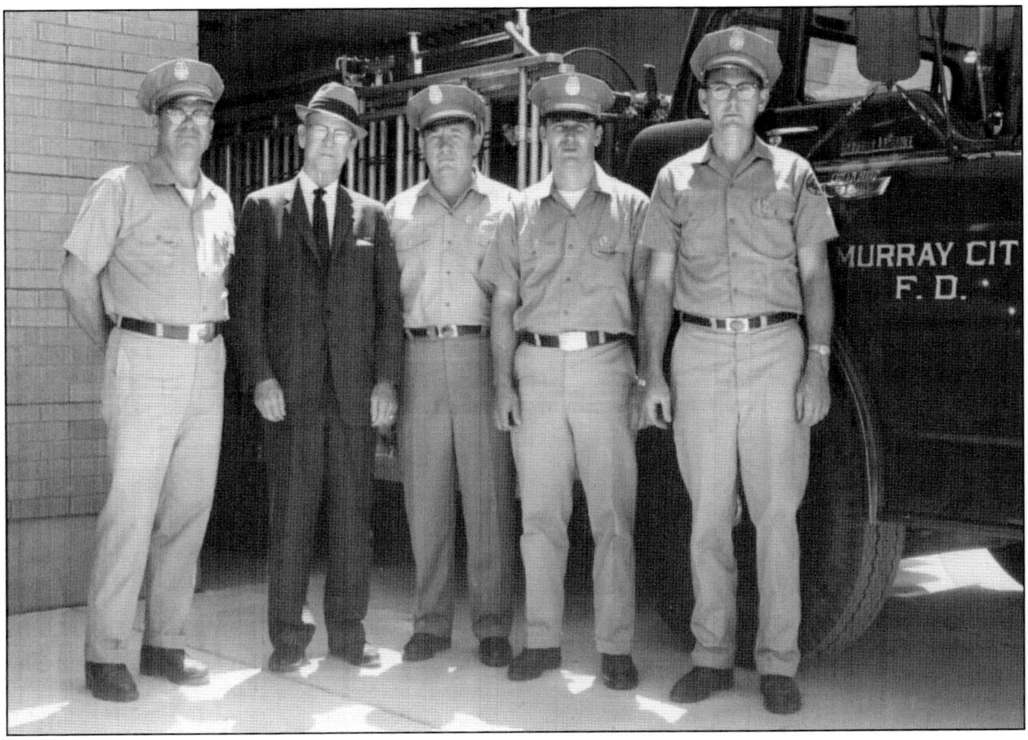

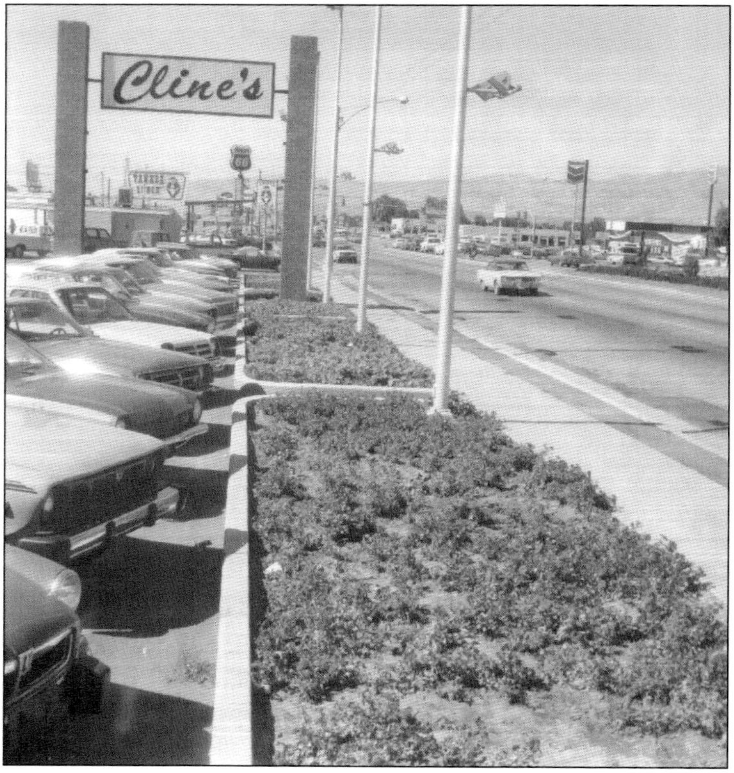

In the 1950s, Murray merchants began using the phrase "Million-Dollar Mile" to describe the commercial business district, and by the 1960s and 1970s, the phrase was extended to include the strip of automobile dealerships, service stations, supermarkets, and fast-food drive-ins along State Street. All of the farmhouses that once lined State Street have disappeared in this photograph taken in the 1970s with a view looking north from approximately 4700 South. (MCM.)

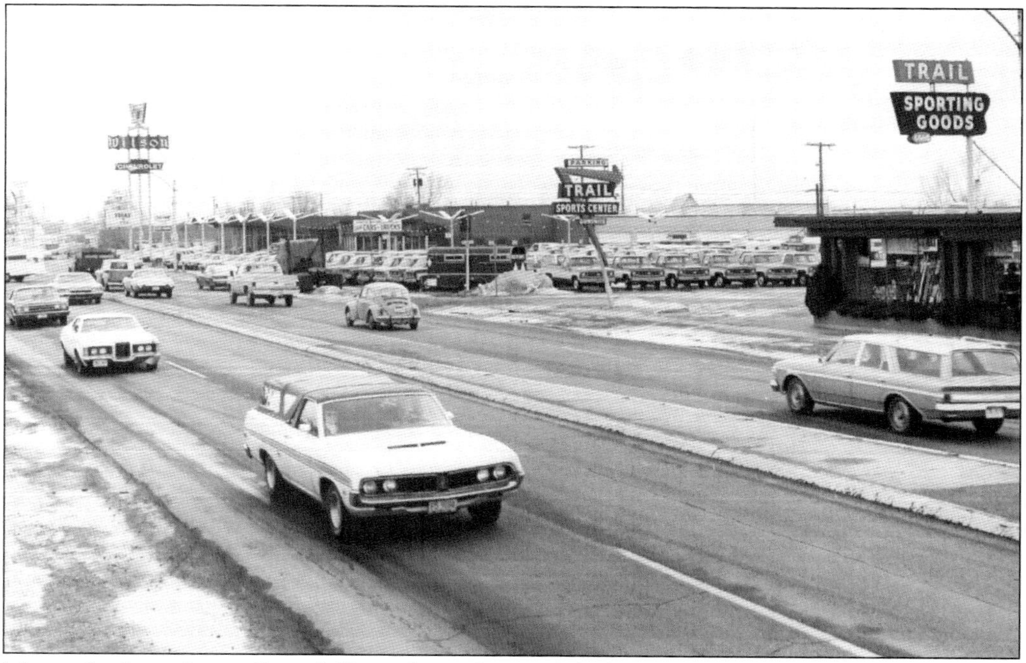

Murray had another million dollar mile in the south half of the city. This photograph of State Street taken in the mid-1970s with a view looking south from Wilson Avenue (5550 South) features adjacent Chevrolet, Toyota, and Dodge dealerships. Today, this section of State Street is promoted as Murray's "Auto Row" and mostly owned by the Larry H. Miller Automotive Group. (MCM.)

Approximately 60 Murray homes between 300 and 500 West were demolished when the Interstate 15 freeway project reached Murray. The 4500 South on- and off-ramps opened in 1964 and the 5300 South ramps in 1966. Pictured here around 1966, Mayor William Dunn (left) poses with an unidentified State Road Commission official. (MCM.)

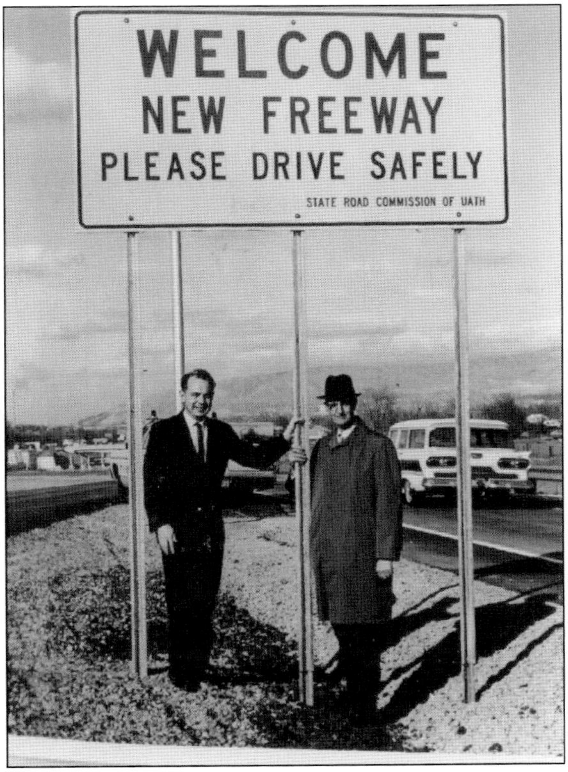

In 1967, Murray City officials pose with executives from Fox Intermountain Theaters Inc. and Miss Fox Olympus (in high heels) at the ground breaking of the Fox Olympus Drive-In on the northeast corner of Vine Street and 5600 South. At completion, the 1,056-car drive-in movie theater featured a cafeteria, playground, and "the latest facilities in screen, sound and projection," as described in the *Murray Eagle*. (MCM.)

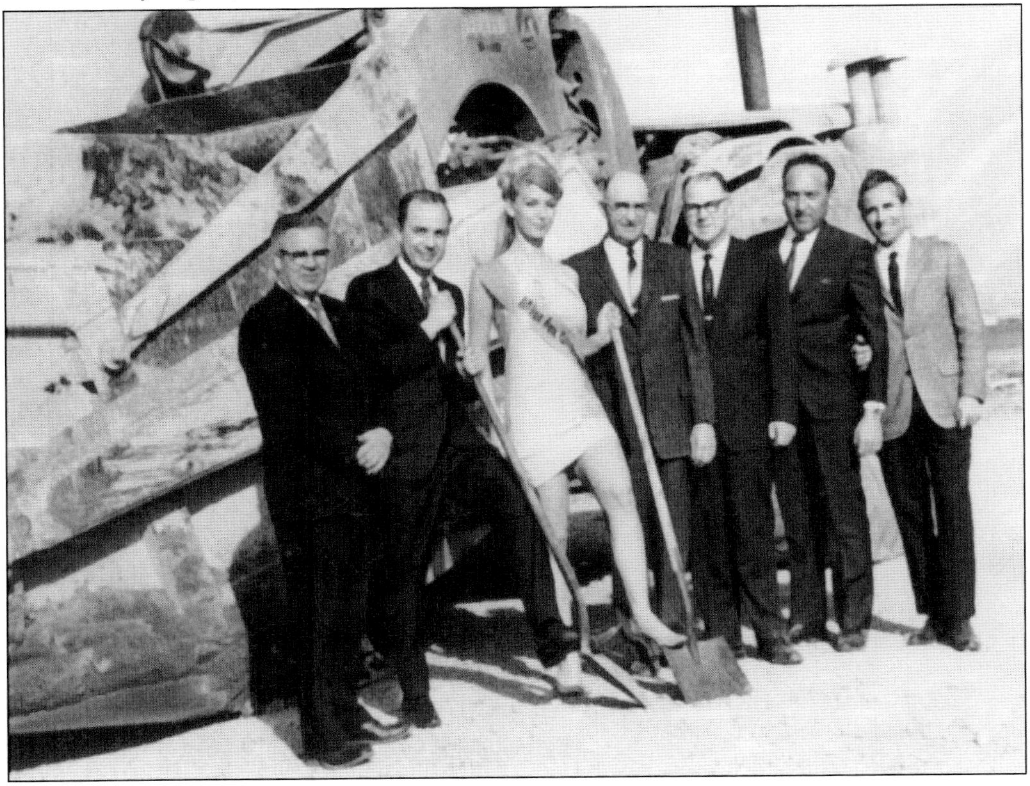

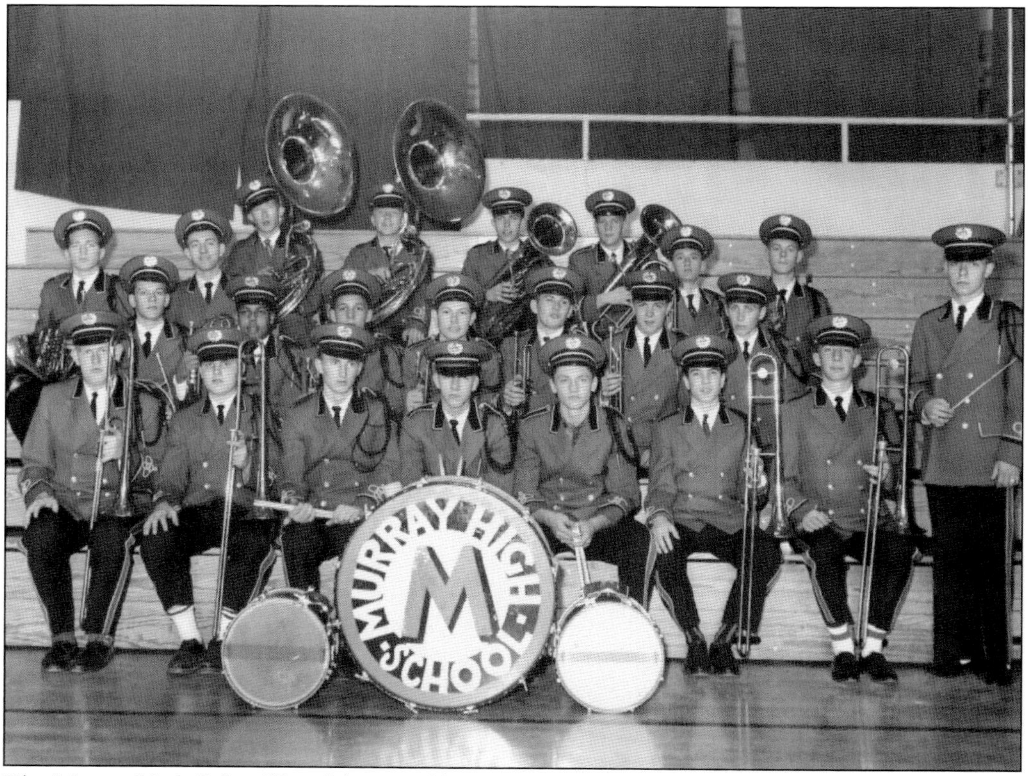

The Murray High School Band (pictured here in 1961) was a popular sight at parades and athletic events. When Riverview Junior High was completed in 1961, the Murray Junior High campus was renamed Hillcrest Junior High. An east-west rivalry existed between the junior high schools that mostly disappeared when students were unified at the high school. (MCM.)

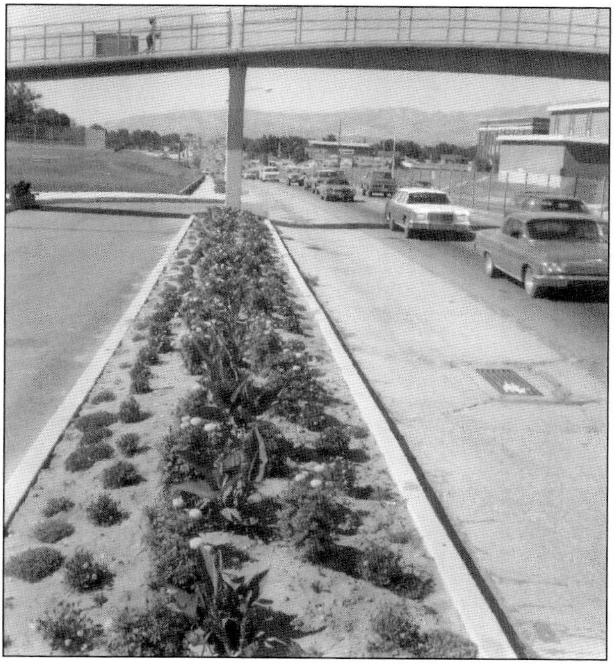

As traffic on State Street increased, Murray City built a skywalk between Hillcrest Junior High (on right) and Murray High School (not shown) in 1971. One of the main reasons for the construction of the Horizon Elementary School in the northwest quadrant of the city in 1981 was the concern from parents whose children had to cross 5300 South. (MCM.)

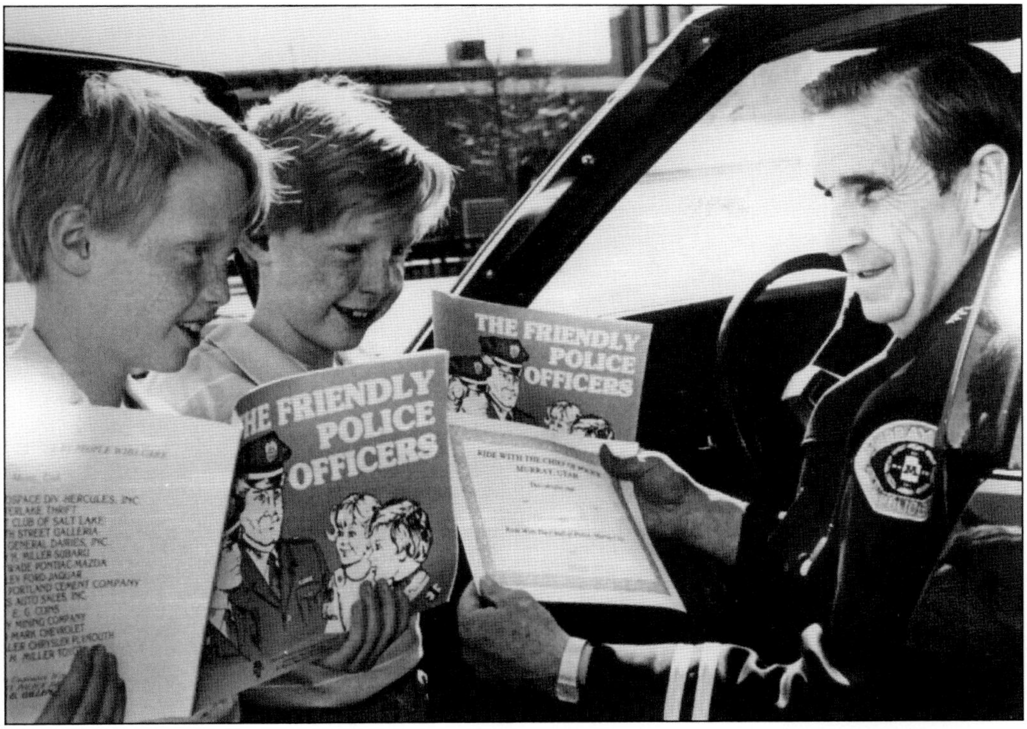

The grandson of Swedish immigrants who worked in the smelter and owned a livery stable, Calvin Gillen joined the Murray police force in 1951 as one of only five officers. Cal Gillen served as chief of police between 1970 and 1988. During his tenure, the department added a K-9 unit, a SWAT team, and numerous school-safety programs. Chief Gillen is pictured here with the Vicchrilli twins in the 1980s. (MCM.)

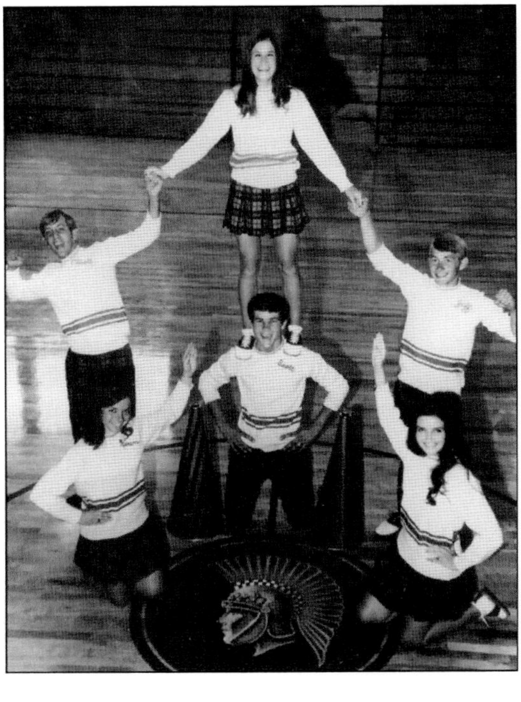

Murray High School cheerleaders form a pyramid to display "Spartan Spirit" in a 1970 yearbook photograph. Clockwise from top are Kathy Erekson, Jeff Hamblin, Kathy White, Scott Wilcock, Karen Oliver, and Elliott Clark. The Murray High class of 1970 commissioned the *Spartan Man* by the famous Utah-born sculptor Avard T. Fairbanks (MCM.)

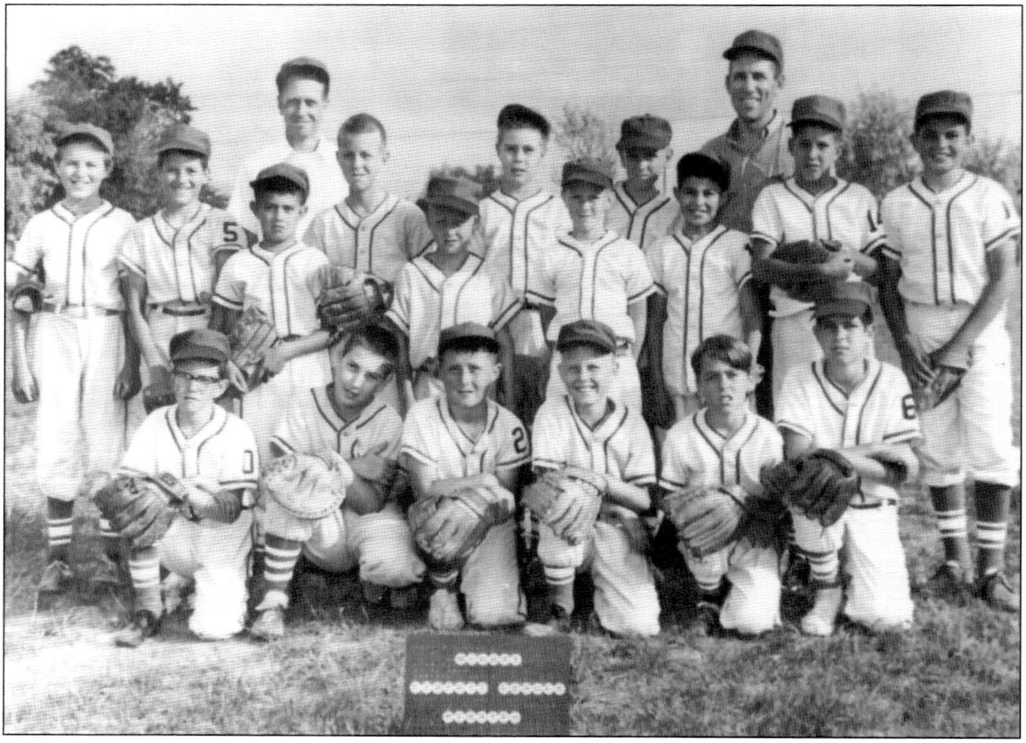

In the 1960s, the number of school-age children in Murray was higher than the city's population prior to World War II. The number of community-based programs for youth increased exponentially. This photograph of the Liberty League Pirates was taken in 1963. Many of these programs, such as the Murray Liberty League, still operate today. (MCM.)

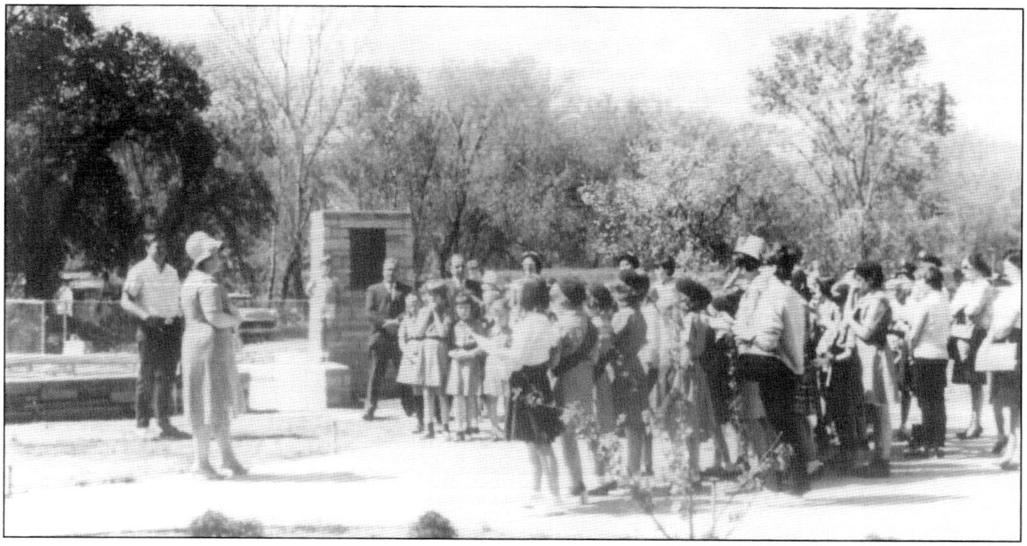

On Arbor Day in 1966, a large group of Girl Scouts planted trees and performed other community service at the Murray Arboretum and Botanical Gardens. The monument in the photograph was the result of the efforts of Joan M. Hardle, a tireless supporter of the arboretum. At the 1982 Arbor Day program, the arboretum was officially renamed the Joan M. Hardle Memorial Arboretum. (MCM.)

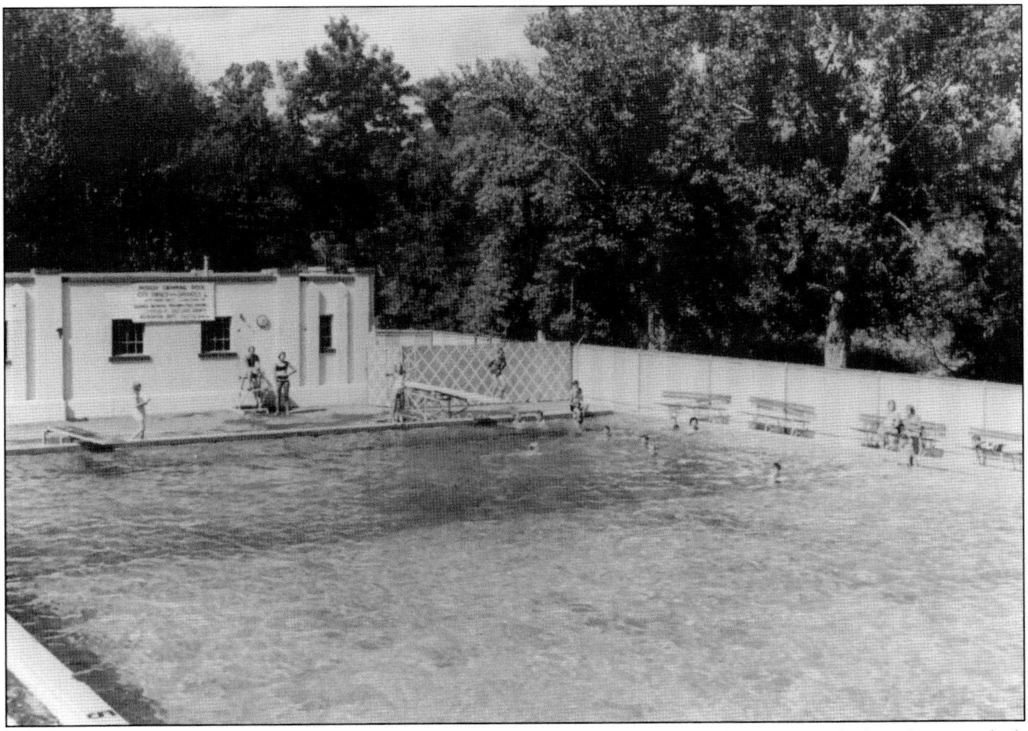

Murray Park's first cement swimming pool was built in 1928, but it was later upgraded and expanded. The swimming pool was first heated in the 1960s (bathhouse and pool pictured above) and had designated times for "boys, girls, and open plunge," according to the *Murray Eagle*. When a new swimming pool complex was built to the east in 1973, the old pool was converted to an ice-skating rink (seen below in the 1970s). Hockey practice and hot chocolate were among the best memories at the rink. The facility was a vast improvement over early winters in Murray, when the softball field would be flooded with water to make a skating pond. (Both, MCM.)

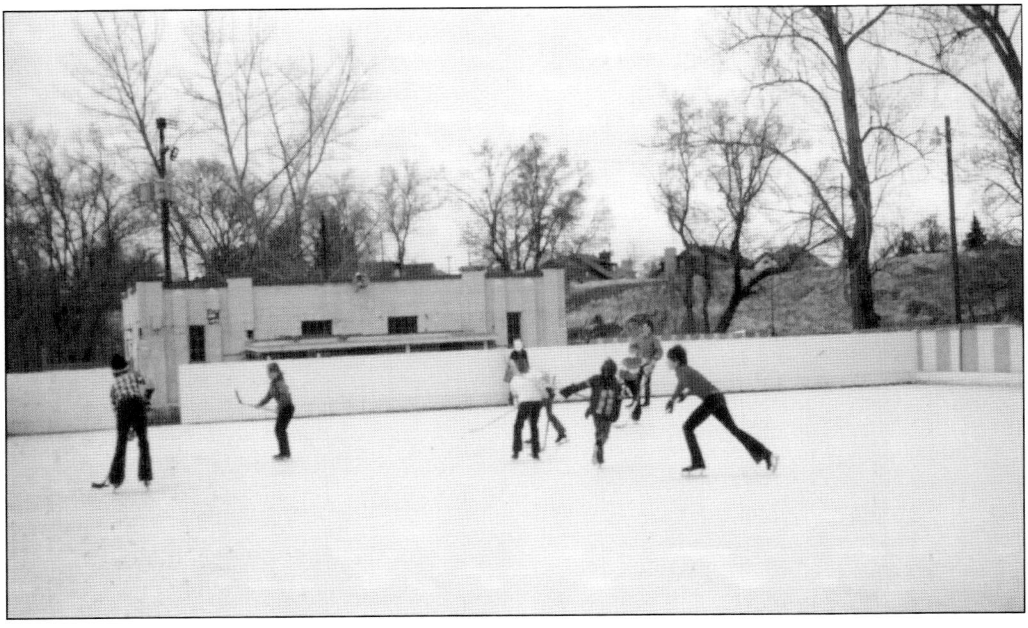

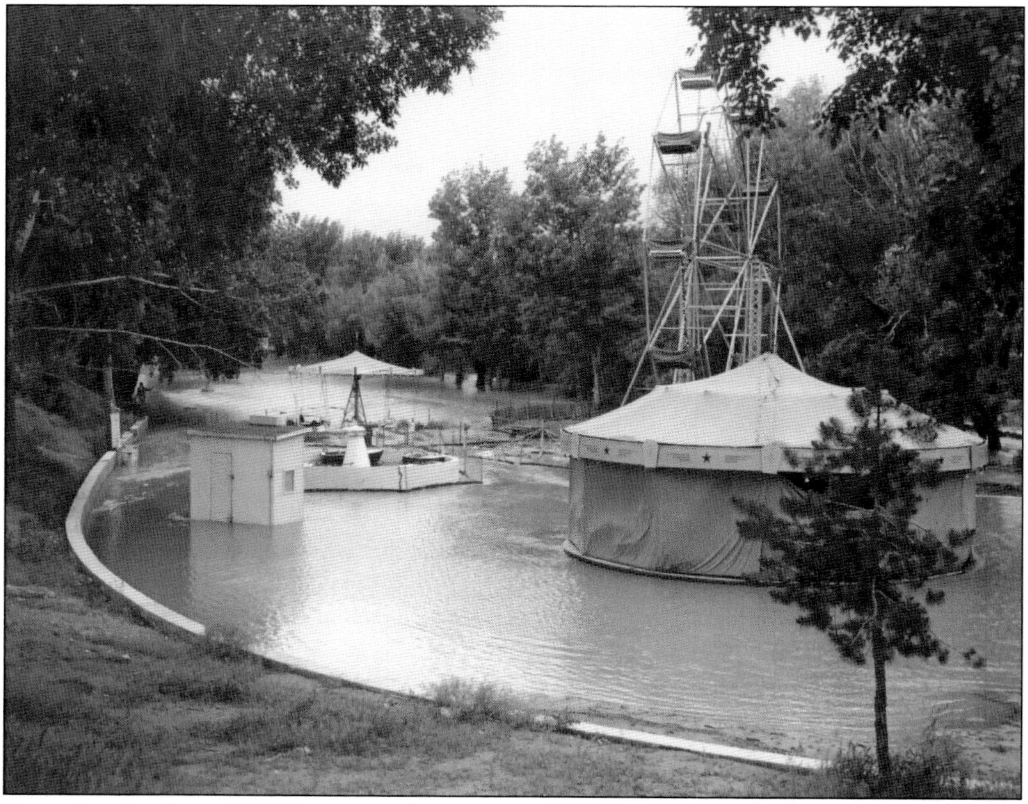

Sometime in the mid-1960s, a traveling circus abandoned a Ferris wheel, merry-go-round, and three kiddie rides in Murray Park. The city operated the amusement-park rides for a few years, but the equipment was not salvageable when the Little Cottonwood Creek overflowed in 1969. (MCM.)

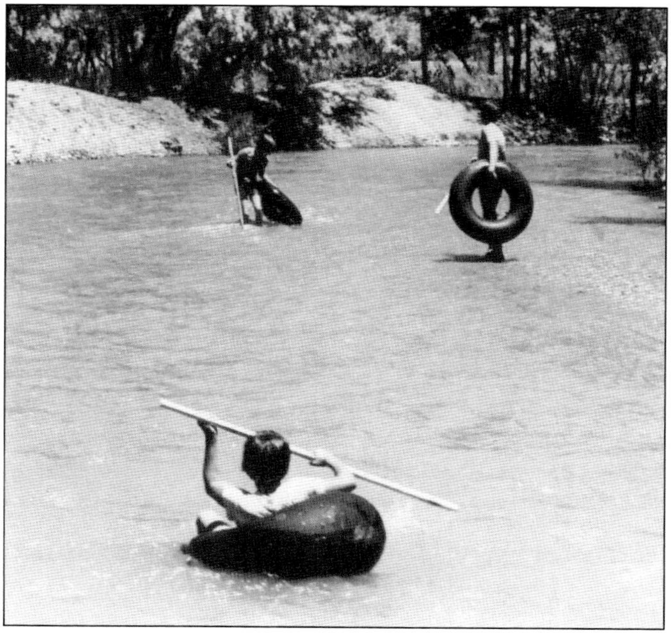

The natural course of Little Cottonwood Creek through Murray Park had been popular with waders, swimmers, and rafters since the arrival of the earliest pioneers. By the 1970s, when these boys were photographed with their inner tubes, the city had placed a grate over the culvert so that adventurous youth, unlike their parents and grandparents, could not navigate the waters under State Street. (MCM.)

In the fall of 1985, Murray residents watched in fascination as Hungarian artist Peter Wolf Toth chiseled two large wood sculptures near the main entrance to Murray Park. Toth sculpted a bust of Chief Wasatch and an eagle (pictured at right with the artist at work) from the trunks of ancient cottonwood trees. *Chief Wasatch* is part of Toth's "Trail of Whispering Giants" series, in which he made at least one similar sculpture in each of the 50 states. The eagle was removed due to tree rot in the 1990s. (MCM.)

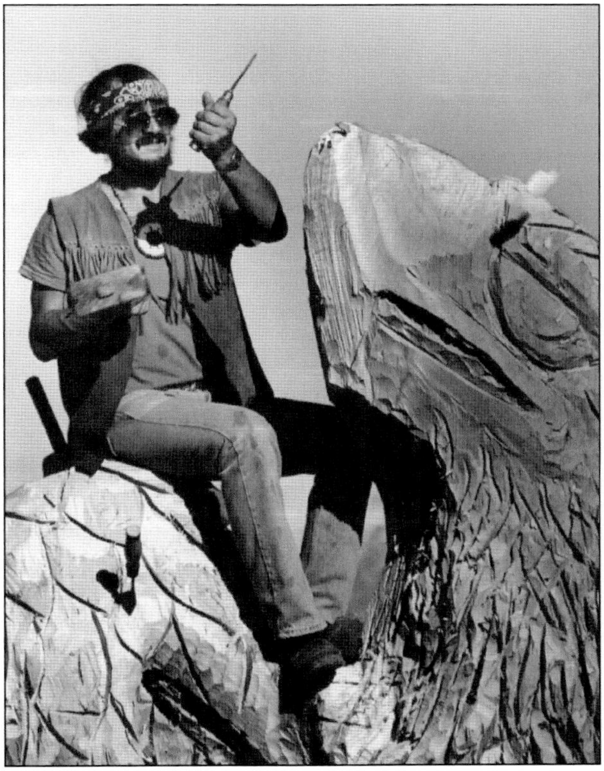

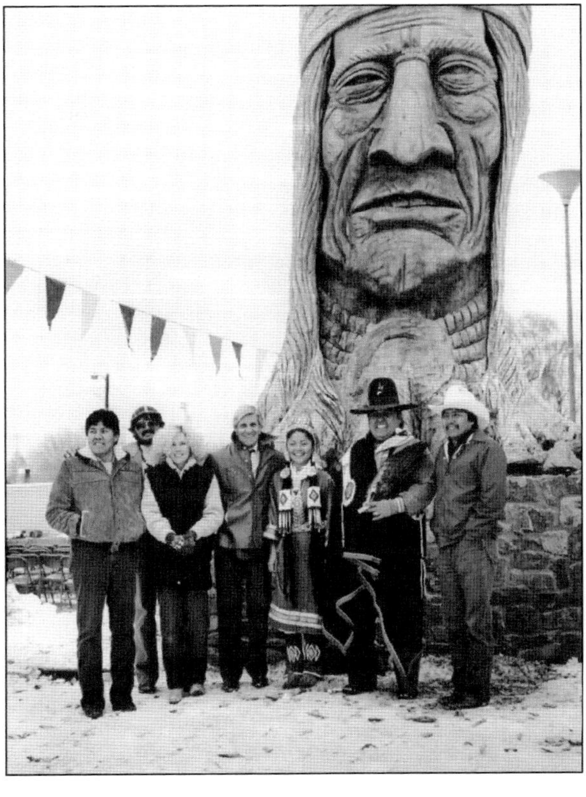

The dedication of *Chief Wasatch* was accompanied by displays of Native American culture and attended by officials of local tribes in the winter of 1985. *Chief Wasatch* maintains his vigil over the park entrance. (MCM.)

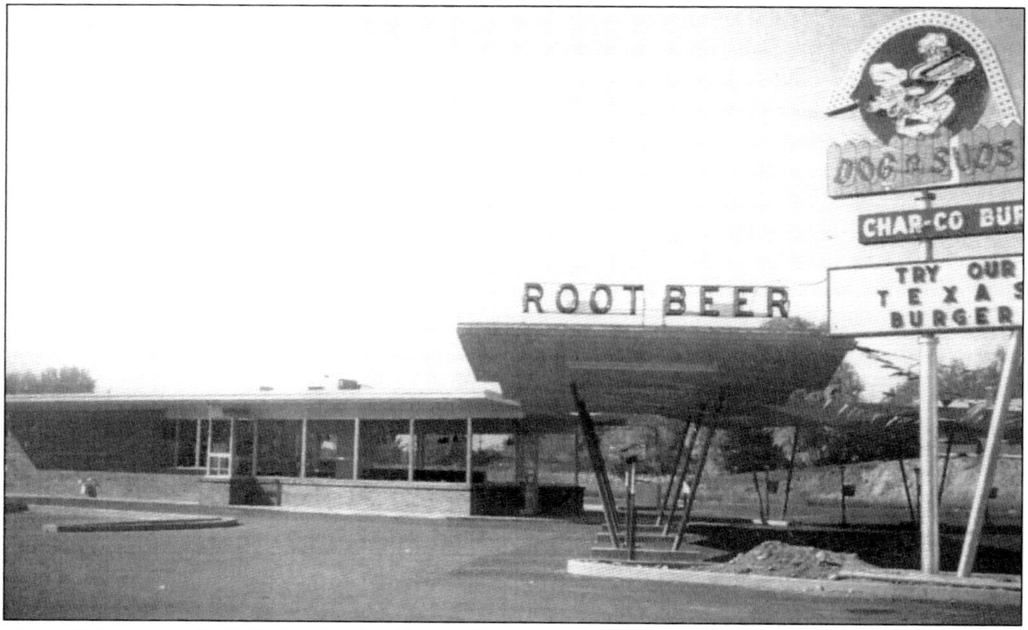

Near 900 East and 5600 South, the Dog 'n Suds was one of many Murray area drive-ins where patrons could order a burger, fries, and a root beer from a carhop. Although the canopy and sign are gone, this building, converted to a martial-arts studio, is a rare surviving example of the architecture of the early 1960s. (SLCA.)

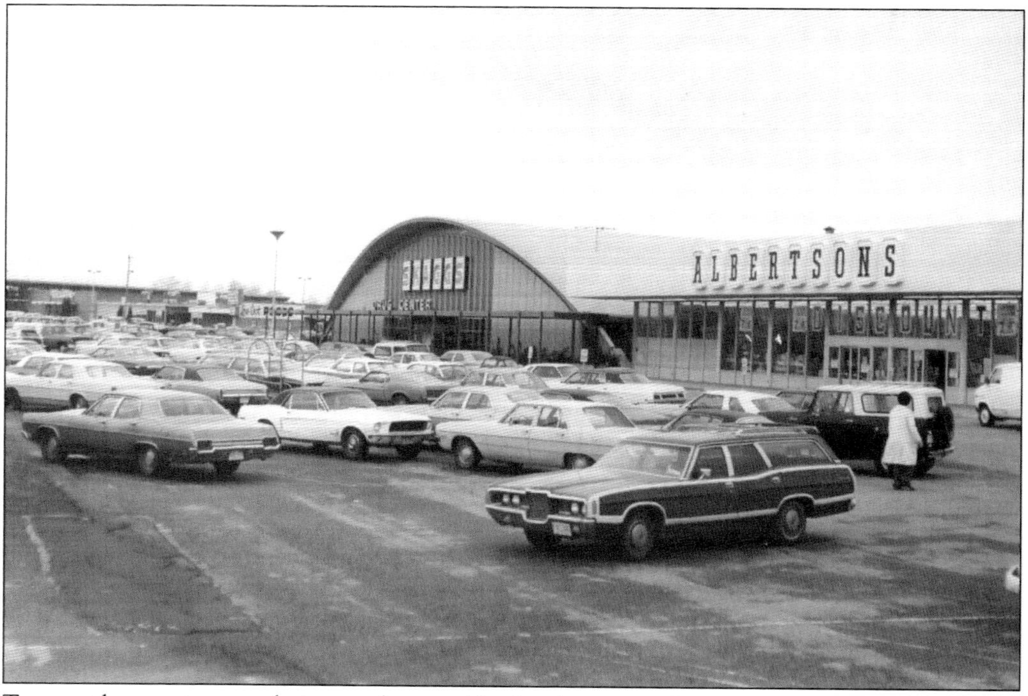

To serve the growing population on the east side, the city annexed new areas to create a commercial district near 5600 South and 900 East. Shown here in the 1970s, the Albertsons supermarket, Skaggs drugstore, and other enterprises were as busy as their State Street counterparts. New businesses have taken over the buildings, but the area is still thriving today. (MCM.)

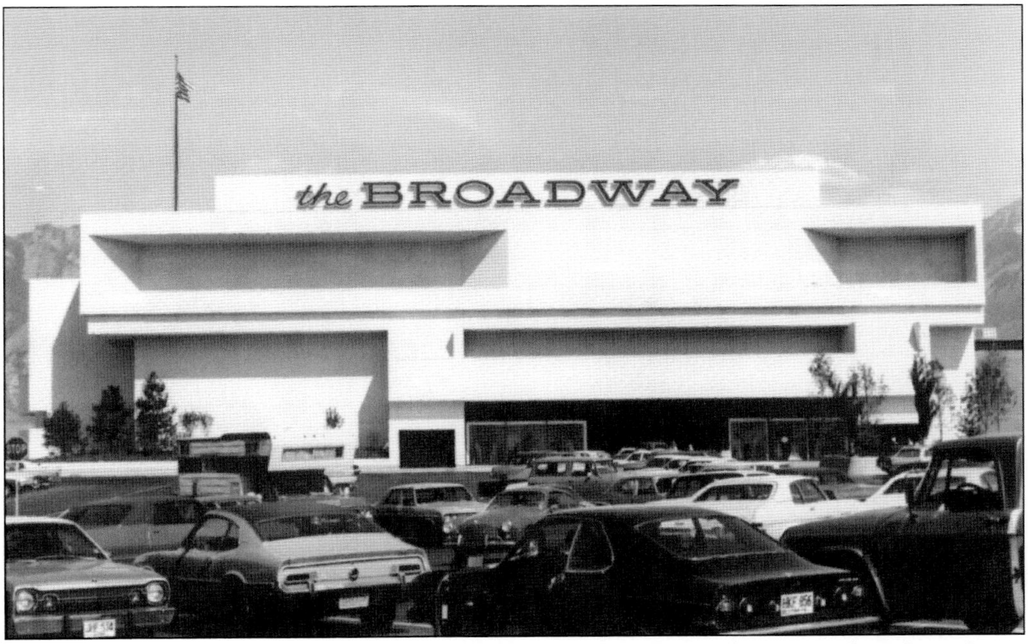

In 1972, Fashion Place Mall opened on a 78-acre site between 6100 and 6400 South on State Street with Sears and Auerbach's as anchor stores. The Broadway extension (pictured) was completed in 1974. The demographics of Salt Lake County had been studied thoroughly before Murray was selected for its central location and solid infrastructure. (MCM.)

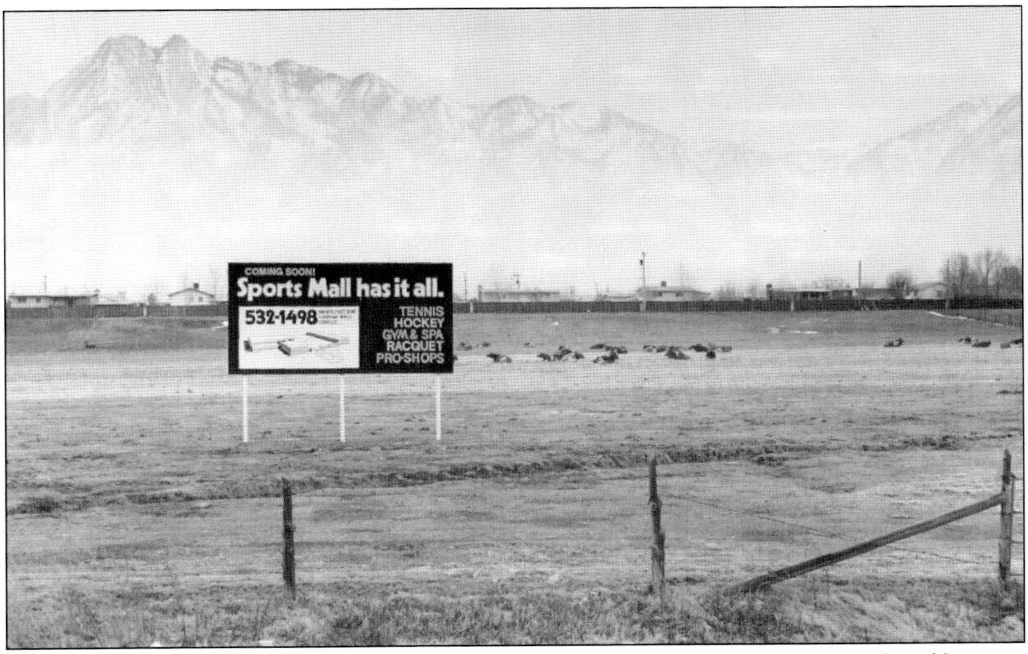

By the end of the 1960s, the rate of single-family subdivisions had slowed and was replaced by more modest apartment and condominium development. Only a handful of Murray's plowed fields and dairy farms remained. In the late 1970s, Arion Erekson sold his dairy farm for the development of the Sports Mall at 5445 South 900 East. The old farmhouse remains, surrounded by commercial development. (MCM.)

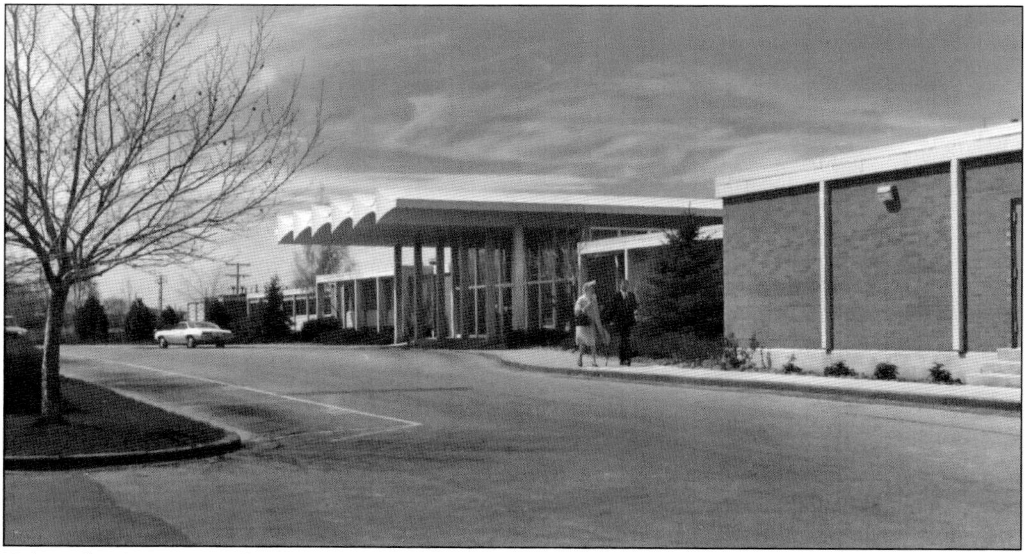

When the Cottonwood Hospital opened in 1963, it was the only large hospital facility in the south half of the valley. Pictured here in 1964, the hospital expanded from 110 to 244 beds in 1975. A specialized maternity wing was built in 1984. After serving the community for 45 years, the general hospital closed and a portion of the complex was converted to the Orthopedic Specialty Hospital (TOSH). (MCM.)

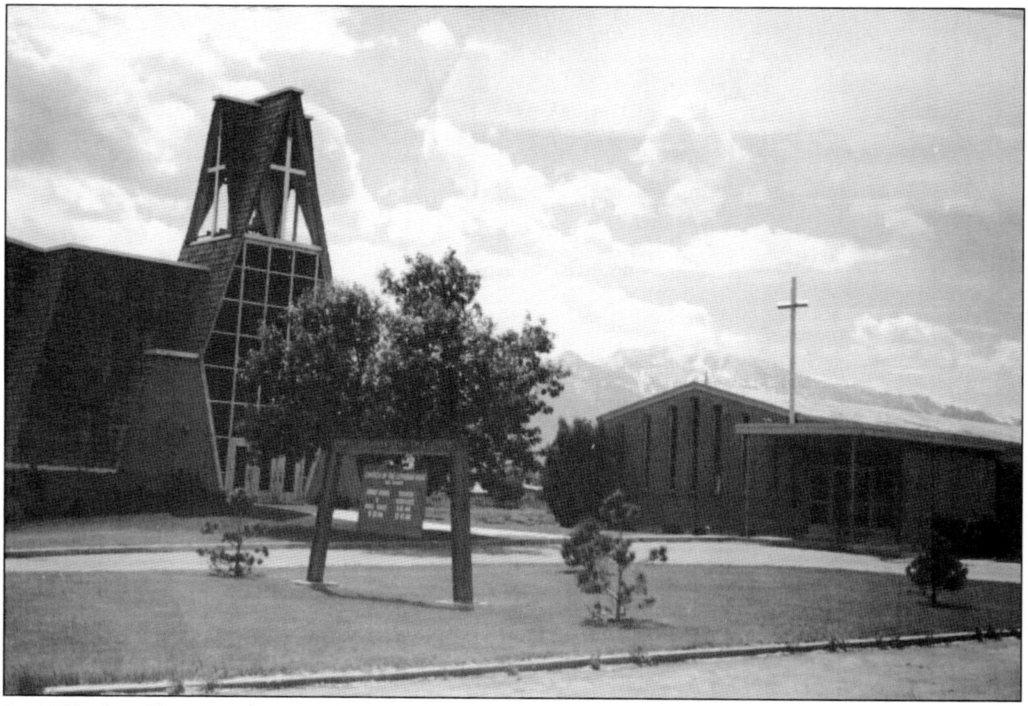

In 1955, the Christ Lutheran Church moved from 4800 South to a new house of worship at 222 East 5600 South (pictured here in the early 1970s). The adjoining Christ Lutheran School, an eight-grade parochial school also built in 1955, was the largest private school in the city until 1975, when the Mount Vernon Academy renovated the old Murray First Ward building on Vine Street. (MCM.)

The late 1970s and early 1980s saw a shift of residential development to newly annexed lands on both sides of the Jordan River. In this 1977 photograph, a carpenter builds a home probably in one of the Walden subdivisions in the area called the River Bottoms. For the growing population in west Murray, two new parks were established—Murray City's Hidden Village and Riverview Park, owned by Salt Lake County. (MCM.)

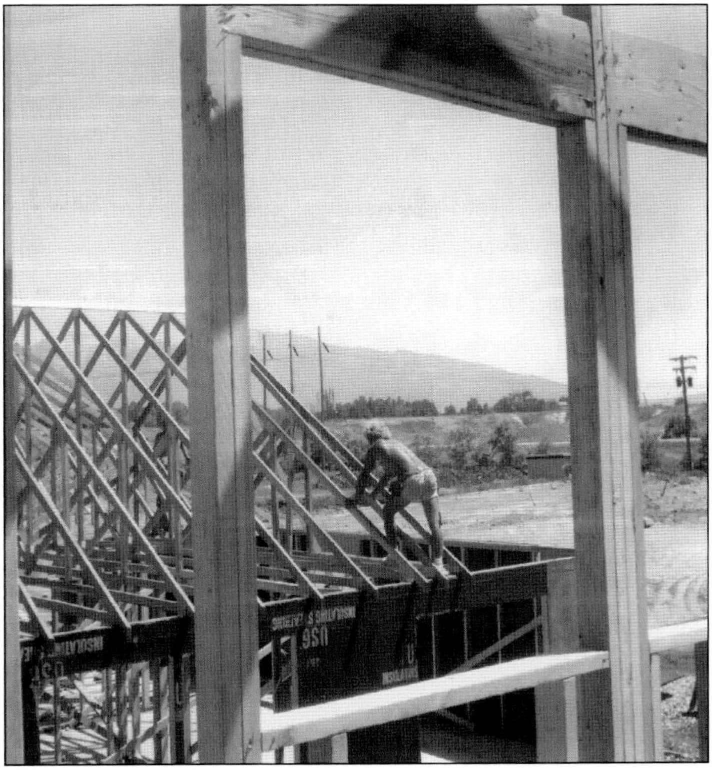

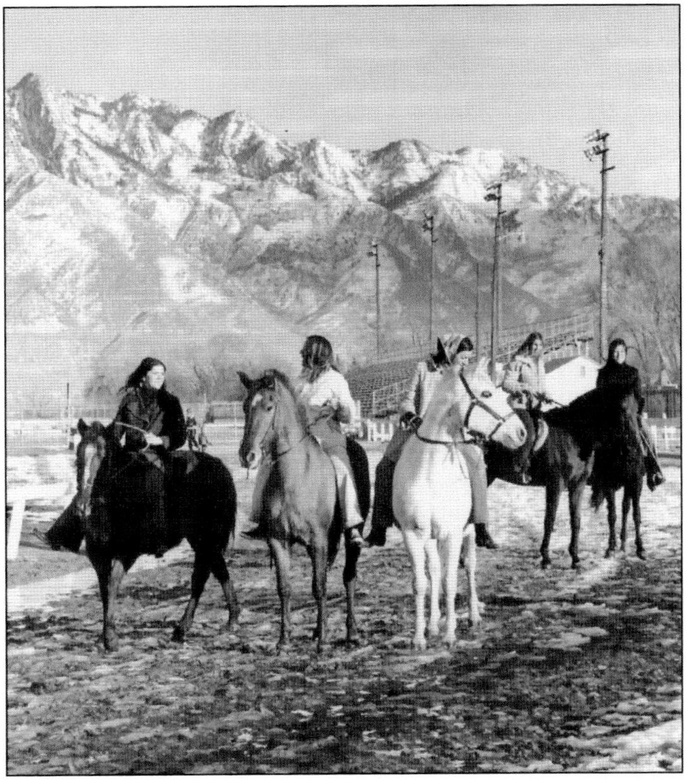

The Salt Lake County Fair and Rodeo remained the biggest August event in Murray, with an annual attendance between 10,000 and 25,000. This photograph of equestrians in the rodeo was taken around 1970. The fairgrounds were moved to South Jordan in 1998. Murray City built a community recreation center on the fairgrounds site called the Park Center, which featured indoor swimming pools, exercise rooms, a gymnasium, and an indoor track. (MCM.)

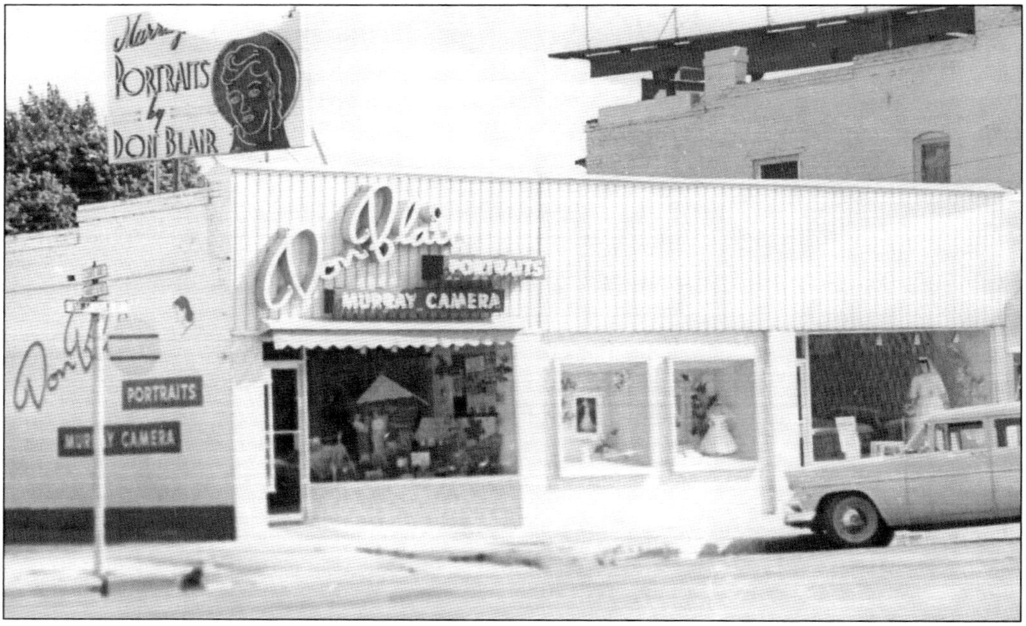

On January 10, 1987, a car crashed into the Don Blair Photograph Studio (pictured in the 1960s) and sheared off a natural-gas meter. Moments after the driver was pulled from vehicle, an explosion leveled the building and damaged the surrounding storefronts on State Street. The loss of the studio's archive included many views of historic Murray as well as decades of yearbook and class photographs. (MCM.)

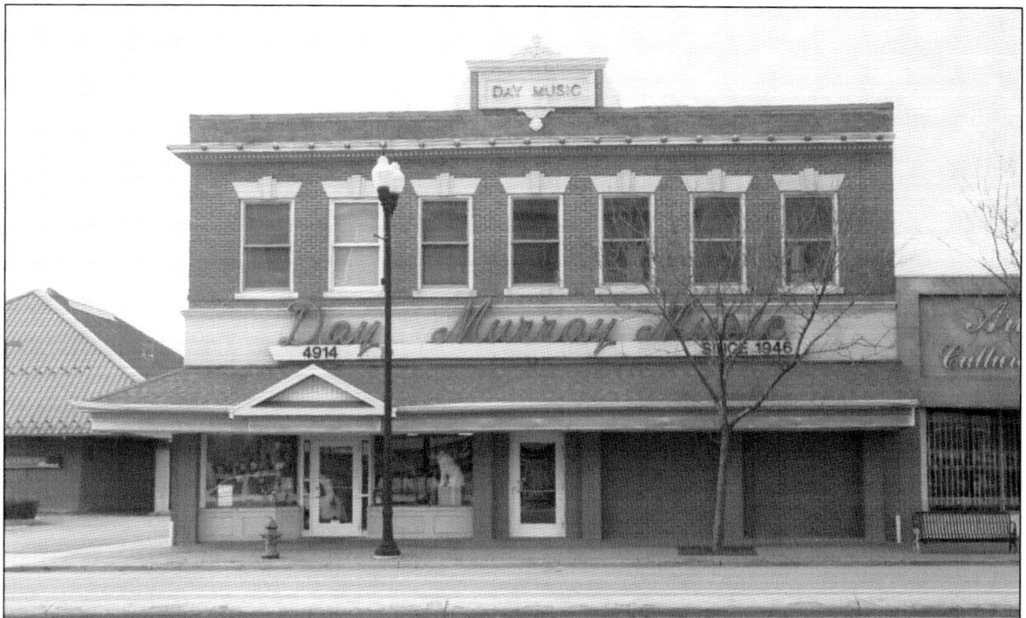

The 1987 explosion shattered the windows of the Waverly Building across the street, but the historic structure was saved by the owners. The remodeled storefront of Day Murray Music was among the many projects in the downtown area supported by the Murray Redevelopment Agency during the administration of Mayor Lavar McMillan. (Photograph by the author.)

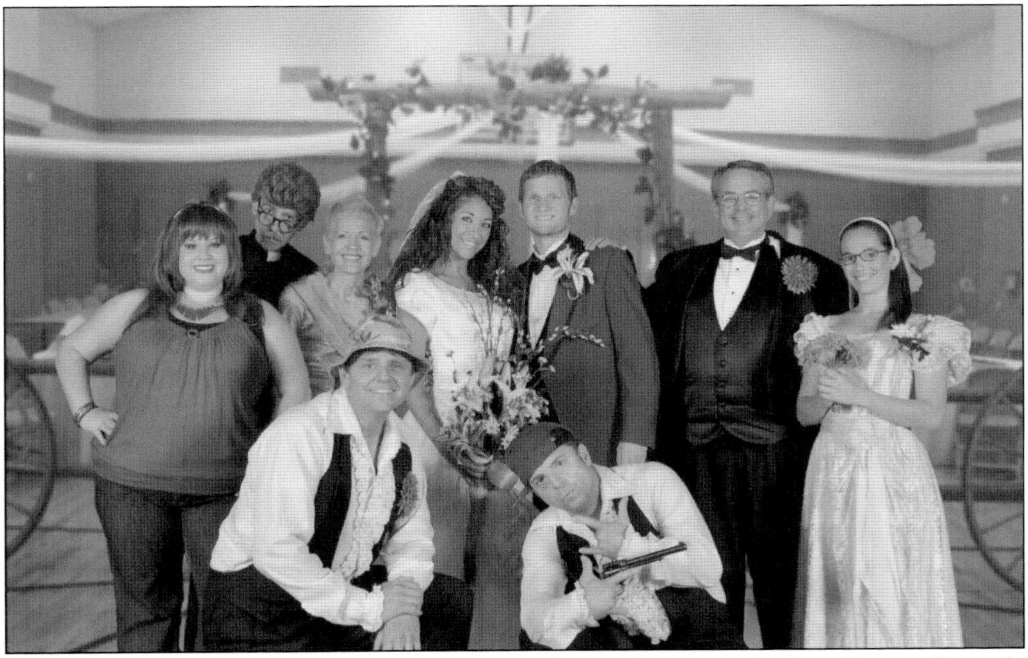

In 1989, Mike Todd began producing melodramas and musical spoofs in the Vista Theater (formerly the new Iris), which he renamed the Desert Star Playhouse. The dinner theater's *My Big Fat Utah Wedding* holds the record as Utah's longest-running live theatrical production. The cast is pictured here with author Scott Holman (front row, left) in 2010. (Desert Star Playhouse.)

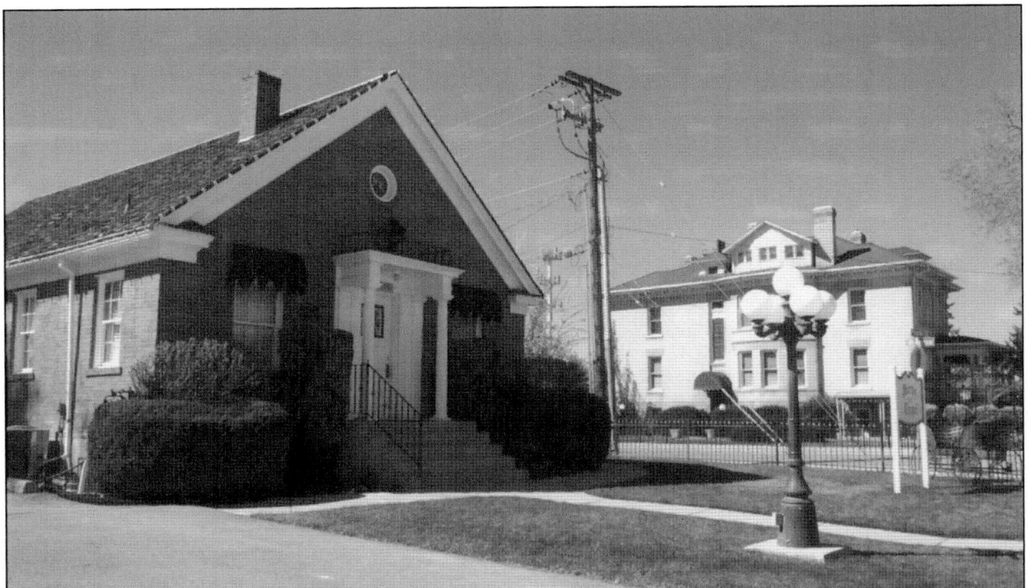

Beginning with the Cahoon Mansion, Bill and Susan Wright purchased several historic buildings along Poplar Street and moved the Baptist church to its current location south of the mansion. The Wrights transformed a former grocery store turned roller rink (complete with hardwood floor) into a ballet studio. The Ballet Centre was originally named for Susan's mentor, choreographer and Ballet West founder Willam Christensen, who taught master classes there. (Photograph by the author.)

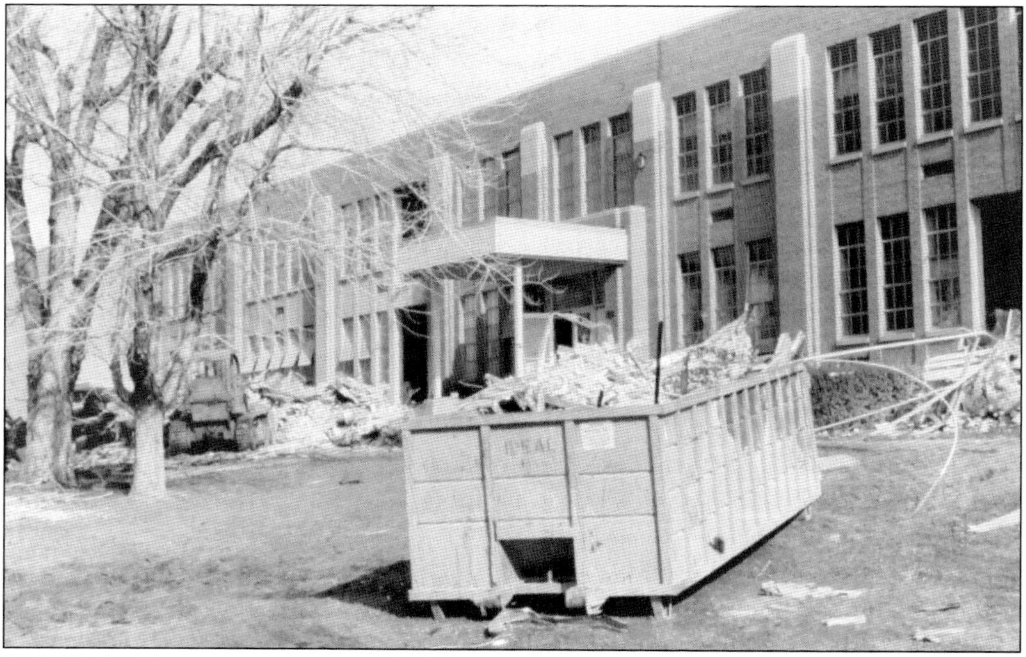

By 1980, the Murray city government had outgrown the municipal building. One of the best options presented was the purchase and remodeling of Arlington Elementary School, if the school district was willing to sell. Arlington's prominent location on busy State Street had been a safety concern for many years, but the site appeared ideal for a new city hall. The school closed at the end of the 1980–1981 school year. The city began moving its offices into the remodeled space in the summer of 1982. The above photograph was taken during the remodel. The image below features Mayor Lynn Pett standing in front of the Murray City Center around 1990. (Both, MCM.)

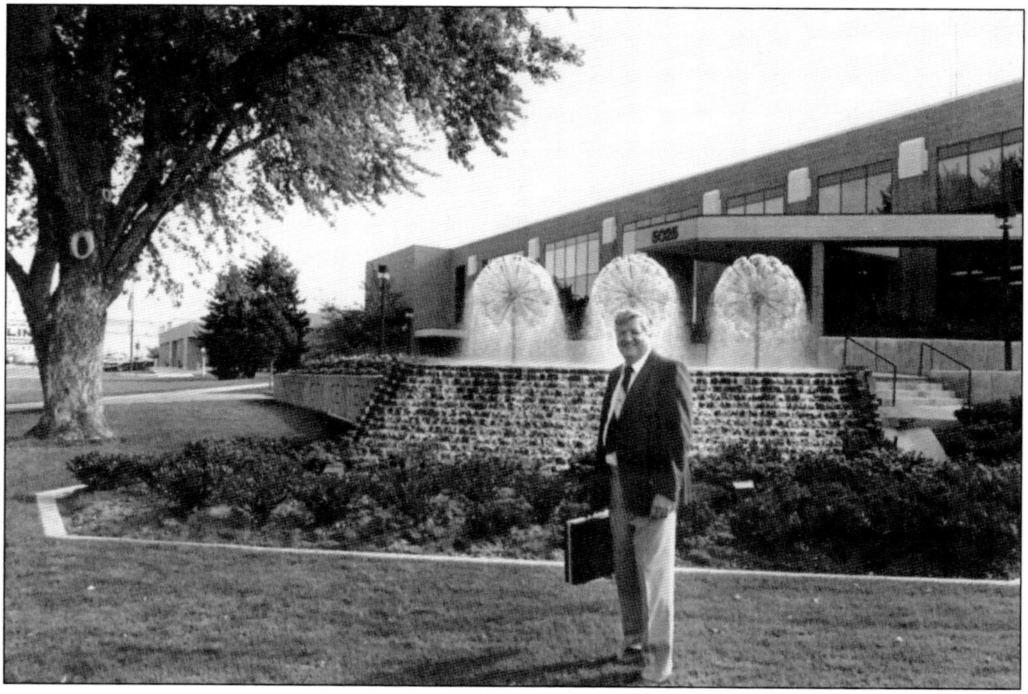

Six

A Century of Progress

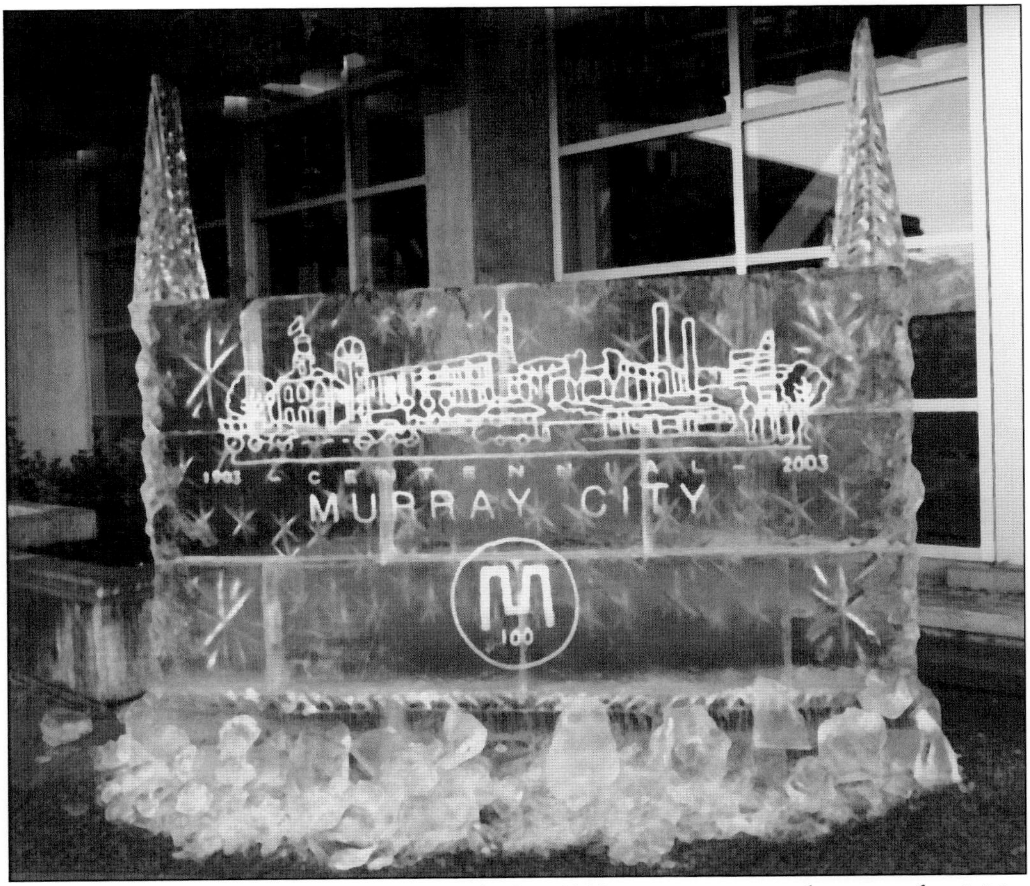

Murray City celebrated the 2003 centennial of its 1903 incorporation with a year of activities and projects, beginning with a two-day celebration on January 3–4, 2003. This beautiful ice sculpture created for one of the events commemorates the icons of Murray City and features the new city logo. (MCM.)

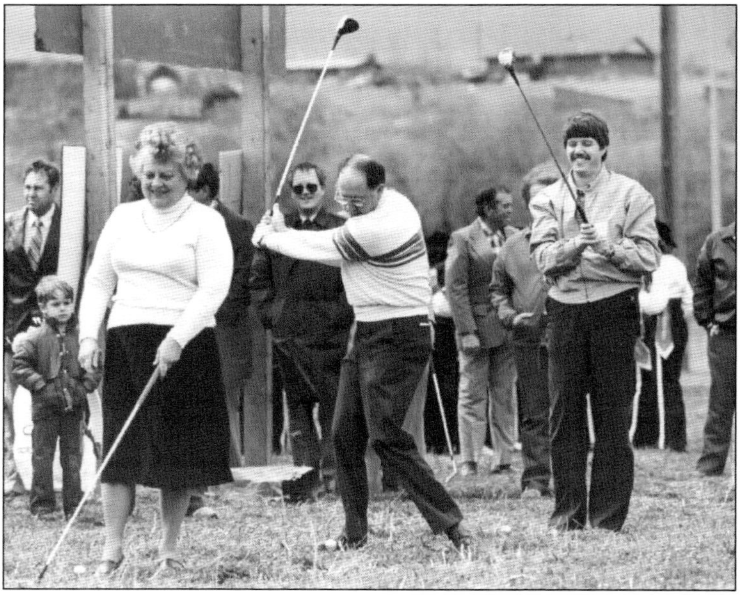

The Murray Parkway Golf Course, open in 1986, was the first phase of a vision of a recreation corridor along the Jordan River. The golf course was the second course in the city. The first was the Mick Riley Golf Course, located north of Murray Park and operated by Salt Lake County. This photograph features former Mayor LaRell Muir (center), and council members Elna Kirkham and Lawrence Cattam. (MCM.)

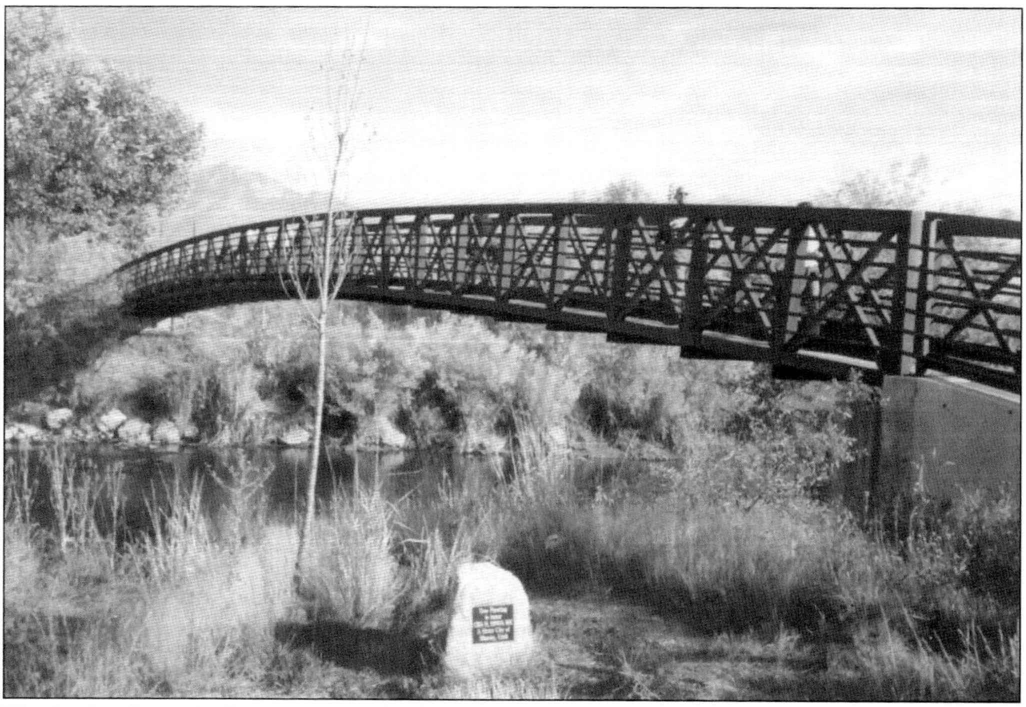

The Jordan River Parkway was a multiphase project that includes trails, a nature center, and five new parks—Arrowhead, Germania, Walden, Winchester, and Willow Pond. This photograph from the 1990s includes one of the bridges built to span the river and a tree-planting monument to Murray's sister city, Chia Yi, Taiwan. (MCM.)

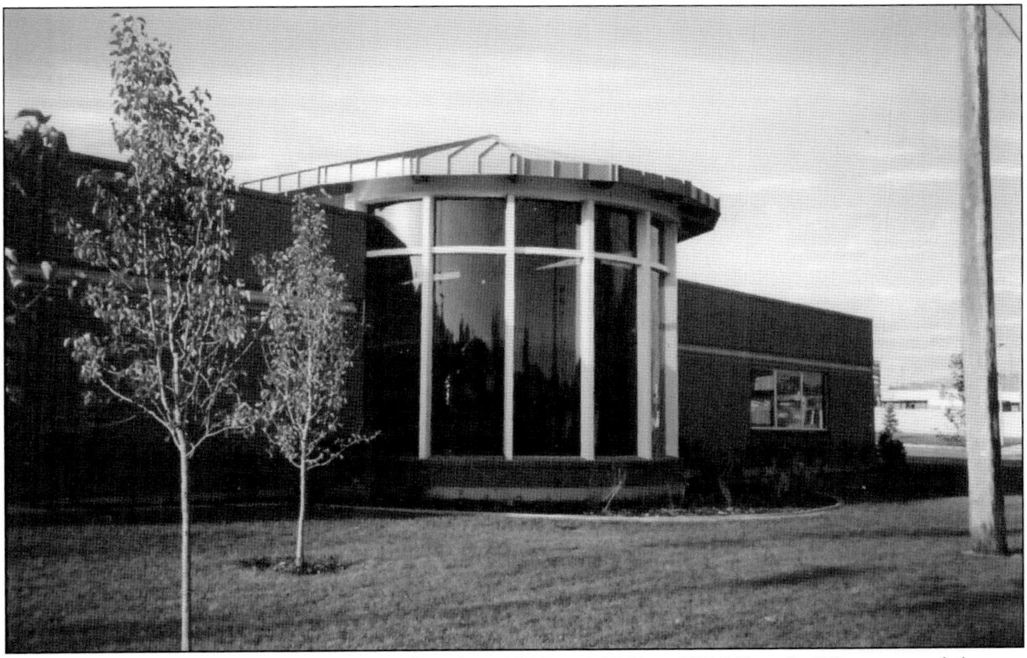

The current Murray Library was completed in 1992 at 166 East 5300 South. The state-of-the-art facility combined the resources of the two previous libraries. The Main Library on 6100 South is now the Early Childhood Education Center, and the Vine Street Library was acquired by the Mount Vernon Academy. (MCM.)

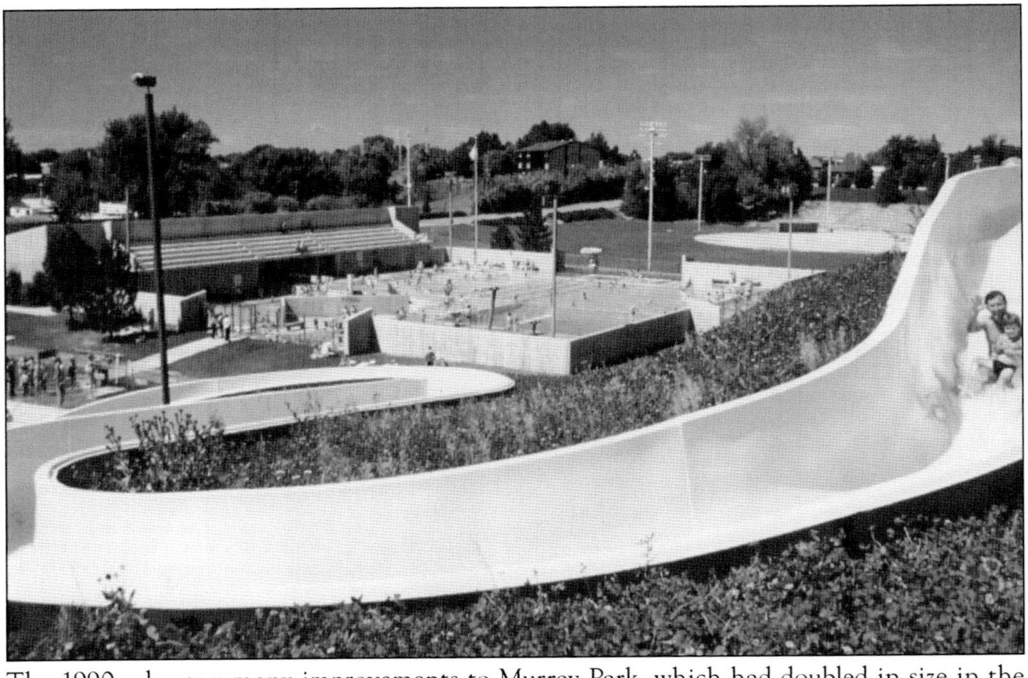

The 1990s also saw many improvements to Murray Park, which had doubled in size in the 1970s. Included in the projects were a waterslide next to the swimming pool (pictured here in foreground) and a restoration of the Depression-era stone bleachers on the softball field (in background). (MCM.)

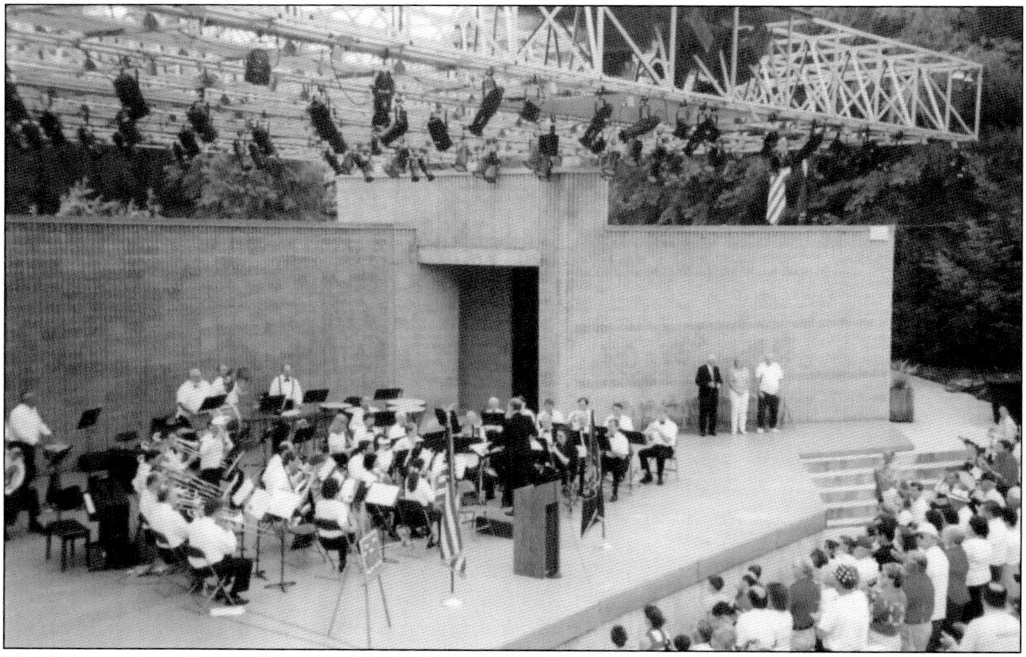

The Murray Arts Council was established in 1977 and in 1980 constructed an outdoor amphitheater at the east end of Murray Park. Each year, the Arts in the Park series produces musicals and concerts for the summer season. A sunrise concert in the amphitheater is the traditional kickoff of Murray Fun Days, Murray City's Fourth of July celebration (MCM.)

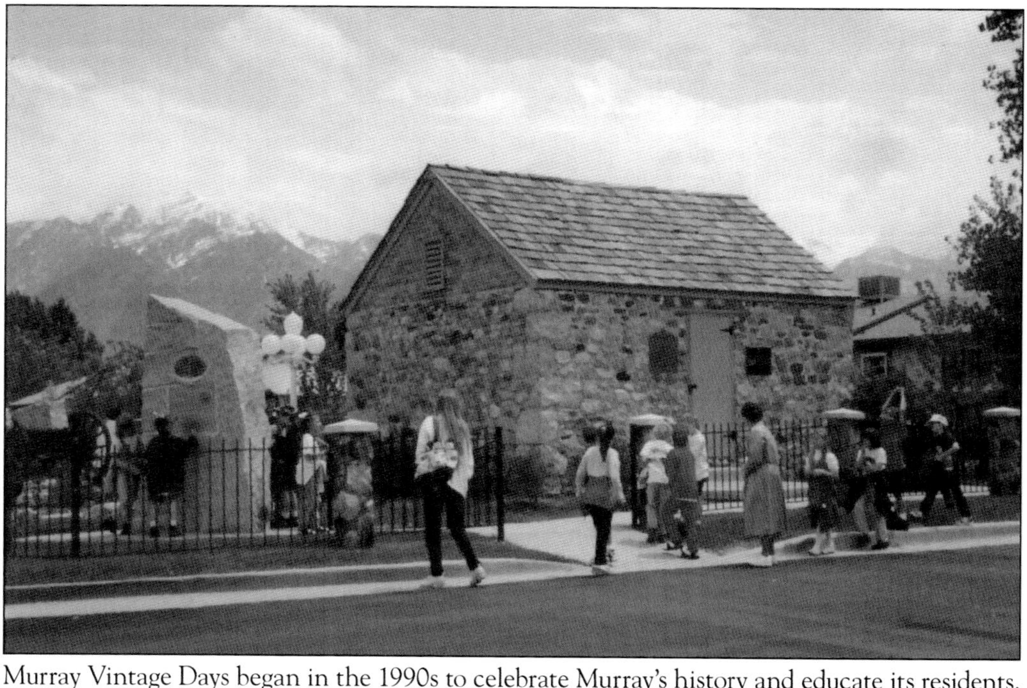

Murray Vintage Days began in the 1990s to celebrate Murray's history and educate its residents. Programs include tours of historic buildings and costumed storytellers in the Murray Cemetery. This photograph taken in May 1996 shows a tour group visiting the stone granary built behind the South Cottonwood Ward around 1878, now preserved as a small park by the LDS Church. (MCM.)

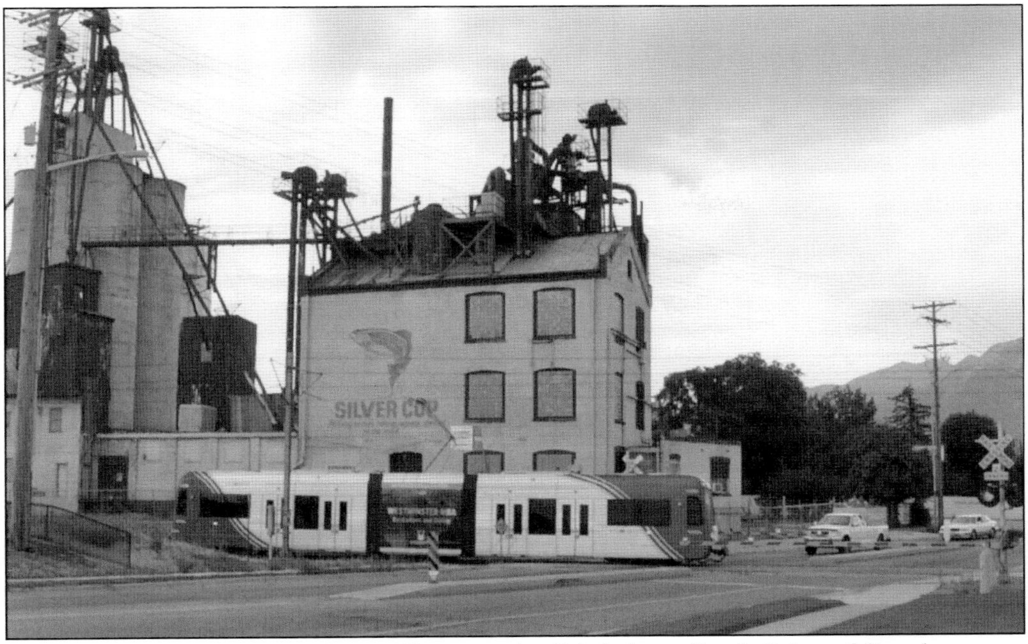

In anticipation of the 2002 Winter Olympics, the Salt Lake to Sandy light-rail line, known as TRAX, was completed in 1999 with three stops in Murray. The Murray Central Station connects to the FrontRunner commuter rail line, which began service in 2012. In this photograph, TRAX glides by the old feed mill on 4800 South. (Photograph by the author.)

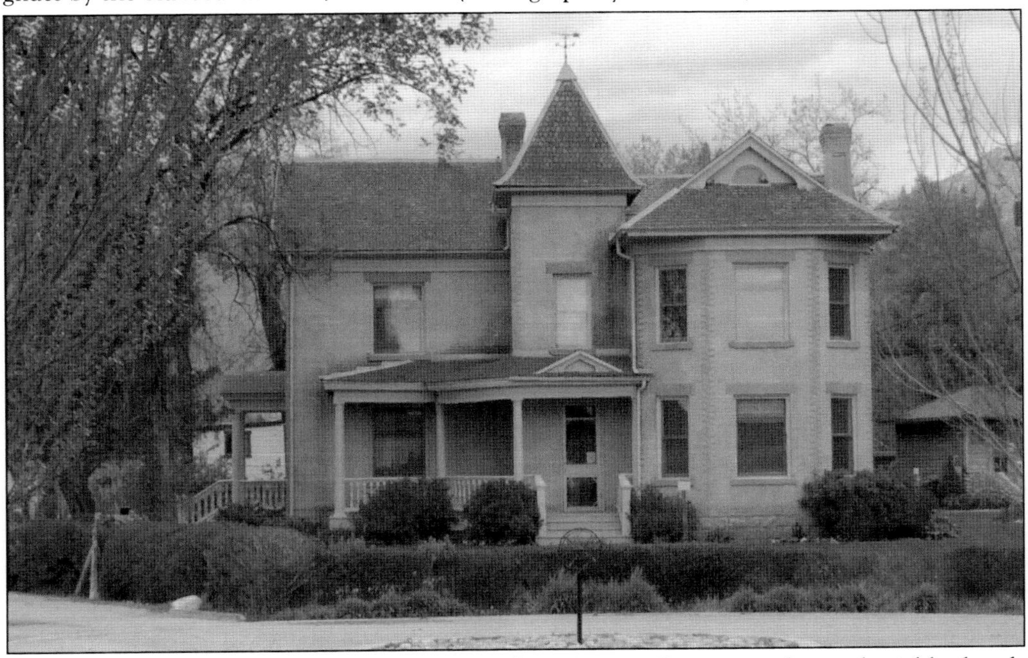

Between 2001 and 2003, at the request of area residents, Murray City annexed several neighborhoods in unincorporated Salt Lake County. Murray City now surrounds the Salt Lake County–owned Wheeler Farm at 6343 South 900 East. The 75-acre farm is the largest intact working historic farm in Salt Lake County and is open year-round to visitors. Henry J. and Sariah Pixton Wheeler built the farmhouse in 1898. (Photograph by the author.)

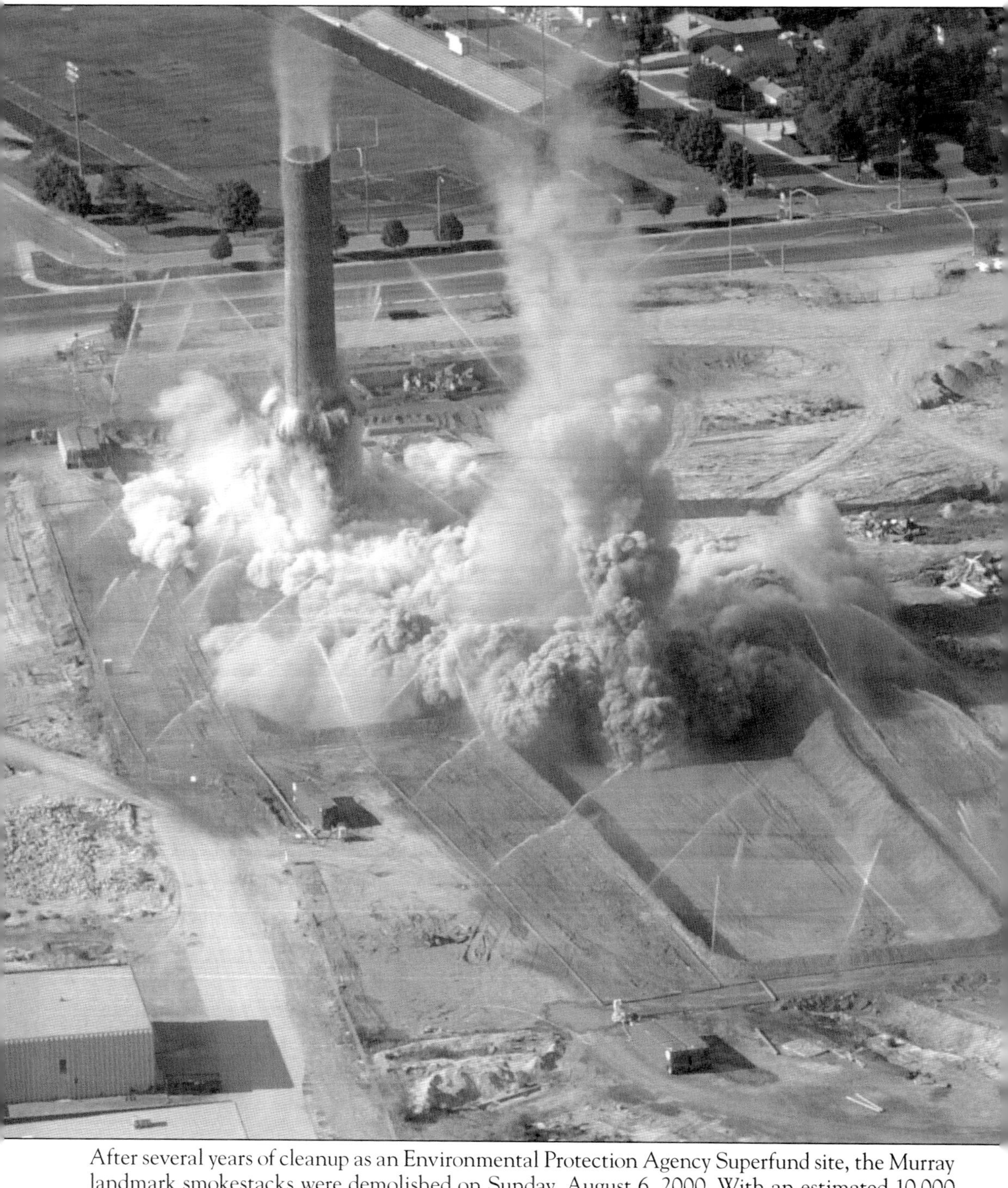

After several years of cleanup as an Environmental Protection Agency Superfund site, the Murray landmark smokestacks were demolished on Sunday, August 6, 2000. With an estimated 10,000 spectators kept at a safe distance, the taller stack was imploded, followed by the shorter stack. This bird's-eye view of the event features the water cannons used to control the contaminated dust of the explosion. (Photograph by Scott G. Winterton, Deseret News Publishing Company.)

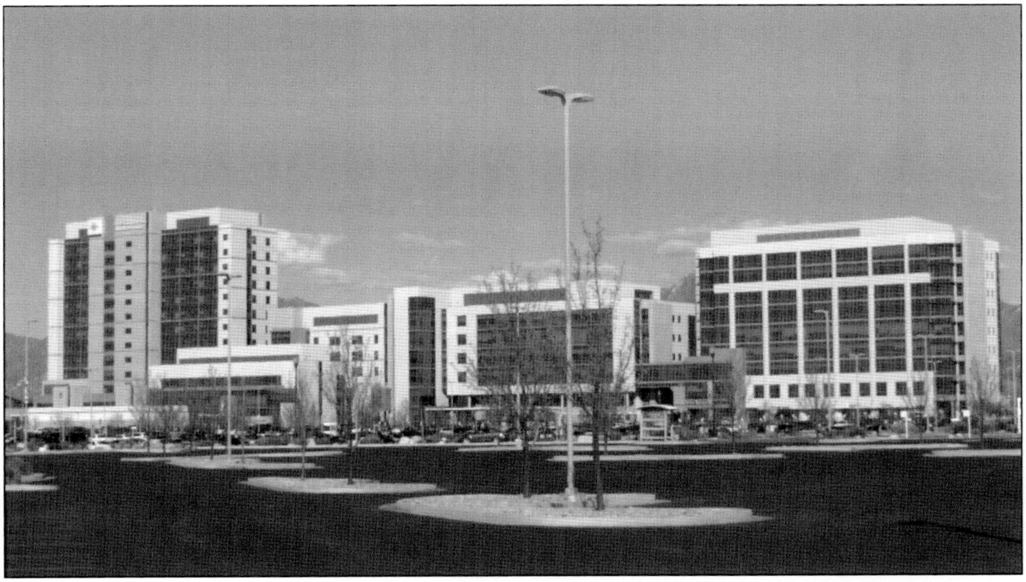

After the rubble was cleared away, the Intermountain Medical Center (IMC) was built on 100 acres of the former smelter site. The flagship hospital of the Intermountain Healthcare system officially opened on October 29, 2007. The complex includes a Level 1 trauma center, life-flight home base, patient tower, cancer treatment center, heart and lung hospital, and a women and newborn center. (Photograph by the author.)

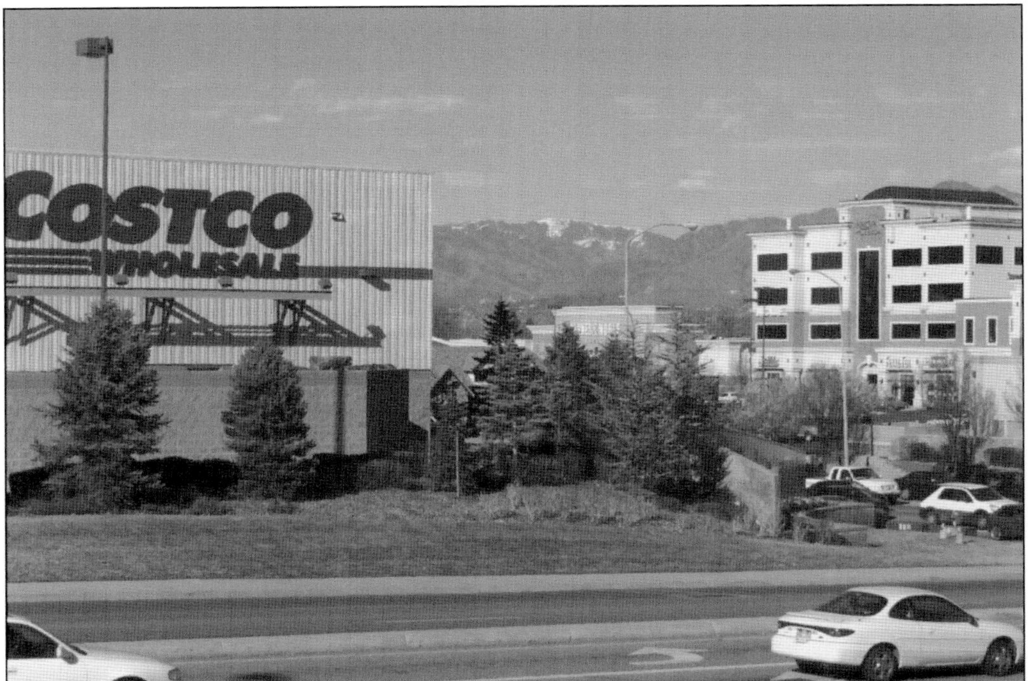

The intersection of State Street and 5300 South has become one of Murray's busiest retail centers. Costco is on the northwest corner near the IMC. The northeast corner is home to a Best Buy, a Barnes & Noble, an office tower, and several other businesses and restaurants. (Photograph by the author.)

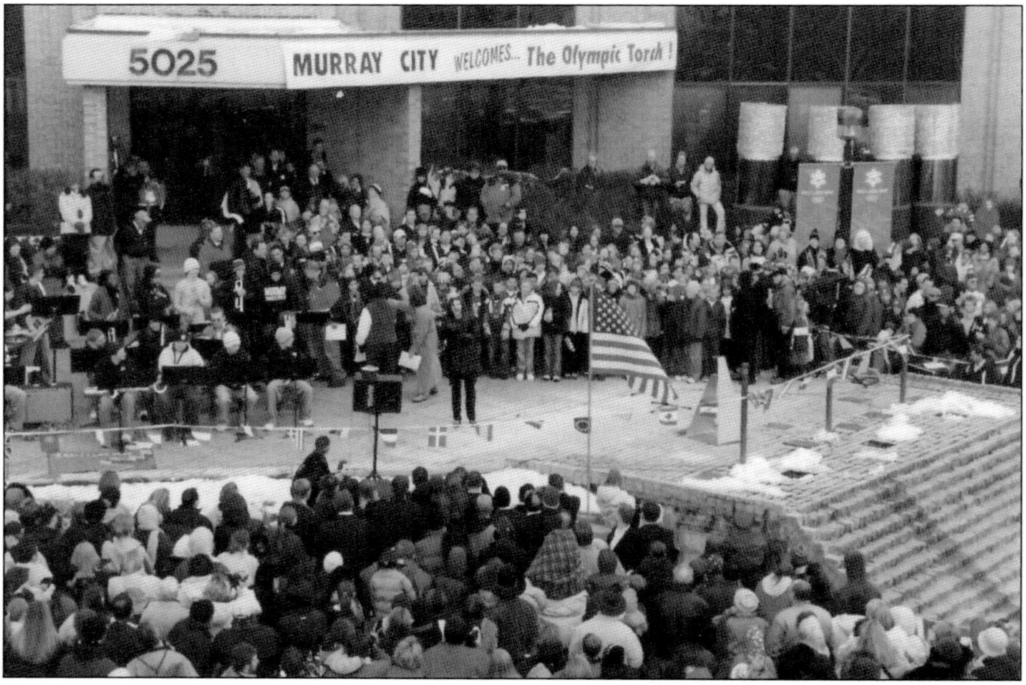

Two days before the opening of the 2002 Winter Olympics in Salt Lake City, on February 8, Murray residents gathered on the steps of city hall to welcome the Olympic torch (pictured). Although no competition events were held in Murray, volunteers from all over the city pitched in to lodge, feed, direct, and transport the Olympic visitors. (MCM.)

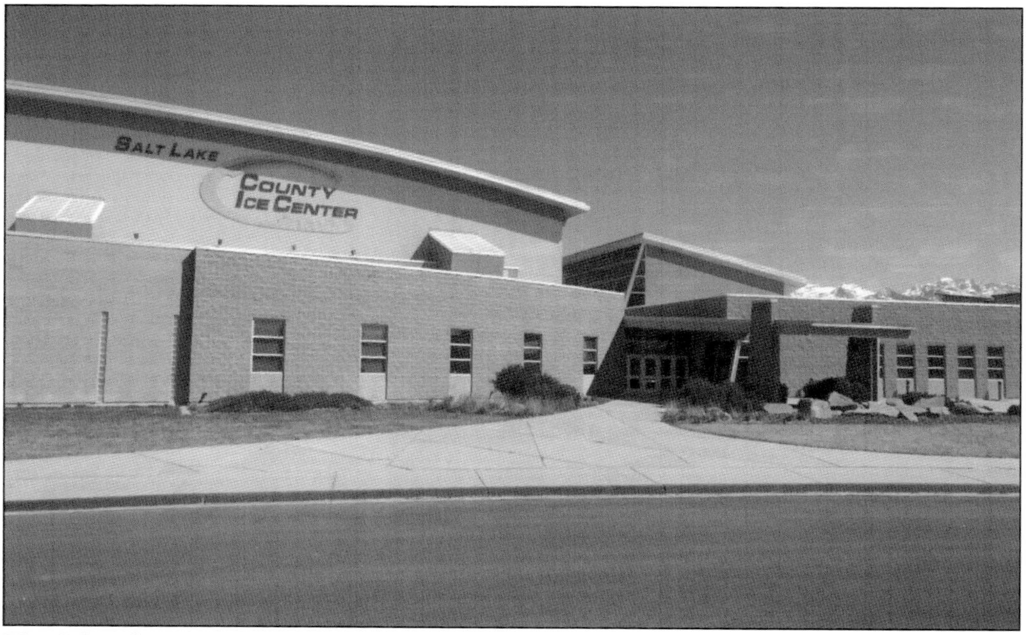

The Salt Lake County Ice Center was built in 1999 as a year-round indoor ice-skating rink on a portion of the former fairgrounds site (on right). The Olympic-sized ice surface was used as a practice venue during the 2002 Winter Olympics. The building also houses the offices of Salt Lake County Sports. (Photograph by the author.)

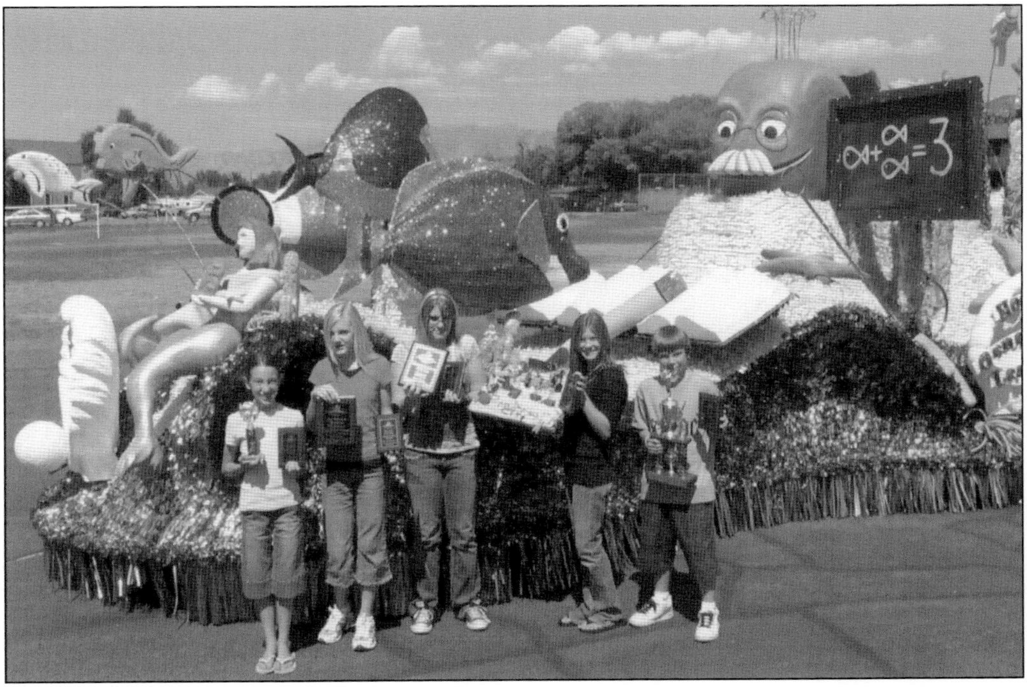

To commemorate its centennial year in 2006, the Murray School District sponsored a design contest for a float to represent Murray in several summertime parades. The winning entry was a "wavy-fish float" titled "Hooked on Generations of Learning." It combined the district's centennial theme, "A Legacy of Learning", and the Days of '47 parade theme, "Pioneer Dreams; Stepping Stones for Generations." The float won numerous awards. (MCM.)

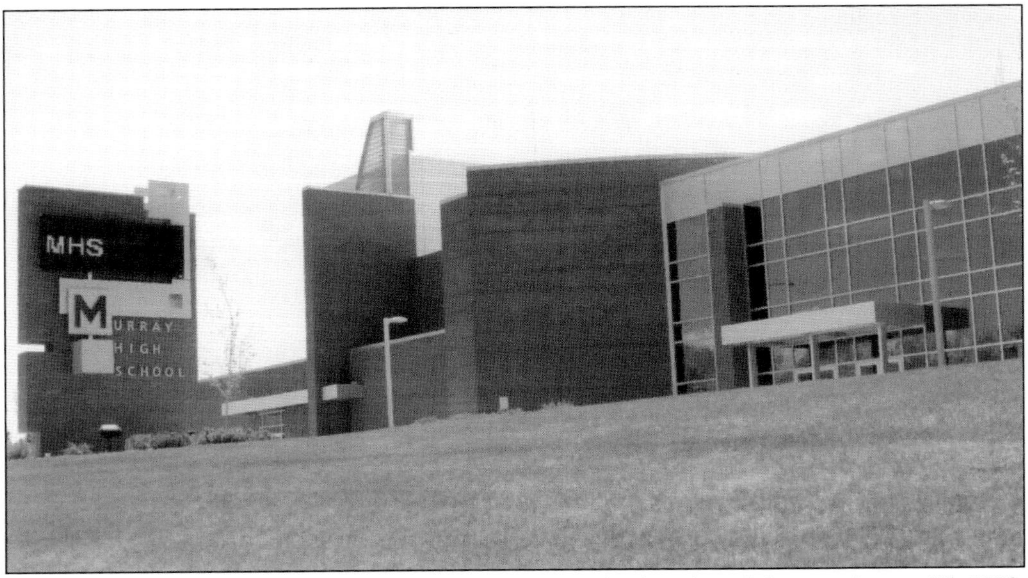

A new Murray High School was completed in time for the first day of class on August 25, 2003. The building was both state-of-the-art and innovative. Separate climate control for each classroom was made available through a geothermal loop heating and cooling system. Natural light was provided for almost all of the classrooms, with extra lights for whiteboards and a fiber-optic network with wireless Internet access. (MCM.)

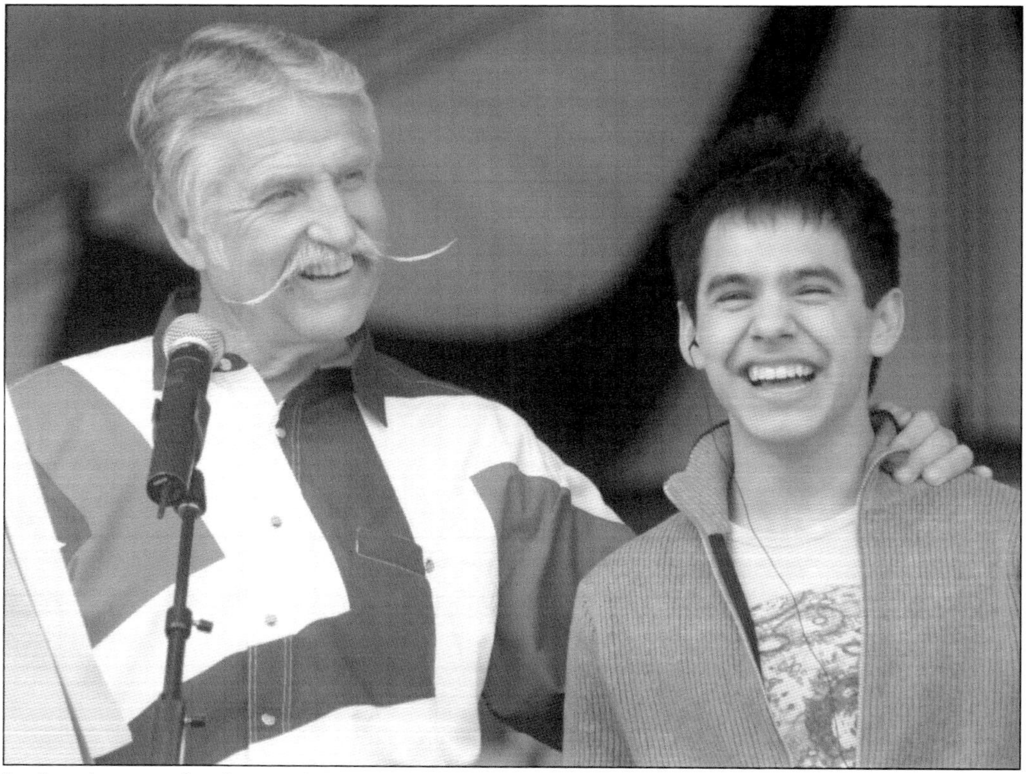

In this photograph taken on May 9, 2008, Mayor Dan Snarr (left) proclaims David Archuleta Day during a pep rally for the *American Idol* Season 7 runner-up. Archuleta was a Murray High School student at the time. Snarr made national news the following year when Murray residents donated money to charity to see their mayor cut off his signature handlebar mustache. (Photograph by Keith Johnson, Deseret News Publishing Company.)

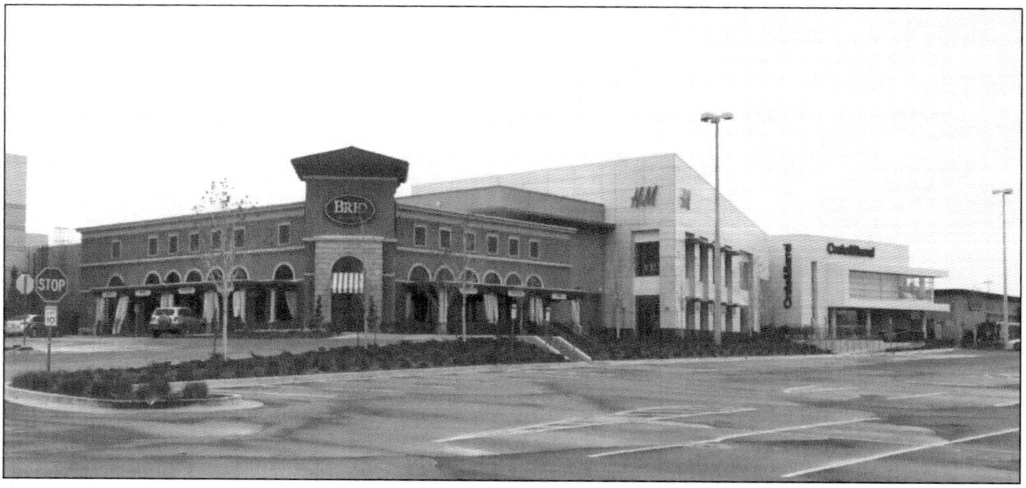

An important contributor to the tax base of Murray since 1972, Fashion Place Mall saw an increase in patronage after the 2007–2008 demise of Cottonwood Mall in neighboring Holladay. The administration of Murray's current mayor, Ted Eyre, has helped facilitate an unprecedented program of expansion and modernization at the mall and in the surrounding area. (Photograph by the author.)

The Murray Museum began in 1976 when residents donated artifacts to celebrate the nation's bicentennial. Most of the collection remained in a storage unit until the late 1990s, when the Murray Museum was given exhibition space in the city hall. Today, the museum exhibits artifacts such as cabinets and merchandise from the Madsen Hardware Store and the semicircular window from the Murray Opera House. (Photograph by the author.)

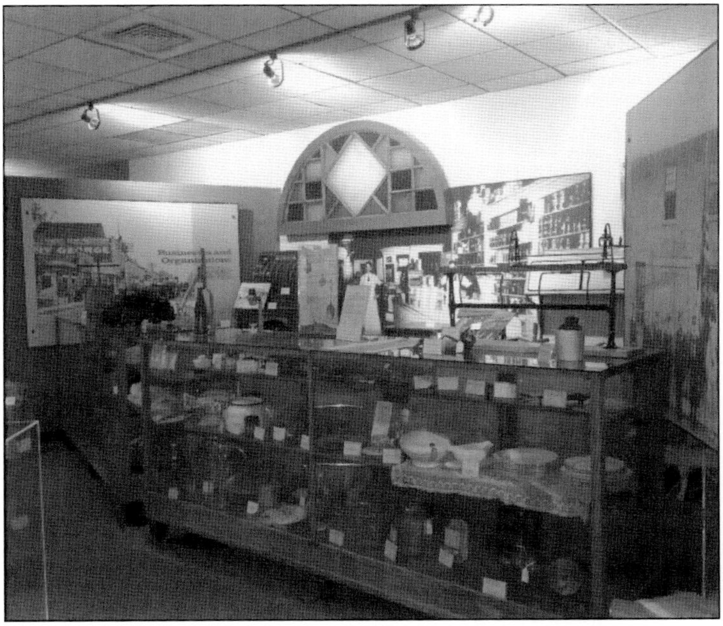

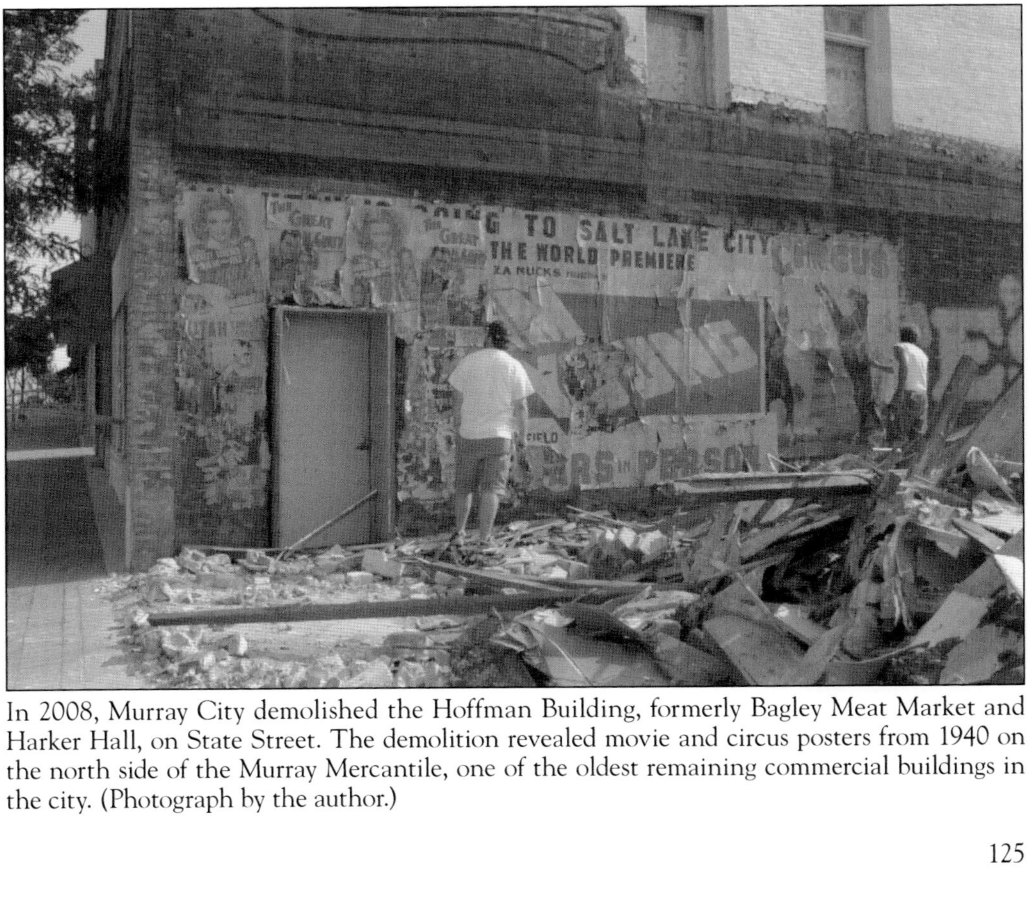

In 2008, Murray City demolished the Hoffman Building, formerly Bagley Meat Market and Harker Hall, on State Street. The demolition revealed movie and circus posters from 1940 on the north side of the Murray Mercantile, one of the oldest remaining commercial buildings in the city. (Photograph by the author.)

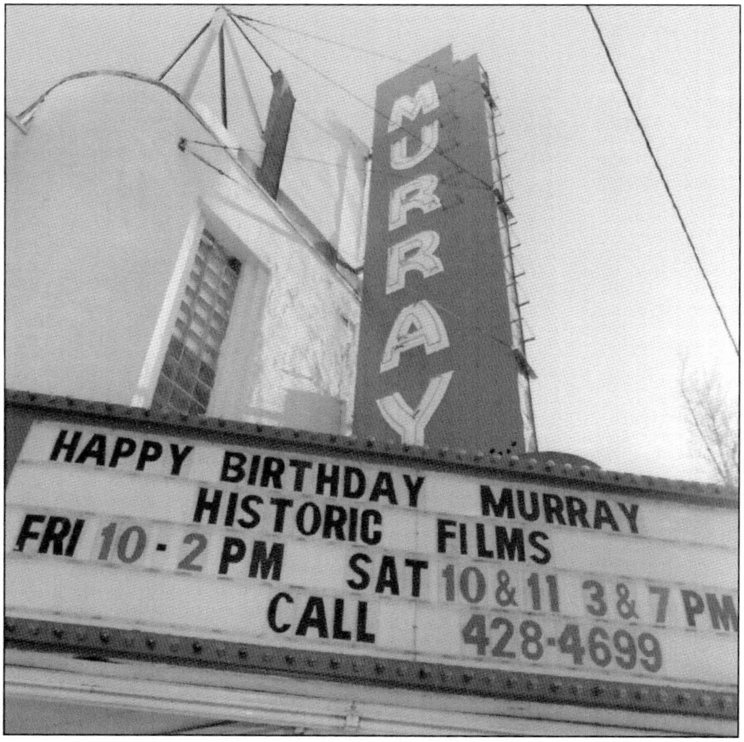

The Murray Theater marquee wishes Murray City a happy birthday during the 2003 centennial celebration. In addition to historic films shown in the theater, the Murray City Corporation published two books on the history of Murray City. The Murray Historic Preservation Advisory Board is currently working on a mobile telephone app walking tour of the historic downtown city center. (MCM.)

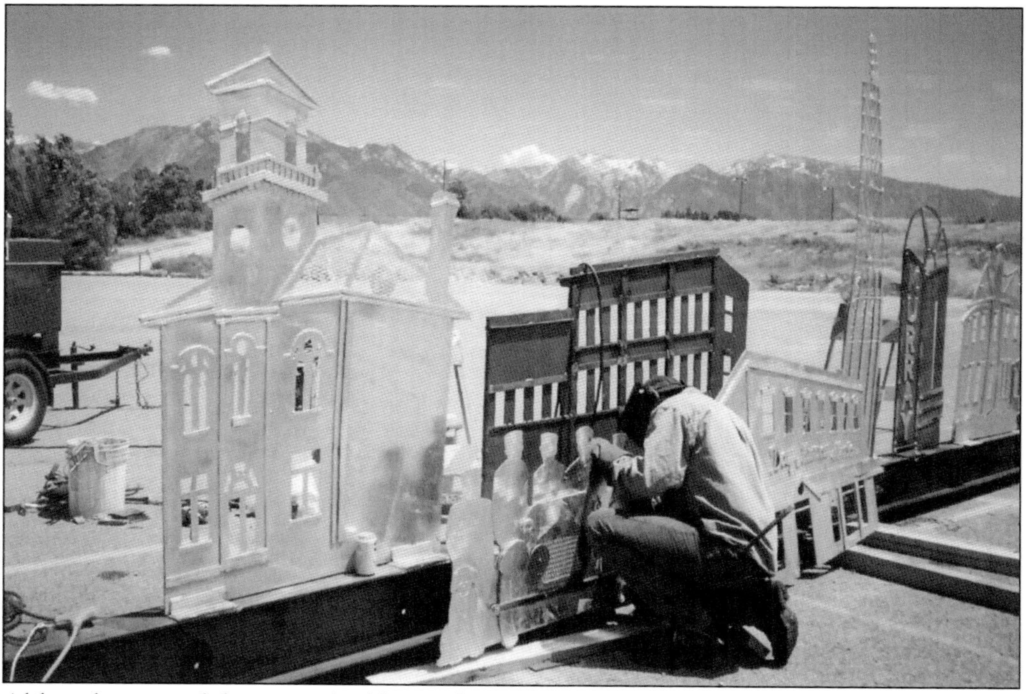

Although many of the iconic buildings of Murray are gone, many are commemorated on the *Over the Cottonwoods Arch* on display in Murray Park. The metal sculpture was created by artists William R. Littig and Paul Heath. One of the artists is pictured here at work in 1997. Littig and Heath also created works of art for the three TRAX stations in Murray in 2001. (MCM.)

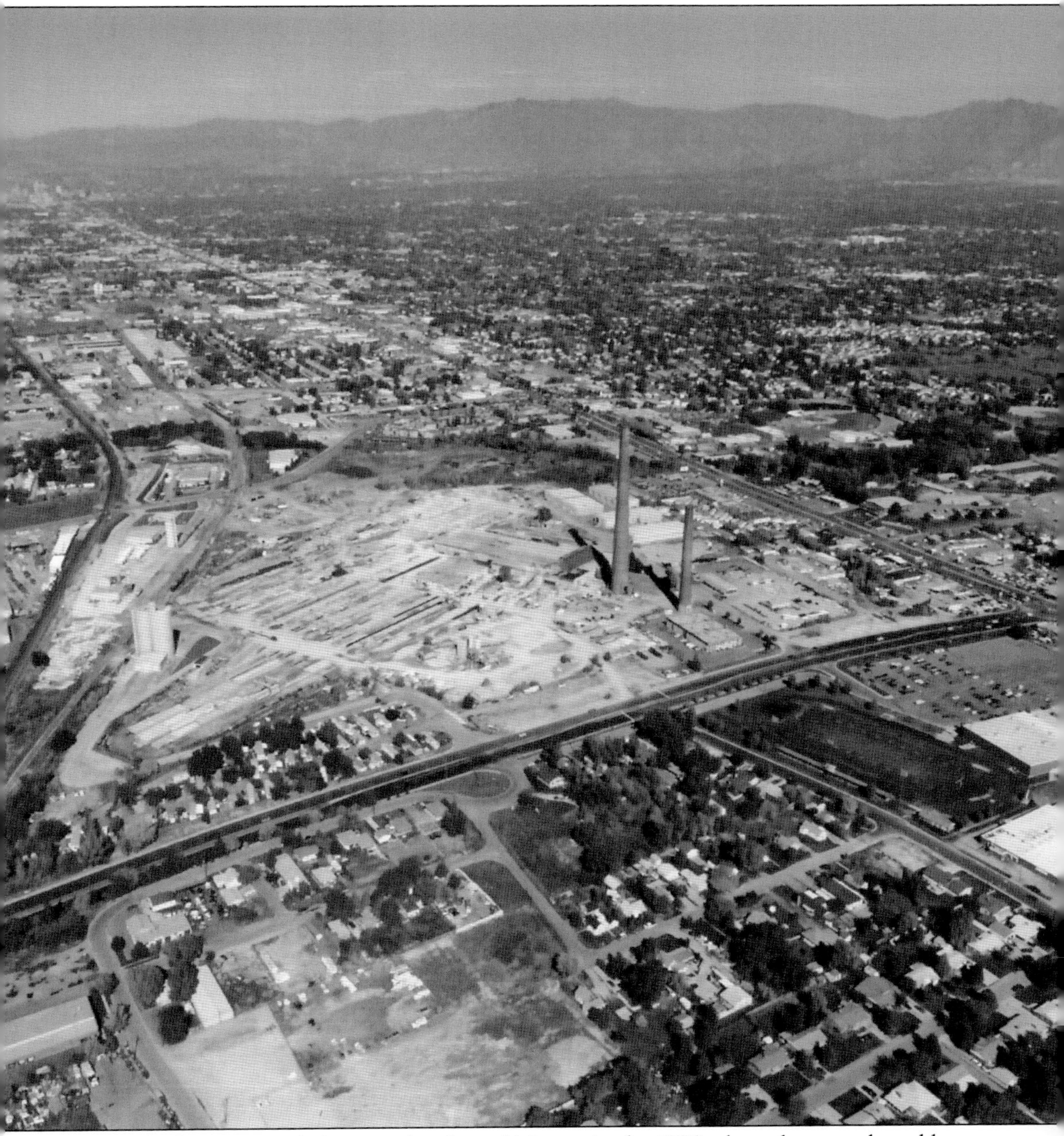

One last look at an aerial photograph taken of Murray in the 1990s shows how much and how little the city has changed in 100 years. Just as the arsenic- and lead-belching smokestacks have been replaced by a state-of-the-art medical facility, Murray City just keeps getting better and better every year. (MCM.)

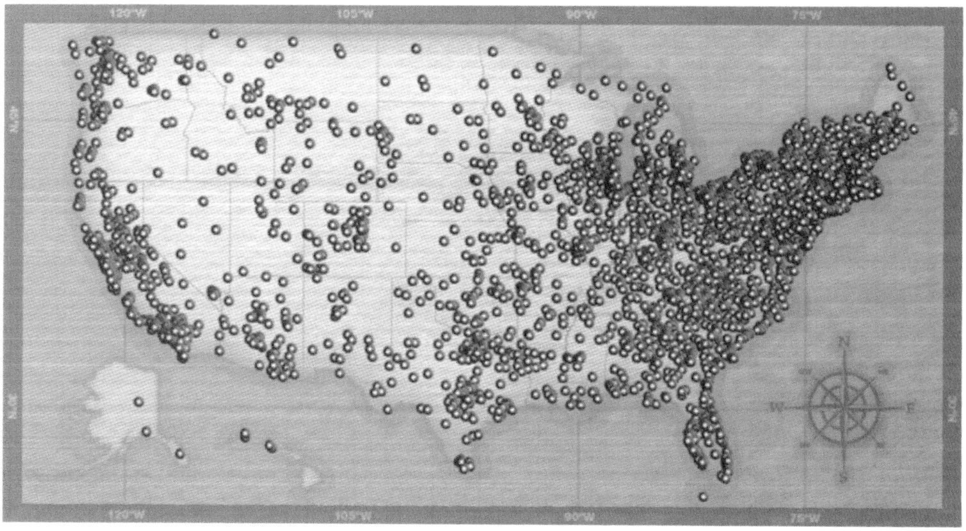